The
STRESS
CURE

Other books by Patrick Holford

Balance Your Hormones

Boost Your Immune System
(with Jennifer Meek)

Burn Fat Fast (with Kate Staples)

Food GLorious Food
(with Fiona McDonald Joyce)

*Food is Better Medicine than
Drugs* (with Jerome Burne)

Hidden Food Allergies
(with Dr James Braly)

*How to Quit Without Feeling
S**t* (with David Miller and
Dr James Braly)

Improve Your Digestion

*Optimum Nutrition Before,
During and After Pregnancy*
(with Susannah Lawson)

Optimum Nutrition for the Mind

*Optimum Nutrition for Your
Child* (with Deborah Colson)

Optimum Nutrition Made Easy
(with Susannah Lawson)

Say No to Arthritis

Say No to Cancer
(with Liz Efiong)

Say No to Heart Disease

Six Weeks to Superhealth

Smart Food for Smart Kids
(with Fiona McDonald Joyce)

Solve Your Skin Problems
(with Natalie Savona)

Ten Secrets of 100% Healthy People

Ten Secrets of Healthy Ageing
(with Jerome Burne)

*Ten Secrets of 100% Health
Cookbook* (with Fiona
McDonald Joyce)

*The Alzheimer's Prevention
Plan* (with Shane Heaton and
Deborah Colson)

The Feel Good Factor

The Homocysteine Solution
(with Dr James Braly)

The 9-day Liver Detox
(with Fiona McDonald Joyce)

The Low-GL Diet Cookbook
(with Fiona McDonald Joyce)

The Low-GL Diet Counter

The Low-GL Diet Bible

The Optimum Nutrition Bible

*The Optimum Nutrition
Cookbook* (with Judy Ridgway)

The Perfect Pregnancy Cookbook
(with Fiona McDonald Joyce
and Susannah Lawson)

*500 Health and Nutrition
Questions Answered*

Foreign editions are listed at
www.patrickholford.com/
foreigneditions

patrick
HOLFORD
& Susannah Lawson

WITHDRAWN

The
STRESS
CURE

HOW TO RESOLVE STRESS, BUILD RESILIENCE AND BOOST YOUR ENERGY

piatkus

PIATKUS

First published in Great Britain in 2015 by Piatkus

3 5 7 9 10 8 6 4 2

A CIP catalogue record for this book
is available from the British Library.

ISBN 978-0-349-40548-3

Typeset in Calluna and The Sans by M Rules
Printed and bound by CPI Group (UK) Ltd, Croydon, CR0 4YY

Papers used by Piatkus are from well-managed forests
and other responsible sources.

MIX
Paper from
responsible sources
FSC® C104740

Piatkus
An imprint of
Little, Brown Book Group
Carmelite House
50 Victoria Embankment
London EC4Y 0DZ

An Hachette UK Company
www.hachette.co.uk

www.piatkus.co.uk

Patrick Holford, BSc, DiplON, FBANT, CNHCRP, is a leading spokesman on nutrition in the media, specialising in the field of mental health. He is the author of over 35 books, translated into more than 30 languages and selling over a million copies worldwide.

Patrick started his academic career in the field of psychology. He then became a student of two of the leading pioneers in nutrition medicine and psychiatry – the late Dr Carl Pfeiffer and Dr Abram Hoffer. In 1984 he founded the Institute for Optimum Nutrition (ION), an independent educational charity, with his mentor, twice Nobel Prize winner Dr Linus Pauling, as patron. ION has been researching and helping to define what it means to be optimally nourished for over 25 years and is one of the most respected educational establishments for training nutritional therapists. He was one of the first promoters of the importance of zinc, antioxidants, high-dose vitamin C, essential fats, low-GL diets and homocysteine-lowering B vitamins and their importance in mental health and Alzheimer's disease prevention.

Patrick is Chief Executive Officer of the Food for the Brain Foundation and director of the Brain Bio Centre, the Foundation's treatment centre that specialises in helping those with mental issues. He is an honorary fellow of the British Association of Nutritional Therapy, as well as a member of the Complementary and Natural Healthcare Council. He is also Patron of the South African Association of Nutritional Therapy.

Susannah Lawson, DiplON, mBANT is a nutritional therapist, HeartMath practitioner and health journalist. She has been supporting clients to achieve better health since 2003, working with a range of issues from stress and fatigue to infertility and digestive problems. She is a member of the British Association for Nutritional Therapists and is registered by the Complementary and Natural Healthcare Council.

The Stress Cure is the fourth book she has written with Patrick Holford, following *Optimum Nutrition Before, During and After Pregnancy*; *Optimum Nutrition Made Easy* and *The Perfect*

Pregnancy Cookbook. She also contributes to newspapers and other media, including *Healthy* magazine, *Zest* and *The Times*, as well as radio shows for the BBC and regional stations.

Passionate about sharing her knowledge, Susannah regularly participates in educational events for both healthcare professionals and the wider community. These include healthy pregnancy workshops for the National Childbirth Trust, seminars on perinatal mental health for the NHS and training courses on optimum nutrition on behalf of the International Institute of Anti-Ageing. She was part of the academic team at the Institute for Optimum Nutrition from 2005 to 2008, working as a tutor with first and second-year students. Before becoming a mother, she was also part of the expert team advising clients for in:spa retreats.

Contents

Acknowledgements

First off, we'd like to thank the many inspirational scientists, doctors and psychologists who've uncovered new approaches to help us thrive in difficult, stressful and challenging times – Bruce Lipton, Candace Pert, James Wilson, Martin Seligman, Robert Emmons, Stephen Palmer and Cary Cooper, to name a few. We're also very grateful to the pioneering work of Doc Childre and the inspirational HeartMath team, both in California and London.

At Piatkus, we'd like to thank our editor Jillian Stewart for being so calm, flexible and helpful, Philip Parr for his meticulous copy editing, and Tim Whiting for his support and encouragement to publish this book and to make it available to as many people as possible. We'd also like to thank Fiona McDonald Joyce for generously allowing us to use some of her delicious recipes in this book.

On a personal level, Patrick would like to thank his wife Gaby and his manager Jo for their support and encouragement.

Susannah has a lot of additional people to thank because writing this book on top of running a nutrition practice, fulfilling corporate work obligations and being a hands-on mum to a busy toddler has certainly provided the opportunity to put myself in the shoes of the over-worked, over-tired and over-stressed. Without the support of the following (and putting the Stress Cure Programme into practice for myself), I may not have hit the deadline and stayed sane: my accommodating husband Simon; my inspirational, kind and ever-helpful mother Dinah; my obliging mother-in-law Sue; my understanding clients at npower (Michael, Roz, Sadie and Lorna, to name a few); my caring friends Tim, Lucy and also Sam, for his insight on time management; and my ever-supportive, superstar neighbour Melody. I also want to thank all my nutrition and HeartMath clients for teaching me so much and allowing me the privilege of learning with them.

Introduction

A psychologist walks around a room while teaching stress management to a large crowd. As she raises a glass of water, many anticipate they're going to be asked the 'half empty or half full' question. Instead, she enquires: 'How heavy is this glass of water?' People call out various weights. Then she says, 'The absolute weight isn't really the issue. It depends on how long I hold it. If I hold it for a minute, it's not a problem. If I hold it for an hour, I'll have an ache in my arm. If I hold it for a day, my arm will feel numb and paralysed. In each case, the weight of the glass doesn't change, but the longer I hold it, the more uncomfortable it becomes.' She continues: 'Stress in your life is like this glass of water. Experience it for a short while and the impact is low. Experience it for a bit longer, and it begins to hurt. And if you remain stressed all day, every day, you will start to feel paralysed, exhausted and incapable of functioning.'

The stress epidemic

Many of us fall into the 'all day, every day' category – and the impact is plain to see. A survey of 2050 adults carried out by Mind, the mental health charity, found that one in five working people take time off for stress and one in ten have sought professional help to deal with it.[1] Many of us also perceive that stress is becoming more prevalent, with 59 per cent of British adults saying their life is more stressful than it was five years ago.[2]

In our own 100% Health survey, which involved more than 55,000 participants, 72 per cent said they felt stressed, while two-thirds (66 per cent) experienced frequent anxiety and tension. More than eight out of ten (81 per cent) also complained of having low energy. Most of us ping-pong between feeling wired and tired most of the time.

Of course, our in-built stress response is key to our survival. Without it, we'd have become some predator's lunch thousands of years ago. The problem is that although most of us are far safer than our cave-dwelling ancestors, we still face challenges that trigger the same 'fight or flight' response many times each day. Workplace politics, traffic jams, disagreements at home, money worries, having too much to do and too little time to do it – all of these problems activate the same stress response with the same release of adrenalin. So too does a dip in our fuel levels (blood sugar). Unfortunately, today's high-carb, stimulant-loaded diets create a rollercoaster ride of fuel highs followed by lows, so adding to your body's stress burden and making you feel more stressed, tired and hungry.

As well as reducing your enjoyment of life, ongoing stress is bad news for your health. Every month, new research reveals yet more harmful effects of too much stress. In the past few years alone, studies have shown that those of us who experience regular stress have:

- A fivefold increased risk of dying from heart-related problems.[3]

- Double the risk of developing diabetes.[4]

- A 65 per cent increased risk of developing dementia.[5]

- Double the chance of becoming obese.[6]

- A 12 per cent lower likelihood of conception among fertile women.[7]

- An increased risk of breast cancer.[8]

- A 70 per cent increased risk of disabilities in later life.[9]

While many think of stress as being all in the mind, the reality is that ongoing stressful thinking can be as harmful to your body as smoking, drinking too much or eating a junk-food diet. Indeed, an article in the *Journal of the American Medical Association* found that too much stress can be as bad for your heart as smoking and high cholesterol.[10] This is because, as well as generating unpleasant emotional sensations, stress triggers a cascade of hormones and chemicals that, over time, accelerate ageing, encourage inflammation and degeneration, and increase the risk of disease.

But you probably know much of this already. And hearing it again is only likely to cause you to become more stressed!

Escaping the stress trap

The good news is that there is a solution – a way out of the vicious cycle of stress and fatigue – and you have it in your hands. The first step (Part 1 of this book) is to find out how you got caught in the stress trap and to learn the dynamics of how stress works and why you feel so tired.

The second step, Part 2, shows you that it's possible to boost your energy reserves dramatically with the right diet, drinks and energy-boosting supplements, all of which will also help to rebalance your stress hormones.

The third step, Part 3, explains how to build up your resilience to stress. In this section we show you how to generate vital energy, relax quickly and effectively, and sleep soundly. We also show you a remarkably effective yet simple five-minute-a-day exercise from the HeartMath® system, which trains you to have a new calm and level-headed 'default' setting, rather than getting stressed and freaking out whenever something goes wrong.

The fourth step, Part 4, allows you to reset your mindset by uncovering your stress triggers and disarming unhelpful beliefs, while also developing a more positive mind-frame when situations that need resolving arise. You will also discover practical ways to rearrange your life, your time and your priorities for the better.

Since everyone is different, in Part 5 we look at some of the other issues that can feed into feeling chronically stressed and tired. These include the underlying causes of chronic fatigue syndrome, often linked to digestive and detoxification issues. We also offer natural solutions for low mood, anxiety and panic attacks, as well as advice on how to control your weight, which is often an issue alongside stress and tiredness for reasons that will become clear as you understand how stress works within the body.

Finally, in Part 6, you will have the opportunity to put it all together in your own, personalised, 30-day action plan for stress-free living. Your Stress Cure programme, which includes a simple way to monitor your progress, will help you feel stronger, more energised and more resilient to stress. You will have everything you need – from recipes and a personalised stress-recovery supplement plan to simple stress-reducing exercises – to build into your daily routine. Our goal for you is that, within 30 days, you will notice significant improvements in your energy levels, feel much less stressed and have the means at your fingertips to resolve stressful situations in constructive ways.

We want you to be enthusiastically in charge of your own life, with the energy, skills and resilience to deal with life's inevitable challenges, rather than a worn-out victim of the twenty-first century's pressures. That is the Stress Cure and we wish you well on your journey towards stress-free living.

Susannah Lawson and Patrick Holford

PART 1

The Stress Trap

How did you come to be so stressed? We bet that's a hard question to answer, as it just kind of happens to most of us as life unfolds. In this part of the book we look at the mechanisms that physically manifest stress in our bodies, and how our lifestyles and everyday habits perpetuate a vicious cycle where we ricochet back and forth between feeling wired and tired. But we begin by throwing you a lifeline in Chapter 1 and offering several quick fixes that will help you feel better right now.

CHAPTER 1

Don't Panic – Quick Fixes to Feel Better Now

When you're feeling stressed and tired, the last thing you need is another thing to do or think about. But you are probably also aware that if you carry on as you are, it's unlikely that things will get better on their own. Only by making some positive changes will you start to feel less overwhelmed and better able to cope with life's challenges.

Sometimes it helps to remember a quote from *Hamlet*:

There is nothing either good or bad but thinking makes it so.

Life happens – it's your reaction that counts. So, if you can increase your energy levels, achieve a calmer state of mind and build greater resilience, then you'll be better equipped to deal with the challenges that cause you stress. You're also likely to start enjoying your life a whole lot more than you may think possible now.

For starters, if you are in a fix and you need some instant help, this list is for you. Please remember, these measures are designed to start you off on the road to feeling less stressed. Throughout the rest of the book you will discover the full Stress Cure programme, which will be personal to you and depend on your unique set of circumstances. If you truly want to beat stress and fatigue, embracing a comprehensive approach that addresses the key contributory physical, emotional and mental factors will bring you the biggest rewards.

Seven stress relievers for an instant fix

1. Swap coffee or regular tea for green tea. While you'll still get a caffeine kick, green tea also contains a calming substance called theanine, which can make you more alert without feeling wired.

2. Eat three meals a day and *never* skip breakfast. This helps you keep your blood sugar even. Blood sugar dips either from not eating or as a rebound after eating something too sweet or starchy. This triggers adrenalin release, and hence stress.

3. Eat protein with every meal – for example, eggs, yoghurt, smoked salmon or kippers with your breakfast; and meat, fish, dairy foods, soya or grains combined with pulses for your lunch and supper. For inspiration, see the quick reference table on page 264 of Chapter 23, which also includes a section on what to choose when eating out (page 282).

4. Snack pre-emptively – if you know you have an energy dip before lunch and around 4 p.m., have a snack mid-morning and again mid-afternoon. Avoid sugar-loaded treats and instead opt for energy-sustaining fresh fruit and nuts, an oat-cake with some cheese, nut butter, paté or hummus, a natural yoghurt and berries, or a sugar-free protein bar (see Resources, page 309, for suggestions).

5. Supplement a high-strength multivitamin and mineral, plus the extra energy-boosting and calming nutrients outlined in the core supplement plan in Chapter 22 (pages 256–59).

6. Turn to Chapter 12 and learn the HeartMath® Quick Coherence® technique (page 129), then introduce it into your daily schedule. (It takes only five minutes, but it's important to commit to doing it every day.) This simple technique will help you to reset to a state of calm and reduce levels of harmful stress hormones while increasing beneficial revitalising ones.

7. If you sleep badly, avoid any caffeine after midday and alcohol in the evening, adopt a relaxing bedtime routine (for example,

have a warm bath with lavender or Epsom salts) and do your HeartMath exercise again before going to sleep. (When you're ready, see Chapter 11 for more on sleep.)

Finally, if you feel your situation is particularly complex and requires specialist help, book a nutrition consultation with a therapist who specialises in stress, and get a tailor-made programme to follow with all the guidance you need (see Resources at the end of the book). It will demand only a few hours of your time and you'll benefit from bespoke support that will consolidate what you'll learn from reading this book.

CHAPTER 2

From Wired to Tired ... and Back Again

The sensations of persistent stress and lack of energy are two of the most commonly experienced symptoms of ill-health. In our 100% Health survey of more than 55,000 people, lack of energy was the most common health complaint, with only 4 per cent of respondents claiming optimum energy and 81 per cent reporting low energy. Feeling impatient was the next most common symptom of stress, experienced by 82 per cent of respondents, followed by having too much to do and feeling anxious or getting tense easily.[1]

We define health as an abundance of well-being, characterised by a consistently good level of energy, emotional balance, a sharp mind and the ability to cope with life's stresses. Feeling tired for much of the time, or spending most of the day stressed out with a knot in your stomach, is not healthy.

Yet, in the twenty-first century, this poor state of being has become the norm. For many of us, our performance may be somewhat blunted, the spark in life somewhat dim, but we just get on with it. At the other end of the scale are those with chronic fatigue who can barely function, let alone hold down a job, and those who are so anxious or stressed out that life is a perpetual emotional rollercoaster.

Everyday sources of stress

Stress can take many forms – mental, physical, emotional and environmental – and all of these can contribute to your overall stress load.

Everyday sources of stress

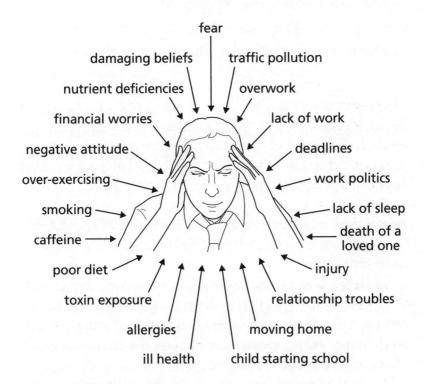

The cascade of stress

So what exactly is stress? Is it a thought, a reaction, or something physical? The answer is all of these and more besides. Let's look at what actually happens to you when you experience an event that you perceive to be stressful:

- Your thought is registered in the cerebral cortex of your brain and carried to the hypothalamus, the brain's 'master gland', which can then stimulate a reaction throughout the body.

- The hypothalamus activates your autonomic nervous system (ANS), which controls essential bodily functions such as breathing and heartbeat. Your ANS has two strands – the sympathetic nervous system (SNS) and the parasympathetic nervous system (PNS). When you register stress, it's the SNS that springs into action, preparing your body for 'fight or flight' – because even if there is no physical danger, you still react to a stressful event as if there is.

- The SNS alerts your adrenal glands to pump out the hormones adrenalin and noradrenalin. These, along with other chemicals released into your blood, trigger an increase in heart rate, boost blood flow to your arms and legs, dilate your pupils to enhance peripheral vision, increase perspiration, stimulate mental activity and concentration, release calcium from your bones to aid blood clotting, and release sugar stores into your bloodstream – all to make you physically ready to deal with the 'danger' you are facing as if it were literally life-threatening.

- The SNS also shuts down non-essential bodily functions and so reduces digestive activity, immune action, repair and regeneration.

- At the same time, the hypothalamus stimulates the pituitary gland (another component of your brain that controls hormones) to release adrenocorticotrophic hormone (ACTH) into your bloodstream. This stimulates your adrenal glands to release another hormone – cortisol – which is longer-lasting than adrenalin. In the short term, cortisol reduces allergic reactions and inflammation while also suppressing immune activity. (In the long term, this leaves you more susceptible to infection.)

- ACTH stimulates your adrenal glands to release another hormone – aldosterone – which increases blood volume; hence, your blood pressure increases.

- Your pituitary gland also releases thyroid-stimulating hormone (TSH) to stimulate your thyroid gland to produce yet another hormone, thyroxine. This increases your metabolic rate, raises the level of sugar in your blood to provide fuel, increases heart and respiration rates, sends your blood pressure up, and increases intestinal motility movement (this can trigger diarrhoea, a common side-effect when you experience a particularly stressful event).

As you can see, just one stressful thought can trigger a whole load of physical reactions. And while this complex cascade is designed to increase your survival chances in the short term, if you keep triggering this response over the long term, you'll move from feeling wired to feeling tired, and eventually you'll become exhausted. The stress response puts you into overdrive to deal with a short-term emergency, but remaining in overdrive is very draining. That's why your body starts to malfunction and you become continually tired and/or more prone to infection. You may find you overreact to stressful situations, feel depressed and find life less enjoyable. Reduced ability to focus and failing memory are also common.

The good news is that it is possible to become more resilient to the stresses of life, feel better and have plenty of energy – to enjoy life again. That is what our Stress Cure programme will give you. Following it requires a whole new understanding of our design as human beings: how we make energy; how we are designed to respond to stress; the nature of our minds; how we have evolved to need certain chemicals or nutrients, and why others tend to throw everything out of balance.

In short, feeling stressed and tired is a sign that you are having difficulty adapting to the myriad challenges that modern life presents – nutritional, chemical, physical, social and psychological. To get a better idea of why this happens, we need to understand how we arrived at this point; and to do that, we need to look back at our human history.

Increasing our chemical load

We need to widen our perspective for a minute to review the chemical history of mankind. For three million years, we were hunter/gatherers, eating 100 per cent natural (and mostly raw) food. As we evolved into peasant farmers, we spent the next 10,000 years eating whole, organic food. Then ... *wham!* The Industrial Revolution occurred and the modern-day diet of refined, processed, high-fat, high-sugar foods was born. Developments in manufacturing and other industries have also flooded our world with man-made chemicals. More than 10 million are now registered with the American Chemical Society: 3500 of which are in our food, with 3000 more in household products, from toiletries to cleaning materials.[2] Then there are pollutants, pesticides, water contaminants and a host of other potentially harmful substances in our immediate environment.

The result of all this is that anyone's blood sample can now contain hundreds of chemicals that were never part of the evolutionary design of *Homo sapiens*. This, in itself, puts stress on the human system. And when you are stressed, your need for nutrients increases. Yet, sadly, as modern methods of intensive farming and food processing continue to advance, the very food that should nourish us is becoming ever more depleted and further removed from what we evolved to eat.

The animals we eat are not fit, but fat. Most vegetables are artificially stimulated to grow fast with chemical fertilisers and sprayed with pesticides. Instead of eating whole fruit, we extract the sugar and eat that, or drink high-sugar juice. Most of the grains we eat are refined, removing many of their nutrients. But that is only half the story: we actually eat half as much as our ancestors because we are less than half as physically active. That means we have less food (and remember our ancestors' diet was all whole, unrefined food) from which to get our nutrients. Most of us fail to get even the minimum recommended daily allowances (RDAs) of essential nutrients, let alone the levels that support optimum health.[3] Is it any wonder most people don't function to their best potential?

Declining physical activity

Human beings were very physically active for 3 million years. We even have a 'fifth gear', triggered by the release of adrenalin, which gives us an energy shot and increases our physical ability to handle an emergency situation (as described in detail on page 12). For our ancestors, stress required this action-supporting response – to fight or take flight from predators.

Today, stress is induced by pressure at work, traffic jams, financial problems, world news, rows with a partner or watching a scary film. On a physiological level, we still perceive these as threats, yet they rarely require a physical response. So how does your body cope with all the hormones released in a state of stress, chemicals that are designed to be burned off by physical activity?

Modern man expends a fraction of the physical energy of our ancestors, while many of us do not have the basic fitness to do more than a few press-ups or sit-ups. We live in a push-button world where many of our former activities have been replaced by an energy-saving gadget. But whose energy are we really saving? There's an old Chinese proverb: 'He who chops wood gets warm twice.' The challenge today is to redesign our physical lives to promote better health and vitality.

Psychological pressures

On a social and psychological level, our complex modern world has changed beyond all recognition. Only three generations ago, a person's life presented two major decisions: who to marry and which profession to follow. Today, on average, 42 per cent of marriages end in divorce, with almost half of these occurring within the first ten years.[4] Most people move from one relationship to another, with all the stresses of new beginnings and separations, especially when children are involved. The same is true for work, with many people changing jobs every four years.

Ironically, while we expect our standard of living to be rising, many of us are working harder than ever before and enjoying less leisure time, while others have to cope with the stress of unemployment. The rapid development of new technologies places us on an endless learning curve just to stand still. Even when on holiday, most of us check our emails several times a day; and one in five young Americans admit to checking their smartphones *during* sex! It isn't rare to wake up with one's mind racing with an endless 'to do' list and to spend most of the day with thoughts spinning like a carousel. Experts estimate we can have as many as 50,000 thoughts a day; but the vast majority of them, an estimated 95 per cent, are repeats.

Maladaptation

Maybe we're good at adapting and everything is fine. Maybe we're not. Our ability to adapt depends on having fully functioning nervous, endocrine (hormonal) and immune systems. So perhaps it's no coincidence that hormonal problems – such as infertility, menopausal and andropausal (male menopause) issues, underactive thyroid, breast and prostate cancer – are rising; that mental health problems, from depression and anxiety to schizophrenia, now affect one in four people each year in Britain[5]; that Alzheimer's is reaching epidemic proportions; that 10 per cent of children are diagnosed with ADHD; that chronic fatigue syndrome, allergies and inflammatory health problems – from asthma to eczema – are increasing rapidly in children and adults alike. These are all signs of maladaptation.

At the very least, an inability to adapt manifests as a lack of energy, poor concentration and memory, feeling tired all the time and being unable to cope with stress. Sadly, the thousands who trudge to their doctor in search of a solution are often sent away empty handed and told simply, 'That's life, I'm afraid.' Or they are given medication to treat the psychological issues that are mistakenly believed to underpin these 'inexplicable' symptoms.

How to adapt and thrive

If this sounds all too familiar, don't lose heart. This book will show you how to adapt and flourish in these stressful times. The twenty-first century requires new and improved ways to communicate, organise and behave for a better world. It also requires a new approach to taking care of our bodies, including adjusting our diet and lifestyle.

Imagine how much better you will feel when you have consistently high energy, emotional balance, a sharp mind and memory, and the ability to deal well with life's inevitable stresses. We know this is well within your reach because we have worked with hundreds of clients and seen them reverse fatigue, build resilience to stress and resolve a host of other health issues they didn't even know were the consequences of stress when they came to see us.

In a pilot study Patrick conducted at the Institute for Optimum Nutrition, which involved giving participants 'optimum nutrition achieved with dietary changes plus supplements', 79 per cent noticed an improvement in energy, 60 per cent had better memory and mental alertness, and 66 per cent felt more emotionally balanced. Over half, 54 per cent, had rated high on a simple stress check (similar to the one shown overleaf), scoring five or more 'yes' answers. But after six months of following an optimum nutrition programme, the number with a high stress rating had dropped to 28 per cent.

So simple nutritional changes almost halved the number of high-stress scorers, even though the questions used to assess stress had nothing to do with nutrition. What this illustrates is that what you put into your body has a very powerful effect on your energy and your ability to adapt to and cope with stress on a mental, emotional, physical and chemical level.

Test your stress

- Is your energy less now than it used to be?
- Do you feel guilty when relaxing?
- Do you have a persistent need for achievement?
- Are you unclear about your goals in life?
- Are you especially competitive?
- Do you work harder than most people?
- Do you become angry easily?
- Do challenging situations trigger anxiety or panic?
- Do you often try to do two or three tasks simultaneously?
- Do you find it hard to relax or switch off?
- Do you avoid exercise because you feel too tired?
- Do you get impatient if people or situations hold you up?
- Do you have difficulty getting to sleep, or staying asleep?
- Do you wake up feeling tired?

If you answer yes to five or more, that's a fair indication you're highly stressed. The higher your score, the greater the negative impact of stress on your life.

Redo this stress test after you've followed the 30-day Stress Cure programme, as explained in Part 6, to see the difference.

The chemicals of communication

The body's adaptive system is based on maintaining a balance in the chemicals of communication, whose job is to keep you 'well tuned' and functioning at your peak. These chemicals are primarily hormones, neurotransmitters and immune cells and signallers, all of which are covered in more detail in the following chapters.

Each of these substances is made from the food that you eat. If you don't have the right supply, the communication network starts to break down. Imagine your body as a city, full of different workers, businesses, trading routes for importing and exporting all the necessary goods, plus communication and delivery networks. If there's a shortage of essentials, or a strike on the transport system, nothing runs smoothly. Everything slows down. Harmony is lost. Stress levels rise. This is what happens to us when our total input – nutritional, environmental, psychological and physical – doesn't meet our needs, or exceeds our ability to adapt. The symptoms are stress and fatigue.

The following chapters explain how this jigsaw puzzle fits together. Certain pieces of the puzzle will be more important for some people than for others. However, somewhere within the overall picture, you will find the key pieces to help *you* improve *your* vitality, sense of well-being and resilience to stress.

CHAPTER 3

Unravelling the Vicious Cycle of Stress and Fatigue

Stress and fatigue are nothing new. Throughout history, man has searched for ways to reduce the negative impact of both. This has led to the concentration of sugar and stimulants – for example, those found in coffee, tea, tobacco, chocolate and sweets – to give us a boost. Consumption of these stimulating substances really took off as 'worker drugs' during the Industrial Revolution.

However, whereas our ancestors struggled through hard, physically demanding lives, toiling in the fields and worrying about putting enough food on the table, these days many of us suffer as a consequence of our fast-paced but sedentary lifestyles and affluent malnutrition. There is an abundance of food for Westerners to eat, but – because much of it is refined and processed – a paucity of the nutrients we need to function at our best. As well as consuming fewer wholefoods, we eat far less than our ancestors did because we don't expend the same energy. As a result, we don't get the same amounts of essential micronutrients. According to a review in the *Journal of the Royal Society of Medicine*, the most practical solution is to supplement the difference.[6] But not many people do, so the result is that most of us are sub-optimally nourished, which means that our bodies' cells cannot make energy efficiently. One of the first signs of sub-optimal nutrition is fatigue.

As we saw in Chapter 2, just one stressful thought can trigger a complex and extensive cascade of biochemical activity throughout your body. This uses up a huge amount of nutrients. So, if you are not ingesting an optimal level of nutrition – and frequent stress is contributing to an even bigger deficit – you are likely to function even less effectively. As a result you will feel more tired, find life's challenges more stressful and suffer a host of other symptoms, from brain fog to loss of libido.

What do most people do to counteract this? They look for a pick-me-up. Or, as we'll see shortly, they just get stressed again, as this triggers the release of yet more stress hormones that deliver a quick burst of energy to keep them going.

The urge to refuel

Ever had an 'I'd kill for a cake' moment? Or perhaps you longed for a double espresso, a bar of chocolate or even a piece of toast? Whatever the object of your desire, the urge to get it probably felt overwhelming at the time. Yet, this is a perfectly normal reaction to low energy, which is often caused by a low level of fuel in your system. For humans, our primary fuel is glucose, commonly known as sugar.

We get this from eating carbohydrates. Your digestive system breaks down carbohydrates into single molecules of glucose, which are absorbed into your bloodstream and then transported into cells to make energy. An ideal scenario is that we eat the right amount of *slow-releasing* carbohydrates to provide a steady flow of glucose to keep our blood sugar stable and supply a ready source of energy for our body and brain. The problem is that most of us don't do this: we eat too much refined, *fast-releasing* carbohydrates and skip meals, resulting in erratic blood sugar levels that peak and trough throughout the day, with our energy and concentration levels mirroring that yoyo pattern.

During the troughs we crave sweet foods or stimulants, or possibly even manoeuvre ourselves into more stressful situations (waiting until the last minute to hit a deadline or not leaving enough time to catch a train comfortably, for example). Sweet foods provide sugar directly, while stimulants and stress stimulate the adrenal glands to pump out hormones that also increase blood sugar. Whichever route you take, you initiate the express delivery of energy-giving glucose to your cells. There is a significant cost to this express delivery, though: it quickly leads to a deficiency in key nutrients and fluctuating blood sugar and energy levels. This is why you may experience a considerable dip in energy and concentration a few hours after taking in sugar or stimulants or finding yourself in a stressful situation. For example, have you ever felt sleepy after eating a bag of sweets or a sugary dessert? And how do many people attempt to combat that? With more sugar, stimulants or stress. And so the cycle continues.

Clearly, many of us wouldn't consciously choose to feel stressed, but we can unconsciously set ourselves up for situations that fuel our adrenalin addiction, as this is how we've learned to operate. Sugar and stimulants are also addictive, and not just because they fuel the highs that pick us up from the lows: they can also trigger a release of the body's own 'feel-good' chemicals – opioids and dopamine.

Addicted to sugar and stimulants

Animals can become addicted to sugar and show all the telltale withdrawal symptoms, including the shakes, when deprived of it, according to research conducted by Dr Bartley Hoebel and colleagues at Princeton University.[7] This is because the more you over-stimulate the release of dopamine, the more insensitive to its effects you become. In a sense, you are becoming 'dopamine-resistant' so you crave something to stimulate your own natural dopamine high – perhaps sugar, alcohol or caffeine. This upsets your blood sugar level, which impacts on your energy, mood and resilience to stress, as well as on your ability to control your weight.

Dr Candace Pert, a former research professor in the Physiology and Biophysics Department at Georgetown University Medical Center in Washington, DC, has said: 'I consider sugar to be a drug, a highly purified plant product that can become addictive. Relying on an artificial form of glucose – sugar – to give us a quick pick-me-up is analogous to, if not as dangerous as, shooting heroin.'[8] Dr Pert was one of a group of scientists who discovered the central role endorphins, which activate opioids, play in addiction. There's certainly plenty of research out there to support her view.[9]

It's clear that consuming sugar, nicotine or caffeine in colas, energy drinks, coffee, tea and chocolate – along with the stresses of twenty-first-century life – can seriously mess with your blood sugar. In our 100% Health survey, a high consumption of sugar-based snacks, added sugar or tea/coffee/cola nearly doubled the likelihood of very low energy levels.

So why do we do it? The answer is that millions of us are caught in the vicious cycle of blood sugar highs and lows, and we feel exhausted and stressed much of the time. Stimulants promise instant energy and short-term resilience, but in reality, of course, they make the problem worse.

We may be eating fast-releasing carbohydrates, devoid of vitamins and minerals. We may be drinking two or three cups of coffee before noon just to deal with our morning weariness. We 'learn' how to cope with the rebound blood sugar low after a meal by having a coffee. If we haven't eaten for two hours, we grab yet another coffee. And when we drag ourselves home after a hard day's work, we may drink even more just to stay awake, and then some alcohol to help us switch off the adrenalin and get a few hours' sleep.

By now you probably understand why stress, sugar and stimulants can be so addictive. (You know you're addicted if you suffer withdrawal effects after 48 hours without any of them.) As well as messing with your energy levels, they can also deplete your health.

Our bodies have a finite capacity to detoxify undesirable substances. Excessive intake of sugar and stimulants, coupled with sub-optimal nutrition, starts to overload the body's detoxification capacity. Once you've exceeded this adaptive capacity, your ability to cope with the otherwise normal stresses of modern living is compromised.

This is the beginning of chronic fatigue, allergies and intolerance, chemical sensitivity, low tolerance of alcohol and smoke, depression, mood swings and feeling out of control. The body is now, effectively, in a state of red alert, and with that comes increased risk of inflammatory diseases such as asthma and eczema, joint pain and headaches, as well as aching, tight muscles that never seem to relax. If left unchecked, these symptoms can mark the start of more serious degenerative diseases.

It's the same with our minds. We have a finite capacity to deal with situations we perceive to be stressful and difficult. If we become overloaded, our ability to deal with new challenges is compromised and we can start to overreact, feel overwhelmed, lose focus and get depressed or overly anxious.

The road to wellness

The road to recovery requires some major dietary, lifestyle and mindset changes. As a result of the body's lack of health reserves, it becomes necessary, for a while, to clean up your act *completely*. This means avoiding all stimulants and toxic substances and focusing on consuming only highly nutritious foods, plus high levels of key nutrients by taking specific nutritional supplements. We also invite you to have a good look at how your beliefs, your attitude and how you spend your time impact on your stress levels. This approach is clearly outlined in the following chapters of this book.

Once you've built up a good health reserve, there's no need to be quite so saintly all the time. A strong body can cope with the occasional indulgence. And once you're back on track, if you're doing something that doesn't suit you, your body is far more likely to let you know about it. By then, with extra awareness based on your experience, you'll be less inclined to override your body's warning signals and more likely to avoid another vicious cycle of stress and fatigue. The tools we share in the Reset Your

Mindset section (Part 4) will also equip you to deal with stressful events both now and in the future.

First, though, we need to get to grips with the vicious cycle of stress and fatigue and learn how to avoid it or recover from it. That means delving deeper into how the body makes and maintains its energy. As we've seen, your body's primary fuel is carbohydrate, which consists of glucose – or sugar. So balancing your blood sugar level is critical to maintaining a high energy level and an ability to cope with stress.

The vicious cycle of stress and fatigue

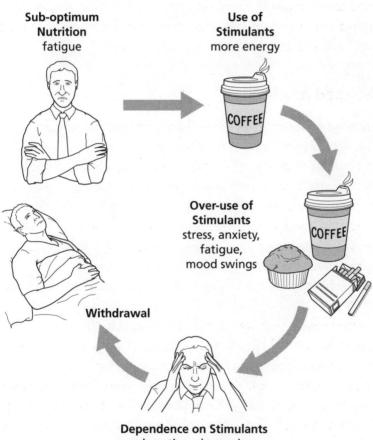

Sub-optimum Nutrition
fatigue

Use of Stimulants
more energy

Over-use of Stimulants
stress, anxiety, fatigue, mood swings

Withdrawal

Dependence on Stimulants
exhaustion, depression, chronic fatigue, can't cope with stress

PART 2

Boost Your Energy Reserves

When you're feeling tired, you are less able to deal with life's pressures. So the first part of becoming more stress resilient is to boost your energy reserves. In this section you'll find out how (and why) what you eat and drink and the everyday habits you've adopted have a direct impact on how you feel. We also look at the complex dance of stress and other hormones that goes on inside your body – and how an imbalance in one area has a knock-on effect on another. We then explain how to gauge where you are in the stress stakes, and what you can do to feel great again.

CHAPTER 4

Beat the Blood Sugar Blues

You are solar-powered. The energy in the food you eat comes from the sun. Plants use that energy to combine water from the soil and carbon dioxide from the air to make carbohydrate. You eat the plant, break the carbohydrate down into glucose and release the sun's energy contained within it.

Almost all of your body's energy is derived from glucose – a single molecule of sugar. This is your main fuel and what you eat determines the quality, quantity and availability of glucose to all your body's cells, including your brain. Consequently, maintaining an even blood sugar level is of paramount importance and is key for energy, resilience to stress and overall good health.

What's more, unbalanced blood sugar – yoyoing from high to low, which is a tendency we see in many of our clients – creates significant stress on your body. The fuel that glucose provides not only ensures you have enough energy to function in your external world; it also ensures your body is able to carry out all of its vital activities in your internal world (digestion, immune response, tissue repair and so on). Your brain, for example, is your body's largest consumer of glucose, as it needs a continuous source of fuel to operate, even when you're asleep. So when your brain detects that your blood sugar is falling, it immediately starts sending messages to rectify the situation, including releasing 'hunger' hormones. This can make you start to feel peckish. A little snack of an apple or some nuts would be ideal, but the chances are that you will push on through this feeling until the message becomes stronger. Then you might go for a coffee or a cigarette – or succumb to a chocolate craving.

The problem here is that all of these substances are stimulants and, as you'll see in Chapter 6, they trigger the release of stress hormones, adrenalin and cortisol. These cause your blood sugar to rise by triggering another hormone – glucagon – to break down the emergency reserves of glucose (in the form of glycogen) that are stored in your liver and muscles. So, even if you have very little external stress in your life, if your blood sugar is imbalanced, you trigger a stress reaction every time it dips too low – and this could happen multiple times during the course of a typical day.

The sugar cycle

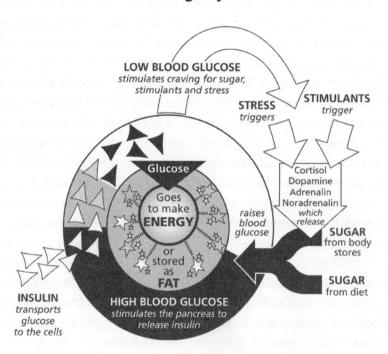

The sugar cycle: Eating sugar increases blood glucose levels. The body releases the hormone insulin to help escort glucose out of your blood and into the cells, to make energy or to be stored as fat. This causes blood glucose levels to fall. Eating will raise levels again. Feeling stressed or consuming a stimulant, such as caffeine, will also raise blood glucose by triggering the release of adrenal hormones to unlock the body's emergency stores of sugar (glycogen). Low blood glucose is perceived as a stress and increases cravings for something sweet or a stimulant.

Regulating our high-octane fuel

While we need sugar to make energy, glucose – the end product of carbohydrate digestion – is a high-octane fuel. Left unchecked, too much of it causes advanced glycation end products (known as AGEs), which damage your cells as well as your arteries, and cause harm all around your body, literally accelerating the ageing process. That's why diabetics, who have an impaired ability to control their blood sugar, are far more susceptible to nerve and eye damage, ulcerated skin and heart disease.

To maintain blood sugar at an optimum level, you produce a hormone called insulin, which is triggered each time your blood sugar rises. Insulin's job is to escort the sugar out of your blood and into your cells, to make energy. When you eat a diet high in sugar and refined carbohydrates, you need to produce more insulin to manage this process. Over time, your cells can become less sensitive to the insulin message. It's as if they become deaf to insulin's cries to 'open the door' and let in the sugar. When this happens, your liver steps in to remove the excess sugar from your blood by converting it into fat and storing it, most notably around your middle. The problem is that you are now making less energy, so you feel tired. When you're tired, you're more likely to reach for something sweet or a stimulant – such as a cup of tea or coffee or a cigarette – to pep you up. And so the cycle continues. Over time, you can end up with something called insulin resistance. According to Professor Gerald Reaven from Stanford University in California – one of the world's leading experts on blood sugar problems – the majority of obese people and 25 per cent of non-obese people are insulin resistant.[1]

If you find yourself feeling tired after eating and also suffering with brain fog, low mood and reduced resilience to coping with stressful situations, you might well be on the path to insulin resistance. This is far more likely if you are also storing your food as fat, rather than converting it to make energy (weight gain is explored in more detail in Chapter 20). Over the long term, insulin resistance can lead to diabetes, which now affects an estimated one in six people over the age of 40 in most developed countries throughout the world.[2]

Are you insulin resistant?

You can get a good idea of where you stand on the road to insulin resistance and loss of blood sugar control by completing the questionnaire below. Score one point for each 'yes' answer.

- Are you rarely wide awake within 20 minutes of getting up?
- Do you need tea, coffee, a cigarette or something similar to get you going in the morning?
- Do you really like sweet foods?
- Do you crave bread, cereal or pasta most days?
- Do you feel as if you 'need' an alcoholic drink most days?
- Are you overweight and unable to shift the extra pounds?
- Do you often have energy slumps during the day or after meals?
- Do you often have mood swings or difficulty concentrating?
- Do you fall asleep in the early evening or need naps during the day?
- Do you avoid exercise because you haven't got the energy?
- Do you get dizzy or irritable if you go six hours without food?
- Do you find you often overreact to stress?
- Do you often get irritable, angry or aggressive unexpectedly?
- Do you have less energy now than in the past?
- Do you get night sweats or suffer with frequent headaches?
- Do you ever lie about how much sweet food you have eaten?

- Do you ever keep a supply of sweet food close to hand?
- Do you ever go out of your way to make sure you have something sweet?
- Do you feel you could never give up bread?
- Do you think of yourself as addicted to sugar, chocolate or biscuits?

If you answered 'yes' to ten or more of these questions, there's a very good chance that you are insulin resistant and struggling to keep your blood sugar level even. The single best way to know where you stand is to measure your level of glycosylated haemoglobin (also known as HbA1c) via a standard blood test, available through a nutritional therapist, your GP or a medical laboratory (see Resources). This is a measure of how often your blood sugar level peaks too high. When that happens, red blood cells effectively become sugar-coated. That's what glycosylated haemoglobin means: sugar-coated red blood cells. And it's the 'glycosylation' of cells that causes long-term damage. (Note: in the US, glycosylation is called 'glycation'.) This test is much better than a single blood glucose test because it provides a long-term measure of your blood sugar control rather than just a snapshot of a single point in time. That's because red blood cells live for three months, so it's a 90-day record of your blood sugar spikes. Ideally, you should have a level below 5 per cent for optimal blood sugar control and certainly below 6.5 per cent. Most diabetics have a level above 7 per cent. If yours is above 6.5 per cent, we recommend you see your GP.

Fuel yourself right

The way to stabilise your blood sugar, reduce any resistance to insulin and increase your energy levels and ability to cope with stress is to eat the right kind of fuel (that is, slow-releasing carbohydrates) in the right amounts.

The mechanisms by which blood sugar control works have an effect on your energy, mood, weight, ability to deal with stress and long-term health. Some carbohydrates are fast-releasing in that they raise blood sugar quickly, while others are slow-releasing. Fast-releasing foods are like rocket fuel: they give you a quick burst of energy but have a rapid burnout. The slow-releasing foods are much more sustaining, giving a consistent energy level. Eating slow-releasing carbohydrates is a vital part of the energy equation.

What makes a food slow- or fast-releasing depends on many factors. Foods contain different kinds of sugars. Most fruits, for example, are rich in slower-releasing fructose. Berries, cherries and plums have the slowest-releasing sugar of all – xylose. By contrast, most puddings and sweet treats are rich in fast-releasing sucrose or glucose. The carbohydrates in some foods are complex in structure, and the body needs a long time to digest them and break them down into simple sugars. This is true for wholegrains, such as wholewheat pasta and brown rice. Oats are especially good because their 'soluble' fibre slows down carbohydrate digestion.

The glycemic index – and why it is only part of the story

The measure of a food's fast- or slow-releasing effect is linked to the degree to which it raises your blood sugar in relation to glucose: the scale is called the glycemic index (or GI). Glucose has a GI of 100. So, if a food has a GI of 50, the kind of sugar it contains raises your blood sugar half as much as the same amount of pure glucose.

You may be familiar with the GI, as there are various GI-related diets and branded products out there. But there is a problem: while the GI of a food is a *qualitative* measure that tells you whether the kind of carbohydrate in the food converts rapidly or slowly into glucose (thus whether it is fast- or slow-releasing), it does not tell you *how much* of that food is carbohydrate. This creates practical problems if you rely only on the GI score of a food. For example, carrots (92), broad beans (79) and watermelon (72) all have high GIs, which means the sugar in them is akin to glucose. But they all contain very small *quantities* of this sugar: an 80g cupful of carrots or broad beans contains only about 5g of carbohydrate, while a big (120g) slice of watermelon has just 6g (roughly a teaspoon of sugar). On the other hand, white rice has a GI of just 56 and a typical chocolate or confectionary bar between 55 and 65. So, relying purely on GI, they seem better than those wonderfully healthy carrots, broad beans and watermelon, all of which are packed full of vitamins and minerals. In fact, a typical 150g portion of rice contains 42g of carbohydrate, and a typical 54g chocolate or confectionary bar has 30–35g (7 teaspoons of sugar). So, you would have to eat six carrots or six large slices of watermelon to get the same amount of sugar as you would find in a single chocolate bar.

This lies at the heart of why the GI alone is rather misleading.

It's the GL that counts

This is where the glycemic load – or GL – comes in. It's the best way to tell how a food will affect your blood sugar, and so impact on your energy levels, your mood and your ability to deal with stress. GL is a simple calculation that takes into account *both* the GI (quality) of carbohydrate in a food *and* the amount (quantity). To get a food's GL, you multiply its GI by the amount of carbo-hydrate in a typical portion. The result will tell you *exactly* what a given serving of that food will do to your blood sugar. We've worked out the GL scores of literally hundreds of foods and you can find a full list in Patrick's *Low-GL Diet Counter* book, or at the back of the *Low-GL Diet Bible*. Alternatively, go to www.patrickholford.com and click on 'low GL' to see the website's GL counter.

The chart overleaf shows a number of high- and low-GL foods. The quantities given all equal 10 GLs: so, for example, two punnets of strawberries have the same GL score as just two dates.

GL scores of common foods

2 slices wholegrain rye bread	1 slice white bread
2 large punnets strawberries	2 dates
1 large bowl peanuts	1 packet of crisps
3 bowls muesli (sugar-free)	1 bowl cornflakes
2 medium carrots	5 French fries
1 carton orange juice	1 glass of Lucozade

All these foods contain the equivalent of 10 GL points, but those in the left-hand column contain more slow-releasing carbohydrate (hence you can eat more of them), while those on the right are fast-releasing.

Knowing the GL score of foods allows you to assess if they will sustain your energy and increase your resilience to stress, or send you on a rollercoaster ride of energy highs and lows that make you more likely to overreact to everyday situations.

Moreover, foods with a higher GL score can lead to weight gain if you eat too much of them (see Chapter 20).

Food combining

It is not just the type of sugar in a food that makes it fast- or slow-releasing.[3] The presence of certain kinds of fibre slows down the release of sugars, so wholefoods are much better for you than refined foods, from which the fibre and many of the vitamins and minerals are removed. It is therefore better to eat wholemeal bread, brown rice and wholewheat pasta than the white versions. And fresh fruit, which contains fibre, is better than fruit juice. The presence of protein in a food also lowers its glycemic load. That's one reason why beans and lentils, which are high in protein and fibre, have such low GL scores.

Combining protein-rich foods with slow-releasing carbohydrates further helps to control blood sugar levels. Protein foods tend to prompt a small and equal insulin release. Carbohydrates, especially fast-releasing ones, prompt a large insulin release. Eating fat has little direct effect on insulin.

The best carbs to choose for energy

By now, you're no doubt beginning to appreciate that eating whole and unrefined foods is the best option for sustained energy and greater resilience to stress. To repeat, you should eat wholegrain bread, rice and pasta instead of white.

But how a food is processed makes a difference, too. When wheat is turned into pasta the GL score is low, especially if it's wholegrain. But when wheat flour is used to make bread, cakes, biscuits or pastry, the GL score increases. This happens because the sugar, yeast and raising agents used create bubbles that help to generate more heat during cooking. This, combined with the longer baking process, turns the more complex sugars into fast-releasing fuel, especially if the wheat flour used is refined (i.e. white). Therefore, wholewheat pasta is far better than white bread for blood sugar balance. The best bread is a Scandinavian-style wholegrain rye bread in which you can still see the wholegrains. It is far closer to raw than a French baguette, and there's a world of difference between their GL effects.

Oats are among the best grains. While the GL of wheat varies depending on how it is processed, oats are the same in every shape and form. Whole oat flakes, rolled oats or oatmeal, as used in oatcakes, all have a low glycemic load.[4]

Fruit and veg

As you will probably understand by now, starchy vegetables, such as potatoes, parsnips, swede and sweetcorn, are more fast-releasing than non-starchy broccoli, spinach, kale, tomatoes and lettuce. Processing and cooking again affect how quickly all of these foods release their energy: baking a potato for an hour in the oven converts much of its carbohydrate content to instantly absorbable sugar, whereas steaming a new potato for 15 minutes leaves more intact for you to digest at a slower pace.

When it comes to fruit, as the taste will testify, all contain sugar. But fruit sugar, fructose, is slower-releasing because it takes longer to break down. Some fruits – such as grapes, pineapples, mangoes and bananas – also contain varying amounts of fast-releasing glucose. That's why a banana may be fine to eat when you've just climbed a mountain and need an instant glucose boost, but it's certainly not the best daily snack while you're sitting at a desk. Berries are the slowest-releasing, which is why blackberries, blueberries, raspberries, strawberries and cherries make such good energy-sustaining snacks; and the same is true for plums. Their main sugar is xylose, which is slower-releasing than fructose. Pears, peaches, oranges, cantaloupe or watermelon and apricots also release their energy more slowly than apples, kiwi fruit and dried fruit.

It should be noted that many so-called 'sugar-free' foods use fruit juice concentrate as a sweetener. Grape juice is akin to pure glucose, so beware. Much better is apple juice concentrate, which is high in fructose and therefore takes longer to break down.

Food frequency

Of course, how often you eat is just as important as what you eat. Eating regular meals and snacks is crucial to ensure you have a consistent supply of energy and don't cause yourself stress from low blood sugar. Breakfast, as the name suggests, is when you break the night's fast. If you've not eaten since 8 p.m. and get up at 7 a.m., that's 11 hours without food. Fail to refuel and you'll start pumping out adrenalin to deal with your low blood sugar. So, always aim to eat a good breakfast. Oats with chopped fruit, natural yoghurt and seeds, or scrambled eggs with rye toast are two good options. Chapter 23 provides many more suggestions.

Lunch and supper are equally important for refuelling throughout the day. Aim for slow-releasing carbohydrates combined with protein (again, see Chapter 23 for ideas). And if you find yourself losing concentration or experiencing energy dips – and especially if you answered 'yes' to ten or more of the questions in our insulin resistance questionnaire – aim to have a mid-morning and a mid-afternoon snack. For example, a piece of fruit and a small handful of fresh almonds, some carrot sticks and hummus, or a piece of cheese with an oatcake all provide energy-sustaining fuel.

Case study: A diet to increase resilience

Lauren was a 32-year-old mother of one when she visited Susannah's clinic for some help with weight loss. Her nutritional questionnaire revealed fatigue, frequent stress and anxiety, which Lauren believed were just normal aspects of modern life. She was amazed to learn that they could all be linked to her diet of refined carbohydrates, low protein intake and addiction to sweets and chocolate.

After learning about blood sugar control, Lauren embarked on a new way of eating and after six weeks, she was 13 pounds lighter and reported *feeling* lighter too, with more energy and less anxiety. 'I feel better able to cope with life and far less troubled when things don't go according to plan,' she said.

Summary

In summary, to avoid the dips in energy and mood that come with fluctuating blood sugar levels:

- Choose slow-releasing, unrefined, whole carbohydrate foods – wholegrains, vegetables, beans and fruit, not fruit juice – over fast-releasing, refined foods.
- Combine carbohydrates with protein-rich food.
- Eat regularly: never skip breakfast, and have a snack mid-morning and mid-afternoon if your energy flags.

CHAPTER 5

The Energy Superheroes

As we saw in the previous chapter, what you eat has a fundamental impact on how you feel and function and on your ability to deal with stress. Taking this one stage further, let's look at how your cells produce energy, and the nutrients you need to make this happen. It is these nutrients that can give you a quick energy boost, especially if you are deficient.

What you experience as energy, whether mental or physical, is the end result of a series of chemical reactions that take place in every cell in your body. The process that turns food into energy is called catabolism. In a carefully controlled sequence of chemical reactions, food is broken down into its component parts, and these are combusted with oxygen to make a unit of cellular energy called ATP, which in turn makes muscles work, nerve signals fire and brain cells function. This magical process was happening inside every single human cell millions of years before humankind's primitive attempts to produce energy, and the only waste products are water and carbon dioxide. First of all, though, the fuel has to be refined.

As we've seen, our primary source of energy is carbohydrate. Although we can also make energy from both protein and fat, carbohydrate-rich foods provide the cleanest kind of fuel. When fat and protein are used to make energy, there can be a build up of toxic substances in the body: protein breakdown produces ammonia, while fat breakdown produces ketones, which can be burned for energy and are therefore the body's back-up system when sugar stores run out. But too many ketones and protein breakdown by-products really tax the kidneys and make the bloodstream too acidic. So carbohydrate is the preferred fuel source, provided you don't have too much of it. Our cells need the simplest unit of carbohydrate, glucose, to make fuel. So the first job of the body is to turn all forms of carbohydrate into glucose. This is the end goal of digestion. By eating foods with a low-GL score, combining carbohydrates with protein and eating regularly throughout the day, your cells will receive an even supply of energy-giving glucose.

Turning glucose into energy

If you feel tired throughout much of the day, your problems are probably due to mitochondria rather than hypochondria.

Within each and every one of our thirty trillion or so cells – including muscle, immune and brain cells – there are tiny energy factories called mitochondria. While the cell's instructions, encoded in DNA, come from both parents, the instructions and DNA within the mitochondria come only from the mother. So, whether you like it or not, you are more like your mother than your father and specifically inherit the same strengths and weaknesses in the energy-producing department.

It is now widely agreed that mitochondria are related to bacteria in how they work. It is highly likely that early single-celled organisms were infected with bacteria and, over time, the two learned to live together to their mutual advantage, with the bacteria providing the energy for the cells. This allowed for the development of more complex cells, such as those of which we are made. Knowing this, you can see why antibacterial drugs, such as antibiotics, could have a harmful impact on your ability to produce energy, as they may affect the bacteria-like mitochondria. Indeed, a recent study has recorded mitochondrial dysfunction as a side-effect of prolonged antibiotic treatment.[5] Maybe that's part of the reason why antibiotics can make patients feel so tired.

Many diseases can be traced back to problems in the body's

ability to process food for energy within these mitochondria (or indeed issues with the functioning of the mitochondria themselves, as we'll see in Chapter 17). On the other hand, if you have super-healthy mitochondria, firing on all cylinders, nothing can stop you. So let's examine in more detail what mitochondria do and how we might tune them up.

The mitochondria turn glucose into another chemical, pyruvic acid, in the process of which a small amount of energy is released, which can be used by the cell to carry out its work. If this step occurs without sufficient oxygen present, a by-product called lactic acid builds up. That's why, the first time you do strenuous exercise using muscles you didn't even know you had, the next day those muscles ache. This is, in part, because you've made them work too hard without supplying them with enough oxygen, causing a build up of lactic acid crystals. This is called anaerobic (without oxygen) exercise and it is what happens when you sprint. The more you exercise, developing larger muscles, the less strain you put on those muscles and the more oxygen they can use. This is what aerobic exercise is all about – providing muscle cells with enough oxygen for them to work properly.

Pyruvic acid then gets turned into acetyl-coenzyme A (AcoA for short). If you're starved of glucose – for example, if you 'hit the wall' during a marathon – you can break down fat or protein to make AcoA, and use this for energy. However, this is rather inefficient, so the body prefers to use carbohydrate for fuel.

From this point on, oxygen is needed every step of the way. AcoA enters a series of chemical reactions known as the Krebs cycle (named after its discoverer, Ernst Krebs), which separates off hydrogen molecules, which then meet oxygen and ... *Bang!* Energy is released. In fact, over 90 per cent of all our energy is derived from this final stage. The waste products are carbon dioxide, which we exhale; water, which goes to form urine; and heat. About a third of all the energy released from glucose is lost as heat. That's why you get hot when you exercise: your muscle cells are making lots of energy, so heat is generated.

How mitochondria turn food into energy

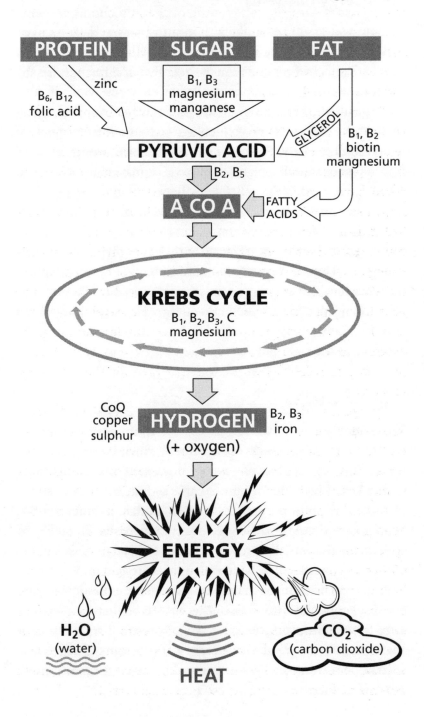

The energy nutrients

By now, you might be thinking that eating slow-releasing carbo-hydrates and breathing will provide you with abundant energy; but that's only half the story. All of these chemical reactions in the mitochondria are carefully controlled by enzymes, which in turn are dependent on nine vitamins and five minerals. Any shortage of these critical catalysts and your energy factories will not function at optimum capacity. The result will be inefficient energy production, a loss of stamina, highs and lows – or maybe just lows. And when you're tired, life's challenges will seem far more stressful.

In our 100% Health survey, 81 per cent of the participants complained of having low energy.[6] In a pilot study at the Institute for Optimum Nutrition, we found that 73 per cent of participants experienced a definite improvement in energy simply by improving their diet and supplementing the thirteen key vitamins and minerals needed to turn food into energy. This strongly suggests that, for many people, the underlying cause of fatigue is simply a shortage of the right nutrients.

Vitamin vitality

The important vitamins for energy are the B complex family, which comprise eight different members, with every one essential for making energy. Glucose cannot be turned into pyruvic acid without B_1 (also called thiamine) and B_3 (niacin). AcoA cannot be formed without B_1, B_2 (riboflavin), B_3 and, most important of all, B_5 (pantothenic acid). The Krebs cycle needs B_1, B_2 and B_3 to work properly. Fats and proteins cannot be used to make energy without B_6 (pyridoxine), B_{12} (cobalamin), folic acid or biotin.

It used to be thought that as long as you ate a reasonable diet, you'd get enough B vitamins. But recent studies have shown that long-term slight insufficiencies gradually result in a depletion of these vitamins in cells, causing early-warning signs of deficiency, such as poor skin condition, anxiety, depression, irritability and, most of all, fatigue.

In reality, many people's diets fall dismally short on these vital vitamins, not even achieving the minimal recommended daily allowance (RDA). What's more, the levels set for RDAs are rarely sufficient to achieve optimum health. Dr Emanuel Cheraskin and colleagues from the University of Alabama made the first attempt to define 'suggested optimal nutrient amounts' back in the 1990s.[7] Over a fifteen-year period, they studied 13,500 people living in six regions of the United States. Each participant completed in-depth health questionnaires and was given physical, dental, eye and other examinations, as well as numerous blood tests, cardiac function tests and a detailed dietary analysis. The objective was to find which nutrient intake levels were associated with the highest health ratings. The results consistently revealed that the healthiest individuals – those with the fewest clinical signs and symptoms – took supplements and ate diets rich in nutrients relative to calories. The researchers found that the intake of nutrients associated with optimal health was often *ten times* higher than RDA levels.

We have continued this research with our 100% Health survey and have identified the intakes of foods and nutrients that are consistent with optimal health.[8] Other studies support our conclusions and confirm that better health is achieved through additional intakes of nutrients above the levels that are possible in the so-called 'well-balanced diet'.

Aren't vitamin supplements a waste of money?

Back in 1982 at the Institute for Optimum Nutrition, Patrick put 76 volunteers on a six-month supplement programme. At the end of this time, 79 per cent reported a definite improvement in energy, 60 per cent spoke of better memory and mental alertness, 66 per cent felt more emotionally balanced, 57 per cent had suffered fewer colds and infections, and 55 per cent had better skin. This study can be criticised because it wasn't placebo controlled or published in a journal, but it is consistent with another research project, which compared the health of over 1000 people. In the latter study, one group took no supplements; another took a basic RDA multi; and a third took high-dose supplements.[9] To quote the study's lead researcher, Dr Gladys Block, 'The greater degree of supplement use was associated with more favorable concentrations of homocysteine, C-reactive protein [a measure of inflammation], high-density lipoprotein cholesterol and triglycerides [blood fats], as well as lower risk of prevalent elevated blood pressure and diabetes.' Those taking the most supplements also had the highest subjective health ratings. There were no downsides, only benefits.

B vitamins

B vitamins are water soluble, so if you take in more than you need, they are simply excreted in your urine. (A few, such as B_6 and B_3, can become toxic if several grams are consumed – but who would want to do that?) Because of their water-solubility and sensitivity to heat, B vitamins are also easily lost when foods are boiled in water, so the best natural sources are raw vegetables, fresh fruit and wheatgerm. Seeds, nuts and wholegrains also contain reasonable amounts, as do meat, fish, eggs and dairy products. But the levels in these foodstuffs decline when they are cooked or stored for a long period of time.

Vitamin C

Vitamin C is another important nutrient that is required for both making energy and increasing resilience to stress. It's a cofactor in the Krebs cycle, a key part of the energy-making process, and is also vital for the manufacture of the adrenal hormones that are crucial when we are under stress. Numerous studies link low levels of vitamin C with increased fatigue. For example, a study at the University of Alabama Medical Center assessed the vitamin C intake of 411 dentists and their spouses, then, using a questionnaire, determined their 'fatigability' score. Researchers found that the 81 subjects who consumed less than 100mg of vitamin C per day reported a fatigability score averaging 0.81. Conversely, the 330 participants who ingested more than 400mg a day reported an average score of just 0.41.[10] The researchers concluded, 'These limited data suggest that individuals consuming the generally accepted RDA for vitamin C report approximately twice the fatigue symptomatology as those taking about sevenfold the RDA.'

Supplementing vitamin C alongside B vitamins can also have a marked impact on how *you* feel and *your* energy levels. A 2011 randomised, placebo-controlled, double-blind trial (what the medical profession refers to as the 'gold standard' for research) gave 198 men between the ages of 30 and 55 in full-time employment either a supplement containing vitamin C, B complex and minerals or a placebo. After assessments at 14 and 28 days, those receiving the supplement were found to have greater physical and mental stamina, concentration and alertness than those taking the placebo.[11]

In addition to the central roles played by B vitamins and vitamin C in the energy-making process, the final key stage – when hydrogen reacts with oxygen – is dependent on a substance called co-enzyme Q (Co-Q). A vital link in the chain, Co-Q provides the spark, together with oxygen, to keep our energy furnaces burning.

Co-enzyme Q

The discovery that Co-Q is present in foods, that levels decline with age, and that cellular levels rise when supplements are taken, has led many nutritional scientists to suspect that this co-enzyme might be the missing link in the energy equation. Technically, Co-Q cannot be classified as a vitamin since it can be made by the body, although it isn't made in large enough amounts for optimum health and energy. It is therefore known as a semi-essential nutrient. The form that humans use is called Co-Q_{10}, which is what you'll find in supplements.

Co-Q's magical properties lie in its ability to improve the cell's capacity to use oxygen. In the final and most significant part of catabolism, when hydrogen is released during the Krebs cycle to react with oxygen, the actual reaction occurs at an atomic level. Components of these elements, electrons, are passed from one atom to the next in what is called the electron transfer pathway. These electrons, which are tiny charged particles, are highly reactive and need to be processed very carefully. They are like nuclear fuel – a very potent, but also very dangerous, energy source. In fact, they are so dangerous that it is thought they might be the initiating factor in turning some cells cancerous, and damaging the cells within artery walls, heralding the beginning of heart disease.

The damage caused to healthy cells by these spare electrons is also a large part of what ageing is all about. The more damaged cells we have, the biochemically older we are. Compounds that contain spare electrons are called free radicals. They are created during normal energy catabolism but also through smoking, eating fried food, breathing in pollution, and radiation from the sun. Co-Q has two key roles to play in the handling of volatile electrons: it controls the flow of oxygen, making the production of energy more efficient; and it prevents damage caused by these free radicals.

Co-Q is safe and effective

No studies have reported toxicity of Co-Q, even at extremely high doses taken over many years. So there is no reason to think that continued supplementation with Co-Q, as is advised for many vitamins, should have anything but extremely positive results. What's more, research shows it can increase resilience and reduce fatigue. Over an eight-day period of supplementing 300mg of Co-Q_{10} a day, participants in one trial were found to have more energy and demonstrated improved physical performance during fatigue-inducing workload trials, where they had to cycle for two hours twice a day on an exercise bike, working at 80 per cent of their maximum heart rate.[12]

Co-Q deficiency: statin-takers beware

Cholesterol-lowering statin drugs knock out Co-Q, and deficiency of the latter has been associated with fatigue, muscle weakness and soreness, and even heart failure.[13] Research in the US has shown that a high-dose supplement of Co-Q_{10} can reverse the muscle pain: fifty patients who had been on statins for two years were taken off the drugs because they were complaining of muscle pains and other side-effects; giving them Co-Q_{10} dramatically relieved their symptoms.[14] There are many studies showing that Co-Q_{10} also has a positive effect on heart and artery health.[15] We recommend taking 30–60mg a day for prevention, and 90–120mg a day if you have cardiovascular disease or are taking statins.

Co-Q exists in many foods but not always in a form we can use. There are also different types of Co-Q, from Co-Q_1 to Co-Q_{10}; yeast, for example, contains Co-Q_6 and Co-Q_7. But only Co-Q_{10} is found in human tissues. It is this form of Co-Q that supports energy production and reduces free radical damage, so only this form should be supplemented.

However, we can utilise the 'lower' forms of Co-Q and convert them into Co-Q_{10}. This conversion process, which occurs naturally in the liver, allows many of us to utilise the various forms of Co-Q found in almost every foodstuff. Unfortunately, though, some people (especially the elderly) lose the ability to do this. For them, Co-Q_{10} is effectively an essential nutrient because the body needs to be given a regular supply of it to avoid suffering deficiency.

Some foods are better dietary sources of Co-Q than others. These include all meat and fish (especially sardines), eggs, spinach, broccoli, alfalfa, potatoes, soya beans and soya oil, wheat (especially wheatgerm), rice bran, buckwheat, millet as well as most beans, nuts and seeds.

Best food sources of Co-Q_{10} (milligrams per gram)

FOOD	AMOUNT	FOOD	AMOUNT
Meat		**Beans**	
Beef	.031	Green beans	.0058
Pork	.024–.041	Soya beans	.0029
Chicken	.021	Aduki beans	.0022
		Soya oil	.092
Fish		**Nuts and seeds**	
Sardines	.064	Peanuts	.027
Mackerel	.043	Sesame seeds	.023
Flat fish	.005	Walnuts	.019
Grains		**Vegetables**	
Rice bran	.0054	Spinach	.010
Wheatgerm	.0035	Broccoli	.008
Millet	.0015	Peppers	.003
Buckwheat	.0013	Carrots	.002

Today many supplement companies offer Co-Q_{10} products. The best dosage is probably between 30 and 120mg a day (the upper end for those with exhaustion), and it is best absorbed in an oil-soluble form.

Elemental energy

The minerals iron, calcium, magnesium, chromium and zinc are also vital for making energy. Calcium and magnesium are perhaps the most important because all muscle cells need an adequate supply of both to be able to contract and relax. A shortage of magnesium, which is very common in people who don't eat much fruit or vegetables, often results in cramp, as muscles are unable to relax.

Magnesium is needed by 75 per cent of the enzymes in your body.[16] It is part of the Krebs energy-making cycle, is vital for carbohydrate metabolism and is essential for nerve cells to send their messages. Symptoms of deficiency include muscle weakness or tremors, insomnia, nervousness, hyperactivity, depression, confusion, irregular heartbeat, constipation and lack of appetite. Most of these are connected with imbalanced muscle or nerve function.

Zinc, together with vitamin B_6, is needed to make the enzymes that digest food.[17] These nutrients are also essential in the production of the hormone insulin, which transports glucose into your cells to make energy. A lack of zinc can also disturb appetite control and diminish the senses of taste and smell, which can result in a preference for meat, cheese and other foods with strong flavours.

The older you are, the less likely you are to be taking in enough chromium[18] – an essential mineral that helps stabilise blood sugar levels by making you more sensitive to insulin,[19] thus reversing insulin resistance. Supplementing chromium has been shown to reduce appetite and promote weight loss,[20] reduce PMS-related mood dips[21] and depression,[22] and reduce fatigue in diabetics.[23] The average daily intake is below 50mcg; an optimal intake, certainly for those with blood sugar problems, is around 200mcg. Chromium is found in wholefoods and is therefore higher in wholegrain flour, bread and pasta than in their refined, white counterparts (white flour has 98 per cent of its chromium removed in the refining process). It is also abundant in beans, nuts and seeds, and especially in asparagus and mushrooms. Since it works with insulin to help stabilise your blood sugar level, when you feel stressed and have erratic energy, you use more – and therefore have a greater need for it. Hence, a sugar and stimulant addict eating a diet high in refined foods is most at risk of chromium deficiency.

It is doubtful that an optimal intake of chromium can be achieved through diet alone. It is therefore wise to take supplements while continuing to eat wholefoods. The best forms of chromium are either picolinate or polynicotinate. Chromium polynicotinate is chromium bound with niacin (vitamin B_3). These two nutrients are used by the liver to make a substance called glucose tolerance factor, which, as the name suggests, makes your body better equipped to deal with glucose. Studies have found that glucose tolerance factor binds to insulin and potentiates its action about threefold, making you more efficient at making energy from your food.[24]

Amazing aminos

In addition to the vitamins and minerals required to generate energy, you need an adequate intake of protein to make adrenal hormones – and specifically an amino acid called tyrosine. Tyrosine helps to improve your resilience to stress, and is also the building block for the energising thyroid hormone thyroxine.

The military has long known that tyrosine improves performance under stress. One study put 21 cadets through a demanding one-week military combat training course. Ten cadets were given a drink containing 2g of tyrosine a day, while the remaining 11 were given an identical drink without the tyrosine. Those on tyrosine consistently performed better, both in memorising the task at hand and in tracking the tasks they had performed.[25] Another study found that the normal decline in thinking straight when very cold is mitigated by taking tyrosine.[26]

Research has also discovered that supplementing tyrosine – or its precursor, the amino acid phenylalanine – can reduce anxiety, depression and sleep disturbance as well as improve mood.[27]

Boosting your tyrosine intake can be particularly helpful if you are very stressed, a stimulant junkie, burning the candle at both ends or doing something that requires endurance. Dietary sources include meat, fish, poultry and dairy products. But as tyrosine can compete with other amino acids, it's worth supplementing 500mg to 1000mg of tyrosine twice a day, ideally with a carbohydrate snack but away from other protein foods, in the early morning and mid-afternoon.

Supplements for energy

Ensuring an optimal intake of all the nutrients that are involved in turning food into energy is a key part of the energy equation, which is also essential in increasing your resilience to dealing with stress. Alongside eating the right kinds of food, one of the easiest ways to guarantee such optimal levels is to take nutritional supplements. That's why we dedicate a whole chapter later in the book to supplements and the appropriate doses (see Chapter 22).

Summary

- Include in your diet foods that are rich in B vitamins (wheatgerm, fish, green vegetables, wholegrains, mushrooms, eggs).

- Eat more sources of Co-Q_{10} (sardines, mackerel, sesame seeds, peanuts, walnuts, beef, pork, chicken, spinach).

- Also include rich sources of magnesium (wheatgerm, almonds, cashew nuts, chia and pumpkin seeds, buckwheat, green vegetables), calcium (cheese, almonds, green vegetables, seeds, prunes), zinc (oysters, lamb, nuts, fish, egg yolk, wholegrains, almonds, chia seeds) and chromium (wholegrains, beans, nuts, seeds, asparagus, mushrooms).

- Supplement the energy nutrients to ensure you are getting an adequate intake, and especially Co-Q_{10} if you take statins or suffer with fatigue. (For more on supplement doses, see Chapter 22.)

CHAPTER 6

Why Stress and Stimulants Keep You Hooked

Stress starts in the mind . . . but it doesn't stay there. Every time you react to a stressful event, you set off a cascade of activity that fundamentally changes your body chemistry (see Chapter 2). The trigger is often a situation that we perceive as requiring our immediate attention: a young child getting too close to the road; a car getting too close to us; a hostile reaction from another person; a financial crisis; an impossible deadline. Rapid signals then stimulate your adrenal glands (situated on top of the kidneys in the small of the back) to produce adrenalin, which in turn triggers the release of the hormone cortisol and other chemical messengers throughout the body. Within seconds your heart is pounding, your breathing changes, stores of glucose are released into your blood, your muscles tense, your eyes dilate and your blood thickens.

What, you might ask, does this have to do with an unexpected call from your bank manager? The answer is very little. But before the days of overdraft limits, most stresses required a *physical* response. That's what adrenalin does: it gets you ready to 'fight or take flight'. The average adrenalin rush of a commuter stuck in a traffic jam provides enough fuel to keep them running for a mile. That's how much glucose is released, mainly by breaking down the glycogen that is held in muscles and the liver. All this can happen as a result of a single stressful thought. The other way to get an adrenalin surge is to have a blood sugar dip, usually as a result of the body overreacting to high-sugar foods. So, combine low blood sugar with a stressful thought or situation and you will really start pumping adrenalin.

Where, you might wonder, does all this extra energy come from? The answer is that the body diverts energy away from its normal repair and general maintenance jobs, such as digesting, cleansing and rejuvenating. So, every moment you spend in a state of stress, essential physical maintenance functions are neglected and the ageing process of your body accelerates. Even thinking about it is stressful! But the effects of prolonged stress are even more insidious than that. Imagine your pituitary and adrenal glands, pancreas and liver perpetually pumping out hormones to control blood sugar that you don't even need, day in, day out. Like a car that is always driven too fast, the body goes out of balance and parts start to wear out.

As a consequence your overall energy level drops, you lose concentration, get confused, suffer bouts of 'brain fog', fall asleep after meals, grow irritable, freak out, can't sleep, can't wake up, sweat too much, get headaches, feel muscles tighten ... Sound familiar?

A quick remedy for energy deficiency

In an attempt to regain control, most people turn to stimulants, as we saw in Chapter 3. Legal stimulants include coffee (which contains theobromine and theophylline as well as caffeine), tea and energy drinks such as cola (both of which contain caffeine), chocolate (which contains caffeine and theobromine), as well as 'psychological stimulants', such as demanding jobs, dangerous pastimes and emotional traumas – all experiences that put you on the edge. Alcohol, cigarettes, remote-control games and scary movies act as both stimulants and sedatives. Illegal stimulants include amphetamines and 'uppers', cocaine, crack and committing crime. Naturally, it becomes increasingly difficult to relax with a regular intake of stimulants, so many people learn to balance their use with relaxants, such as alcohol, sleeping pills, tranquillisers, cannabis and so on.

Addicted to stress

Of course, you can't live like this for ever. At some point, most people burn out and have to head for the beach to recover. As they wait at the airport, many of them will probably buy a novel from the bookshop. The back cover might promise, 'Murder, mystery, greed, lust, gripping suspense!' After a few diverting hours engrossed in the thriller on the beach, it's time for some real excitement – windsurfing, waterskiing, surfing, something exhilarating. What are we looking for when we engage in such activities? An interviewer once asked the stunt rider Evel Knievel, 'Why do you do it?' when he was sitting in the cockpit of his 'rocket bike'. Evel replied, 'There is a moment when I'm flying through the air of absolute peace.' He closed the hatch, pressed the button, and seconds later his rocket bike plummeted to the bottom of the Snake River Canyon.

Thankfully, there is an easier way to feel great – and we are going to show you how to achieve it. But first, it's useful to understand why so many people become addicted to stress, and to the highly physiologically addictive cocktail of chemical 'uppers' and 'downers' we all have at our disposal.

Instead of using our stress response as a back-up, a super-charge to be activated only in times of emergency, many of us exist permanently on adrenalin and cortisol, going from one stressful event to another and surviving on coffee, tea, cigarettes and/or sugar. After a while, the adrenalin and cortisol are the only things keeping us going. If you quit the stimulants or take some time off, you collapse into a heap – depressed and exhausted. That's a sure sign that you've become addicted to stress and/or stimulants.

Are you addicted to stimulants?

Imagine a day with *no* coffee, tea, sugar, chocolate, cigarettes or alcohol. If you shout, 'No way!' there is a very real possibility that you have some level of addiction to these stimulants. This can range from a mild addiction that you can live with quite happily to a major problem that is controlling your life. However, whatever the level of addiction, the net consequence is always less energy, not more.

One of our clients, Bobbie, serves as a case in point. She was already eating a healthy diet and took a sensible daily programme of vitamin and mineral supplements. She had only two problems: a lack of energy in the morning and occasional headaches. She also had one vice: three cups of coffee a day. After some persuasion, she agreed to stop the coffee for a month. To her surprise, her energy levels rose and the headaches stopped.

In making an accurate assessment of your current relationship to stimulants, you need to be honest with yourself about how you use them. So, fill in the stimulant inventory overleaf for three days (or photocopy it and fill that in). Note down how much coffee you consume and when, and do the same for tea, chocolate, sugar (or another sweet treat), cigarettes and alcohol. Also, consider what your relationship is to these substances. Do you, for example, ever buy sweets and hide the wrappers so other people don't know you've eaten them? Do you swoon at the dessert menu in restaurants and always grab a mint or two on the way out? How much do you think about and look forward to that mid-morning cup of coffee? How important is that drink after work? Does everyone really know how much you smoke? Have you become a coffee connoisseur, side-stepping the issue of addiction by focusing on your 'hobby' of sampling yet another variety?

This kind of relationship to stimulants, often cloaked in an attitude that they are just some of the innocent pleasures of life, is indicative of an underlying chemical imbalance that depletes your energy and peace of mind.

Stimulant inventory

	A unit equals	Day 1	Day 2	Day 3
Tea	1 cup*	☐	☐	☐
Coffee (espresso)	½ shot	☐	☐	☐
Coffee (filter or instant)	1 cup*	☐	☐	☐
Green tea	2 cups*	☐	☐	☐
Cola or caffeinated drinks	1 cup*	☐	☐	☐
Caffeine pills (e.g. No-Doz, Pro Plus, Excedrin, Dexatrim)	1 pill	☐	☐	☐
Chocolate (milk)	200g	☐	☐	☐
Chocolate (dark)	70g	☐	☐	☐
Added sugar	1 teaspoon	☐	☐	☐
Hidden sugar (i.e. listed in ingredients)	1 teaspoon/ 5g	☐	☐	☐
Beer, lager or cider (4%)	half pint	☐	☐	☐
Spirits (40%)	25ml measure	☐	☐	☐
Wine (13%)	80ml**	☐	☐	☐
Cigarettes***	1	☐	☐	☐

* One cup = 250ml (8.8 fl oz)

** A small glass of wine (125ml) contains about 1.5 units; a large glass (250ml) contains about 3 units

*** Cigarettes are covered in more detail in Chapter 7

The next step is to reduce your intake, which is discussed on page 62 in the section 'Reducing stimulants without suffering'. But, first, let's look in more detail at why stimulants are bad news.

You don't need stimulants

Stimulants are energy's greatest enemy. Even though they can create energy in the short term, the long-term effect is always bad. The same is true for stress. So an important step in the Stress Cure programme is to cut out, or at least cut down, stimulants. This includes coffee, tea, chocolate, sugar and refined foods, cigarettes, energy drinks and alcohol.

If you eliminate these stimulants for one month, you'll be in a much better position to understand how they really work. The more damage stimulants are doing to you, the greater the withdrawal effect. (Fortunately, by eating a low-GL diet and increasing your intake of energy-boosting nutrients – as outlined in Chapters 4 and 5 and mapped out for you in Part 6 – you can minimise those withdrawal symptoms, which usually last no more than four days.) Once you're clean, you will notice what happens when you take your first hit of tea, coffee, sugar or chocolate. You'll probably experience what stress expert Hans Selye (who first outlined the general adaptation syndrome, illustrated overleaf) called the 'initial response' – in other words, your true response to these powerful chemicals. So hit that strong coffee again and you are likely to experience a pounding head, hyperactive mind, fast heartbeat and insomnia, followed by extreme drowsiness.

If you were then to continue using stimulants (although we strongly recommend you don't, once you've gone through cold turkey), you would adapt – that's phase 2. Keep doing this long enough and eventually you will hit exhaustion – phase 3. Everybody succumbs to this eventually. The only variance is how long it takes you to get there.

The good news is that recovery is not only possible but usually rapid. Most people feel substantially more energised and better able to cope with stress within just 30 days of quitting stimulants (with nutritional support). This is what we advocate in our Stress Cure programme.

The general adaptation syndrome

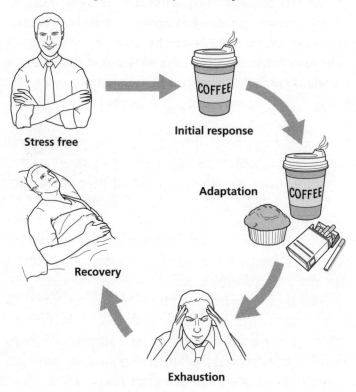

Stress free

Initial response

Adaptation

Exhaustion

Recovery

Know your stimulants

It's worth knowing what each of the main social stimulants contains and how they affect the body.

- **Alcohol** is made by the action of yeast on sugar. As such, it has a similar effect to sugar. In the short term, alcohol actually inhibits the release of reserve glucose from the liver and encourages low blood sugar levels, causing an increase in appetite (that's why kebab shops and curry houses do such good trade late at night). The diseases associated with excess alcohol intake include diabetes, heart disease, cirrhosis and cancer of the liver.

- **Chocolate** contains cocoa as its major 'active' ingredient. Cocoa contains caffeine and significant quantities of the stimulant theobromine, which has an action similar to, although not as strong as, caffeine. Theobromine is also found in cocoa drinks, such as hot chocolate.

- **Cigarettes** contain nicotine as well as 16 other cancer-producing chemicals. Nicotine is the primary stimulant and has a substantial effect even in small doses. In large amounts, it acts as a sedative. It is more addictive than heroin. People in the process of quitting smoking often experience low blood sugar problems.

- **Coffee** contains theobromine, theophylline and caffeine, all of which are stimulants. Caffeine is the major stimulant; however, decaffeinated coffee still contains the other two. Theophylline disturbs normal sleep patterns. Coffee consumption is associated with greater risk of pancreatic cancer, and increased incidence of birth defects and other problems during pregnancy.[28]

- **Energy drinks** usually contain caffeine in varying quantities. Cola, for example, contains around half the caffeine found in a single espresso shot, whereas Red Bull contains about the same amount (80g). These drinks often also contain sugar, artificial sweeteners and colourings, all of which can act as stimulants.

- **Medications** for the relief of headaches may contain caffeine. Other caffeine tablets are available as stimulants. The most common are Pro Plus and the herb guarana.

- **Tea** contains caffeine, theobromine, theophylline and tannin. It is a stimulant and a diuretic with similar, although lesser, effects to coffee. As a general rule, a strong cup of tea provides about as much caffeine as a weak cup of

coffee. Tannin interferes with the absorption of minerals.
Tea drinkers have an increased risk of stomach ulcers.
However, tea also contains the amino acid theanine, which
is a relaxant, so, overall, it is a better choice than coffee.

Reducing stimulants without suffering

Of course, most people would consider cutting out all stimulants
virtually impossible, as well as extremely stressful! But with a
staged approach – and the right nutritional support – it can be
done. The first step is to find out which stimulants are most
important for you. Look at your habits, which you can identify
by filling in the three-day diary on page 58. Which of these stimulants do you have in one form or another several times a day?
Which do you use as a pick-me-up, perhaps to get you out of bed
in the morning or when your energy is flagging at work? Which
would you find the hardest to stop completely for a month?
When was the last time you went for a month without any of
these stimulants?

Although you may intend to stop them for ever, in reality it is
far easier to take one step at a time. Start by picking one stimulant (other than cigarettes) that you use frequently. Could you
realistically cut it out for a month? If not, to what extent could
you reduce your intake? If you consume a lot, a staged reduction
is more realistic: for example, reduce by one-third, then two-
thirds and finally completely over the course of several weeks.
Write down this schedule and stick to it. Set yourself similar
targets for no more than three stimulants. Sometimes they will
overlap. For example, if you use coffee, sugar and chocolate but
can't stand the taste of coffee without sugar, then cutting out
sugar will automatically mean no chocolate and no coffee as well.

Finally, a note about alcohol. Do you know how many units
you drink each week? Many of our clients are surprised when
we add them up. A typical glass of wine, for example, no longer

equals one unit. This is because, over the past few years, the alcohol content in wine has been creeping up, due in part to the use of riper grapes to satisfy more 'international' flavour require- ments and to the switch to modern strains of yeast that are more effective at turning sugar into alcohol. The one glass equals one unit calculation was based on drinking wine at 8 per cent alcohol volume, which you'd be hard pushed to find these days. Many wines now contain 14 per cent, and a typical small (125ml) glass contains 1.5 units while a large (250ml) glass has around 3 units. Many beers and lagers also contain more alcohol these days, with a pint of strong beer (5.2 per cent) containing 3 units. Govern- ment guidelines suggest women should not regularly consume more than 2–3 units each day, and men 3–4 units each day. In practice, this means a *maximum* of one large glass of wine for women and just over a glass for men. A single bottle of wine with 14 per cent alcohol content (typically Shiraz, Cabinet Sauvignon, Merlot, Sauvignon Blanc, Chenin Blanc and Chardonnay) con- tains almost 11 units!

When it comes to reducing your intake of all stimulants, here are some tips to help you along:

- **Sugar** is an acquired taste. Although we are born with a liking for sweet things, research has shown that only those who are fed sweets and sweet foods like high levels of sweetness. So, as you gradually cut down the level of sweetness in *all* the food you eat, you will soon grow accustomed to the taste. This means having less sugar in hot drinks, less on your food, even less dried fruit, and drinking more diluted fruit juice. Also, check what's in the food you buy: some cereals, for example, contain more sugar than a packet of biscuits, and 'diet' foods often load in the sugar as they reduce the fat to provide flavour. If you follow a low-GL approach to eating (as outlined in Chapter 4), however, you'll avoid this trap. When you crave something sweet, have fresh (not dried) fruit. Sweeten sugar-free cereals and desserts with fruit. And if you're really desperate, have a sugar-free, low-carb protein bar (see Resources, page 309). Be aware, though, that many standard sugar-free products containing 'natural' sweeteners such as honey, dates and concentrated fruit juices can still give you a sugar high. For a truly sugar-free alternative, try fresh coconut (supermarkets often sell it ready-prepared for instant snacking) or a sugar-free nut butter on an oatcake – both can satisfy a sugar craving. Also, don't be tempted to use sugar substitutes. These may not raise your blood sugar levels, but they stop you changing your habits. It takes about a month to acquire the preference for less sweet foods. Let your taste buds be the judge of how sweet a food is – but do check the labels for all those disguised forms of sugar.

- **Coffee** is strongly addictive. It takes, on average, four days to break the habit. During this time, you may experience headaches and grogginess. These are strong reminders of how bad coffee is for you. Decaffeinated coffee is half as bad (or good, depending on which way you look at it), but drinking it doesn't help you break your addiction to drinking coffee. You are better to switch to a different kind of drink altogether. The most popular coffee alternatives are Caro, Barleycup, Yannoh and Symington's dandelion coffee. When you have been off coffee for a month, you may decide to allow yourself the occasional cup. Have this as a treat, perhaps when you are eating out. Do not use it as a pick-me-up.

- **Tea** is not as bad for you as coffee, unless you're the sort of person who likes your tea well stewed. Start by decreasing the strength of your tea, and perhaps use a smaller cup or teapot. Tea has such a strong flavour that you can dip in a tea bag for just a few seconds and still have a strong-tasting drink. Try Moringa tea, which is caffeine-free, high in nutrients and gives a natural energy boost. Remember that green tea also contains caffeine, but it can be useful to bridge the gap to caffeine-free teas as it contains a substance called theanine which can help you to feel calmer and more alert. There are also hundreds of varieties of delicious, caffeine-free herbal teas. You are bound to find one you like (see Resources for some recommended brands and our favourites). Also try red bush (or rooibosch) tea, which is caffeine free and has a taste closer to 'normal' tea, and can be served with milk.

- **Chocolate** contains both sugar and the stimulants caffeine and theobromine. Start by having chocolate-free snacks, like Siesta carob bars (the mint flavour tastes quite like mint chocolate, and carob is naturally sweet, so there is no added sugar) or GoLower bars (see Resources, page 309). Then avoid even these, keeping them strictly for emergencies. Instead, eat fresh fruit or coconut if you feel you need something sweet.

- **Alcohol** is an easy habit to acquire because of its key role in social interaction. Start by limiting when you have alcohol: for example, don't drink at lunchtime. You'll certainly work better in the afternoon. Then limit what you drink: for example, stick to wine, avoiding beer and spirits. Next, limit how much you drink by setting yourself a realistic target: for example, no more than seven glasses of wine a week. This allows you to have quite a few at that party on Saturday night and compensate by having little throughout the rest of the week. Then cut it out completely for at least two weeks, and preferably four. If you find this hard to do, take a close look at your drinking habits and, if necessary, seek professional help. Once you've got your energy back on track, and have built greater resilience to stress, you can start to reintroduce alcohol as a social enjoyment rather than a crutch to compensate for low energy and high stress.

- **Smoking** is one of the hardest habits to kick. The average smoker is addicted not only to nicotine but to smoking itself when tired, hungry, upset, on waking, after a meal, with a drink and so on. Improved nutrition decreases the craving for cigarettes, so it's best to leave kicking this stimulant until you've followed the Stress Cure programme set out in Part 6 for at least a month. Thereafter, follow the guidelines provided in the next chapter.

Summary

In summary, here are some practical steps to help you break your addiction to stress and stimulants:

- Identify the stimulants to which you are addicted.

- Determine which stimulants you like the most and avoid or considerably reduce your intake of them until they are no longer a daily requirement.

- Identify alternatives you can enjoy instead, so you have something ready to fill the void. Try Moringa tea.

- Support yourself by eating a low-GL diet (see Chapter 4) and supplementing key energy nutrients (see Chapter 5).

- If you smoke, follow the guidelines in Chapter 7.

- Monitor your patterns of stressful behaviour and replace these with a more positive way of responding (see Chapters 13 and 14).

Finally, if you are struggling with other addictions, including illicit and medical drugs, Patrick's book *How to Quit without Feeling S**t* (Piatkus) offers practical guidance out of addiction to almost every addictive substance.

CHAPTER 7

How to Quit Smoking

Many smokers insist that smoking helps them to cope with stress. Clients often tell us: 'I'll think about quitting as soon as I'm over this stressful period.' Yet research conducted by scientists at the universities of Birmingham, Oxford and King's College London has debunked this myth, finding that quitting smoking can actually relieve stress.[29] Their study, published in the *British Medical Journal* in February 2014, analysed 26 studies that focused on a wide range of mental health issues in people who stopped smoking. As well as reducing stress, they also found that quitting can be as effective as taking antidepressants when it comes to improving your mood.

This is certainly good news for those who want to quit. But even with the reassurance a smoke-free life can help rather than hinder your stress levels, quitting can still seem a daunting challenge.

The chances are, if you smoke, you've already tried to give up. Indeed, Mark Twain is reported to have said: 'It's easy to quit smoking. I've done it hundreds of times.' Unless you follow a comprehensive approach that includes more than willpower alone, cigarettes can be extremely difficult to give up for good. The reason for this is that nicotine, the primary mood enhancer in cigarettes, is more addictive than heroin. In small doses it has a stimulant effect, while in large amounts it acts as a sedative. That's why it is so attractive: on the one hand, it gives you an immediate lift; on the other, it calms you down. Before a meal it can stop you feeling hungry and after a meal it can stop you feeling drowsy.

All of these effects are due to nicotine's action on adrenal hormones, blood sugar and brain chemicals. By strictly following the advice outlined in the earlier chapters of this book, your craving for cigarettes will diminish as a direct consequence of stabilising your blood sugar and hormone levels. So, before attempting to quit, we recommend following our dietary and supplement guidelines for at least four weeks, preferably with the guidance and support of a nutritional therapist. The aim is to get you to a stage where you no longer consume any other stimulants – such as tea, coffee, chocolate and sugar. Instead, your diet will support your energy levels via regular meals and snacks, with an emphasis on slow-releasing carbohydrates combined with protein-rich foods. Once you have achieved this, you will be ready to move on to reducing your cigarette intake.

Breaking the associated habits

The average smoker reaches for a cigarette at specific moments: when they are tired, hungry or upset, when they wake up in the morning, after a meal, when they have a glass of wine and so on. Before giving up smoking altogether, it is advisable to break these mental associations.

Without attempting to change your smoking habits, keep a diary for a week, writing down every occasion when you smoked, how you felt before and how you felt after the cigarette. On page 299 you'll find a one-week smoking diary to photocopy and use. The example opposite demonstrates how to fill it out.

At the end of the week, add up how many cigarettes you smoke in each situation. Your list might look something like this:

- With a hot drink – 6
- After a meal – 3
- With alcohol – 4
- Difficult situation – 4
- After sex – 3

Sample smoking diary

Day: _Thursday_		Feeling before	Feeling after
Time	**Situation**		
9am	outside work	down	perkier
11am	coffee break	tired	less tired
1pm	after lunch	still hungry	no longer hungry
3pm	coffee break	tired	more energy
5pm	boss checking up	stressed	calmer
7pm	with beer	tense	more relaxed
7.30pm	with second beer	relaxed	relaxed
8.30pm	with third beer	merry	merry
8.45pm	outside pub	bored	more sociable
10pm	after curry	heavy and full	heavy and full
11pm	watching TV	bored	bit more energy

Now set yourself a series of fortnightly targets. For example, for the first two weeks, smoke as much as you like whenever you like aside from when you drink a hot drink. For the two weeks after that, smoke as much as you like whenever you like aside from when you drink a hot drink *and* within 30 minutes of finishing a meal. Continue in this vein until, when you have a cigarette, all you do is smoke, without the associated habits.

Following this approach will be tremendously helpful for you when you quit. Most people start again because the phone rings, presenting you with yet another problem to solve, someone brings in a coffee, another offers you a cigarette ... and before you know it, you're smoking again.

Reducing your nicotine load

Now it's time to gradually reduce your nicotine load. Week by week, switch to a brand that contains less nicotine until what you smoke contains no more than 2mg per cigarette. In addition to the supplements recommended in Chapter 22, supplementing 1000mg of vitamin C, 100mcg of chromium and 50mg of niacin with each meal will help to reduce your cravings. You may experience a blushing sensation when first taking niacin. This is harmless and usually occurs 15 to 30 minutes after taking it; then it lasts for about 15 minutes. The blushing is less likely to occur if you take niacin with a meal and it will diminish and, in most cases, stop completely if you take 50mg three times a day. You can buy no-flush niacin (inositol hexanicotinate or niacinamide), but the most effective form is (the flushing) nicotinic acid. (You may have noticed that this sounds a little like nicotine, and indeed it is thought to have a similar, albeit far milder, effect, which may explain why many smokers find it so helpful when giving up.) When choosing a niacin supplement, be sure to check the ingredients for nicotinic acid rather than one of the non-flush versions, as new legislation means that all three will probably be labelled 'niacin' on the front of the packet. Another word of caution: if you have any liver problems or are taking medication, consult a nutritional therapist before taking niacin, so that any possible contraindications can be assessed first.

Increasing the alkaline balance of the body can also help to reduce nicotine cravings. A way to achieve this is by eating a diet that is high in vegetables, fruit and seeds. In addition, consider supplementing calcium (600mg) and magnesium (400mg) daily as these are alkaline minerals and can help to neutralise excess acidity. Having a bath with Epsom salts (magnesium sulphate) will also help.

Whenever you feel the need for nicotine, first eat an apple or a pear. This will raise a low blood sugar level, which is often what triggers such a craving.

Regular exercise also helps, so this is a great time to schedule in regular walks or other light exercise (see Chapter 9). Beware anything too strenuous, however, as this can have a negative impact on your stress hormones – and the one thing you don't need right now is extra stress, even if it's only in the form of vigorous activity!

The next step is to reduce the number of cigarettes you smoke until you are down to no more than five a day, each with a nicotine content of 2mg or less. If you wish, stop smoking now and start using nicotine gum as an intermediate step. Gums come in two strengths – 4mg and 2mg.

You should be down to a maximum of 10mg of nicotine a day before quitting, so five pieces of 2mg gum, or five 2mg nicotine cigarettes. You could also try e-cigarettes as an alternative to both.

Time to quit

By the time you reach this stage, you have laid the groundwork to quit for good. But to be sure of a positive outcome, you should gather all the support you can. Make sure your friends and work colleagues know what you are doing so they can help you by taking care not to stress you out and not overreacting if you are not at your best. It's also great to have a buddy to talk to whenever you crave nicotine. They can boost your resolve.

The withdrawal effects from nicotine are a direct result of its action on your blood sugar, adrenal hormone levels and key chemicals in the brain. It is incredibly helpful to follow a really

good nutritional programme during the first month after quitting, which we outline below in the summary of this chapter.
Make sure you always have a good breakfast, lunch and dinner
and ensure that low-GL snacks (see Chapter 23 for ideas) are
available throughout the day for when your blood sugar level
dips.

Chromium also helps to even out your blood sugar, as does
cinnamon. Take a 100mcg chromium supplement with breakfast,
and ideally one that contains the cinnamon extract cinnulin.
You could also add cinnamon to your cereal and other foods and
drink herbal teas containing cinnamon, such as liquorice and
cinnamon (see Resources).

You may also find it helpful to take a 5-hydroxytryptophan
(5-HTP) supplement. This is an amino acid that the body converts
into serotonin, an important brain chemical that controls mood.
Nicotine withdrawal tends to lower serotonin levels,[30] which can
lead to depression and irritability. By supplementing 200mg of
5-HTP, which is available in health-food stores, you can prevent
this happening. Start with 50mg twice a day and build up slowly
(but always consult your GP or a nutritional therapist if you are
also taking serotonin reuptake inhibitor antidepressant drugs, as
a combination of the two could push your levels too high). 5-HTP
is best absorbed when it is taken away from protein foods and
with carbohydrate foods, so take it either on an empty stomach
or with a piece of fruit or an oatcake. If you find that you have difficulty sleeping, you may want to try taking 5-HTP an hour before
bed, as serotonin is converted into the sleep hormone melatonin
at night, aiding a good night's sleep.

Detoxifying your body

An important factor in helping to reduce cravings is to boost
the body's ability to detoxify and eliminate harmful substances,
including nicotine. There are five key things you can do to speed
up this process:

- exercise

- sweat

- drink plenty of water

- supplement vitamin C, and

- supplement niacin.

Putting these together is a winning formula for rapid and effective detoxification.

Most gyms have either a sauna or a steam room (also look out for infrared saunas in health spas, which facilitate detox at lower temperatures). Here's how to make the best use of them:

- Take 1 gram of vitamin C and 100mg of niacin.

- Go for a power walk or undertake some other form of gentle cardiovascular exercise that raises your heart rate and stimulates circulation.

- Once you start blushing as a consequence of the niacin, enter the sauna or steam room. The sauna should never be at a temperature above 27°C (80°F). If you start to feel too warm, come out and take a cold shower to cool down, then re-enter, building up to an overall duration of half an hour. Always finish with a cool shower, as this washes away any toxins excreted through the skin (warm water opens up the pores, so they can be reabsorbed).

- Drink a litre of water and keep drinking at regular intervals.

Aim to repeat this every day for at least a week, and preferably for a fortnight. However, please note that this routine is not recommended if you have a history of cardiovascular disease, unless under proper medical supervision. While no danger is anticipated or reported, the combination of exercise, niacin and saunas can act as a substantial stimulation to circulation, and hence cellular detoxification, which is the purpose of this routine.

Beware of smoking cessation drugs

The attraction of simply taking a pill to solve your nicotine addiction is obvious. But as with many drugs, prescription medications to aid smoking cessation have not been found to be especially effective, and they also carry the risk of unpleasant – or even deadly – side-effects. For example, the American Food and Drug Administration (FDA) ruled in 2009 that varenicline (marketed as Champix in the UK, Europe and Canada, and Chantix in the USA) must carry a 'black box' warning (the FDA's strongest safety alert) due to the drug's potential to increase risk of suicide. It has also ruled that varenicline may be associated with an increased risk of cardiovascular events, such as heart attacks and strokes. More common side-effects include nausea, vivid dreams, constipation and flatulence. But even if you get through the treatment, its effectiveness is not especially impressive – in a trial sponsored by its manufacturer, Pfizer, 77 per cent of those taking varenicline had resumed smoking a year later. This is probably because the drug aims to replicate nicotine receptor stimulation in the brain, albeit in a far milder way, without addressing all the other issues that underpin addiction. By taking the optimum nutrition approach outlined in this chapter instead, you will cover all the bases and dramatically increase your chance of success.

Summary

- We recommend you follow the Stress Cure programme (see Part 6) for a month *before* you embark on quitting smoking. That way you will be on the way to better blood sugar balance, you will have eliminated your intake of other stimulants and you will have had a good supply of energy-supporting nutrients, so you will be in a more stable place when you start to reduce your nicotine intake.

- In the week before you get ready to quit, keep a smoking diary (see page 299): note down when you smoke and how you feel before and after each cigarette. This will help you identify the habits that accompany your smoking.

- Break these habits one at a time, over the course of several weeks.

- Next, reduce your nicotine *load* – either via a weaker brand of cigarettes or by using nicotine gum or e-cigarettes. Then reduce the *number* you smoke, over the course of a few weeks, until you are down to just five a day. Once you achieve that, you are ready to quit.

- Enlist help and support from those around you to help you boost your resolve.

- Supplement wise, keep taking the core supplement regime of the Stress Cure programme, using the 'extra energy hit' and 'calm in a capsule' formulas as and when required (see Chapter 22).

- Add extra chromium to aid blood sugar balance – take 100mcg with each meal, and look for a formula that also contains cinnamon. Also supplement 50mg of niacin (the flushing variety – nicotinic acid) with each meal to reduce nicotine cravings.

- Eat a diet high in vegetables, fruit and seeds to alkalinise your body. If you crave a cigarette, have a fruit snack, which should help. Supplementing 600mg of calcium and 400mg of magnesium can provide further alkalinising support.

- Regular light exercise can help (see Chapter 9).

- If you feel depressed and irritable, supplement 50mg of 5-HTP twice a day, and build up to a total intake of 200mg.

- Consider a week's daily sauna and supplement programme (as outlined above) to aid nicotine detoxification.

CHAPTER 8

Rebalance Your Stress Hormones

By now you have probably realised that what you eat and drink (and smoke) has a profound effect on how you feel. But how exactly does this process work? What are the mediators of your mood? What are the molecules of your emotions? The answer is hormones. They affect key chemicals in the brain that change your whole perception of your life and your environment.

There are two main biochemical reasons why people become addicted to stress or stimulants. The first is that these can raise a low blood sugar level, thus temporarily improving a person's energy. The second is that they can stimulate the release of adrenal hormones, providing a motivating kick-start to keep you going through the day. Understanding how these chemicals work provides a big clue to solving the stress syndrome.

The dance of the hormones

Hormones are biochemical messengers. They are special chemicals, produced in specific cells, collectively known as endocrine glands (e.g. the adrenal glands or thyroid gland), that are released into the bloodstream to deliver their instructions to targeted body cells.

We've already met a few of them:

- Insulin, which helps carry sugar out of the blood and into the cells to make energy.

- Glucagon, which raises low blood sugar by calling on sugar reserves stored as glycogen and fat.

- Adrenalin, which raises blood sugar by breaking down glycogen.

- Cortisol, another adrenal hormone, which has multiple functions, including regulating blood sugar by stimulating the liver to make more glucose from protein.

There's one more adrenal hormone worth a mention to get a complete picture of how the body maintains energy and stress resistance: DHEA (dehydroepiandrosterone), the rejuvenating, anti-ageing cousin of cortisol.

When all of these hormones are in sync, so are you. Your energy is good, your mind is sharp and so-called 'stress' becomes simply another problem to solve. Before explaining how they all link together and how you can bring them into balance, it's worth knowing how they relate to each other chemically.

Insulin, glucagon and adrenalin are proteins. This means they are made from a particular arrangement of amino acids, the constituents of protein in food. Other nutrients are also used in the manufacture of these protein hormones: for example, insulin requires zinc and vitamin B_6, while adrenalin requires vitamins C and B_{12}, among others.

Cortisol and DHEA are fat-based compounds known as steroid hormones. They are made from cholesterol: you get this from your diet and it is also manufactured every day by your liver. These two hormones are chemically very similar and they have a profound effect on each other. Knowing how much cortisol and DHEA a person produces helps to identify where they are in the stress cycle. (The sex hormones progesterone, oestrogens and testosterone are also made from cholesterol, which is why excessive stress can lead to other hormone-related problems in both men and women.)

The hormone chain

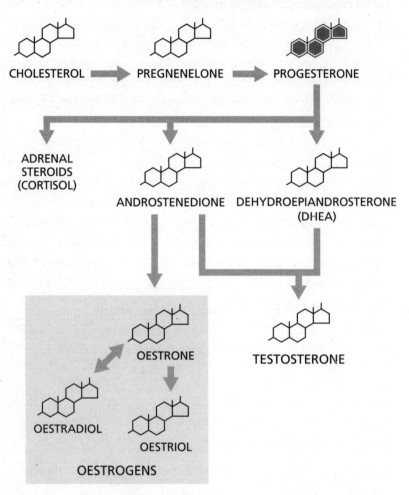

Both stress and sex hormones are made from cholesterol. In times of stress, cortisol is prioritised, so depleting other hormones such as revitalising DHEA, motivating testosterone and the female hormones progesterone and oestogens.

How hormones affect your blood sugar level

Just like the pieces in a chess game, each hormone can affect another in a specific way.

For instance, if you eat a meal containing carbohydrate, it's digested down to glucose and your blood sugar rises. Insulin is then released to get the glucose out of the blood and into the cells as fuel or into storage as fat. If your blood sugar level isn't quite high enough, perhaps on the rebound after a sugary snack or because it's been a while since you last ate, glucagon is released, which makes more glucose available. It does this by breaking down short-term reserves of glycogen, which are held in your liver and muscles.

If your blood sugar level drops very low, this stimulates the release of adrenal hormones, which perceive this lack of vital fuel as an emergency – and therefore a stress. The adrenal hormones have one main mission – ensuring your survival. If this is threatened, they leap into action. They do this if you injure yourself, undergo surgery, are shocked (perhaps by the flash of a speed trap), skip a meal or have a serious rebound in blood sugar after eating the wrong kind of food. The body first releases adrenalin, the effects of which last only a short period of time (up to an hour), then cortisol and DHEA. Between them, these chemicals have many effects, all designed to make sure you've got the fuel and physical resources to 'fight or take flight'. So, whenever your blood sugar level dips too low, the adrenal hormones are released to get it back up again. Most of us rely on these dynamics – albeit often unconsciously – and help the process along by stimulating the release of adrenalin when our blood sugar is low by having a coffee.

The problem is that the extra energy liberated by adrenal stimulation comes at a cost. Ultimately, over the long term, it suppresses your immune system and slows down the body's rate of repair and its metabolism. In other words, the cost of going into the survival mode of stress is rapid ageing. For instance, living in a state of stress for an extended period of time results in weight gain and a greater risk of osteoporosis and degenerative disease.

As we learned in Chapters 2 and 3, we can't keep doing this for ever. The body adapts to stress and then finally maladapts, entering a state of exhaustion. At this point you will not be able to cope with stress and you'll feel exhausted. Knowing where you are in the cycle is key to finding the best way out of it.

The stress cycle

Stage 1 – The initial response (alarm stage)

What we think of as stress – for example, working to a tight deadline – stimulates the pituitary gland in the brain, which releases ACTH, a hormone that, in turn, stimulates the adrenal glands to release cortisol and DHEA. The brain stops producing ACTH only when they reach sufficiently high levels. Once the stress is over, cortisol and DHEA levels return to normal. This is often the point when we reach for that coffee.

The stress cycle

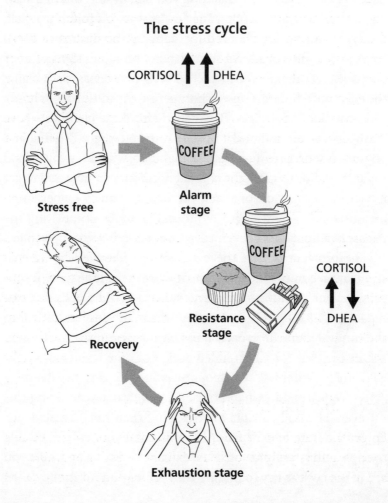

Stage 2 – Adaptation (resistance stage)

With repeated stress, the body becomes tired and less responsive to the effects of cortisol. This calls for more of it to be produced. Since DHEA can be turned into cortisol, the body makes the extra cortisol at the expense of DHEA, so levels of the former rise while levels of the latter fall. As it takes more time for these adrenal hormones to raise blood sugar levels to normal, you feel tired and less able to keep on an even keel as far as energy is concerned. At this point those stimulants look even more attractive, making us feel we need a coffee *and* something sweet to keep going.

Over time, adaptation turns to maladaptation. Your cortisol level keeps going up, while your DHEA level keeps falling since the body can no longer produce adequate quantities of both. You start to suffer from chronic fatigue and shows signs of poor immunity. This is because the adrenal hormones shut down your immune system. Now you will be more prone to infections and find them harder to overcome. In this stage you react more strongly to stress and find it hard to return to normal. Being in a permanent state of stress becomes your way of life.

Stage 3 – Exhaustion

Eventually your body can't even produce enough cortisol, so levels of both this and DHEA will be dangerously low. In this stage you fall to pieces when facing even the slightest stress, get irritable, can't concentrate, have no energy and feel depressed. You may also suffer headaches, find it harder to tolerate alcohol and be more prone to inflammatory and degenerative conditions and diseases.

Stress and the thyroid

To get the full picture of this hormonal game of stress, we also need to understand the role played by the thyroid gland. Situated at the base of the throat, the thyroid produces a hormone called thyroxine, which effectively tells cells to speed up their energy production (i.e. increase their metabolism).

In the initial stages of stress, thyroxine levels rise to support the 'state of emergency'. But when you continue to experience stress over a prolonged period and cortisol levels remain high, thyroxine levels fall. This is because cortisol is directly antagonistic to thyroxine: it tries to conserve energy by slowing down metabolism in what it perceives as a longer-term emergency situation. As a result, thyroxine levels fall, as does body temperature.

Thyroid tests measure two things: the level of thyroid stimulating hormone (TSH) and the level of thyroxine. The pituitary gland produces TSH, which in turn stimulates the thyroid gland to produce more thyroxine, of which there are two kinds: T_4 and T_3. T_4 is a kind of 'pre-hormone' that is converted into T_3, the active hormone. It's the T_3 level that counts.

When cortisol levels are raised under stress, TSH levels fall, so there's less stimulation of the thyroid gland. Also, cortisol inhibits the process in which the inactive T_4 turns into the active T_3. So low TSH and low T_3 is another indicator of prolonged stress. See 'Is your thyroid impacting on your weight?' (page 222) for more details of how you can test yourself at home.

The thyroxine pathway

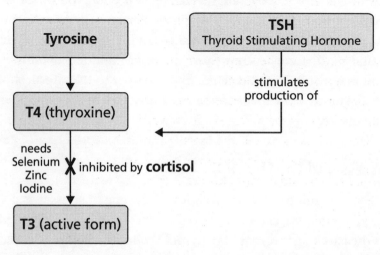

Test your stress

Exactly where you are in this cycle of stress can be pinpointed by measuring your levels of the stress hormones via an adrenal stress index test, which analyses saliva samples over the course of a day. Analysis of salivary hormone levels rather than blood can be more effective. The reason for this is that, once hormones are released, most of them attach to proteins in the blood. Only a small amount of the hormone remains 'free', unattached and able to deliver its message, and this 'free' hormone level is thought to be reflected better in saliva than in blood.

The levels of and relationship between cortisol and DHEA allow you to gauge where you are in the stress cycle. Nutritional therapists, who have been trained to devise the most effective regime to rebalance your stress hormone levels, can usually arrange an adrenal stress index test.

Other useful indicators are your heart rate and blood pressure, which are directly influenced by adrenalin levels. When you are unstressed and lying down, which is the state you should be in before rising after sleep, your pulse will naturally be lower, as will your blood pressure. Simply the act of standing up raises adrenalin and consequently pulse and blood pressure. If your blood pressure is high and there is no change in it when you stand, or if your pulse upon waking is high (80-plus beats a minute), you are probably highly stressed. Feeling cold is another common symptom, due to the suppressive effect of high levels of stress hormones on the thyroid gland.

Supported by knowledge of how you feel and any stress-related symptoms, you can establish where you stand in relation to stress, which is one of the most common reasons for chronic fatigue. The chart overleaf shows the symptoms and hormone levels a test would identify for each stage of stress.

Stress test: which stage are you?

	STAGE 0	STAGE 1	STAGE 2	STAGE 3
	No stress	Normal stress	Prolonged stress	Chronic stress
	–	Normal response	Poor adaptation	Can't adapt
DHEA	Normal	High	Low	Low
CORTISOL	Normal	High	High	Low
	Stress free	Stressed	Stressed out	Can't cope
	Even energy	Energy OK	Always tired	Chronic fatigue
	Good concentration	OK concentration	Poor concentration	Unclear thinking
	Mood good	Irritable	Anxious and depressed	Depressed
	Sleep good	Sleep OK	Disturbed sleep	Always tired

How your mood impacts on your hormones

By now, you will understand how depleting long-term stress can be. When we react stressfully to life's events, we also tend to generate negative emotions – anxiety, anger, fear, irritation and hostility, for example. But the opposite of stress is not necessarily being super-relaxed. You can be firing on all cylinders and in a positive emotional state – and although your sympathetic nervous system activity is high, you won't be generating adrenalin or cortisol. Equally, you can be in a low-energy state but feeling negative emotions, such as depression, despair, boredom or apathy, that can damage your overall health.

The chart below illustrates the role emotions play in stress hormone balance. For greater health and resilience, ideally you should spend the majority of your time in the right-hand quadrants and avoid the top-left quadrant: stressed and unhappy, with emotions such as anger, irritation, frustration, fear and anxiety. These negative emotional states all increase your risk of suffering a heart attack.

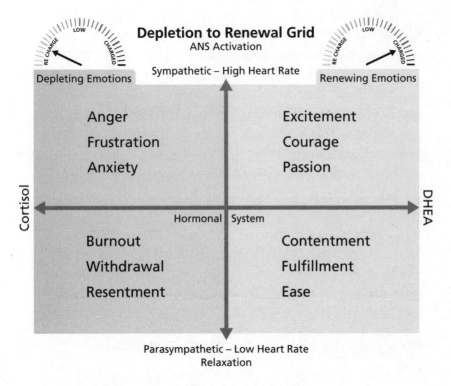

Source: *HeartMath 2014, Depleteion to Renewal Grid™*

The HeartMath® system, which we explore in Chapter 12, includes a technique to help you feel fewer negative emotions and more positive emotions.

Rebalancing your stress

Needless to say, everything discussed in earlier chapters will help you to restabilise your stress response: weaning yourself off stimulants; avoiding sugar and refined foods; increasing your consumption of low-GL foods and eating them with protein; and supplementing key energy nutrients. Ensuring you are getting enough sleep is also important (see Chapter 11, especially if sleep is a problem for you). It's also worth making some time to include regular activities that help to increase your resilience to stress and increase your overall well-being. The HeartMath system, for example, is a simple technique that takes only five minutes each day, yet it can help to rebalance stress hormones remarkably quickly. So, if you are feeling stressed, tired and short of time, you should consider adding it to your daily routine (see Chapter 12 for more information).

If you already exercise (and indeed if you don't), you should consult Chapter 9, which explains why certain types of exercise are better than others when you are feeling stressed. Just 15 minutes of restorative activity every other day can help you feel better faster. Understanding more about your stress triggers – and how you can adapt the way you react to them to develop a more positive attitude to life's challenges – is also important. We look at this topic in more detail in Chapters 13 and 14. Finally, we bring all this together in an action plan for you in the Stress Cure programme (Part 6).

Stress relief in a bottle

You might be tempted to look for the solution to stress and low energy on the shelves of a pharmacy or health-food shop. Indeed, various specialist supplements offer very effective support, especially if you know where you are in the stress cycle. But these will be effective in the long term only if they are incorporated into a holistic strategy that also addresses diet and stimulant addiction, introduces regular de-stressing activities, such as the HeartMath

Quick Coherence® tool or yoga, and promotes adequate rest and down time. For example, adrenal glandulars can help to revitalise overworked adrenal glands; supplements containing theanine and the amino acid GABA can help to make you feel more relaxed and less 'edgy';[31] and adaptogenic herbs such as Siberian ginseng, rhodiola rosea, ashwaganda and schisandra have been found to alleviate fatigue and other symptoms of stress.[32] The three most reputable adaptogens are the ginseng family, reishi mushroom (also known as lingzhi in China) and rhodiola. In Asia, especially China and Japan, reishi has been revered for 5000 years. Chinese reishi mushroom (*Ganodermum lucidum*) is often used to modify or enhance the effects of other stress-fighting herbs. It also helps to lower insulin levels.[33] Moringa also gives you a natural energy boost.

Beware of energy tablets that contain caffeine or guarana, a natural form of caffeine. Like stimulants, these provide a short-term fix that leave you more tired and imbalanced in the long run. Liquorice is often touted as a tonic for stress, but it can raise cortisol levels, which is not ideal if you are already in stage 2 of the stress cycle, as it can fast-track you to the final, 'exhaustion' stage. However, if you are already in stage 3 – and your cortisol is no longer high – then it can help to slow down the breakdown of cortisol, so making it last longer.[34] Choose liquorice powder in capsules, rather than eating a highly sugared liquorice sweet. Siberian ginseng is probably OK in any circumstances. While it can raise cortisol, it seems to work as an 'adaptogen', helping you to adapt by stabilising the stress response and reducing fatigue.[35]

If an adrenal stress index test indicates low DHEA, don't be tempted to supplement it (although you will probably find it difficult to do this anyway, as DHEA supplements are not available in the UK). Instead, follow the advice in this book, and especially look at the HeartMath exercise outlined in Chapter 12. This simple breathing and focus technique is a surprisingly effective means of increasing low DHEA levels.

Summary

In summary, the fastest way to rebalance your stress hormones is to:

- Avoid adrenal stimulants, eat a low-GL diet, and take nutritional supplements to support energy production and balance your blood sugar. All of this is set out in detail in the Stress Cure programme in Part 6.

- Do the right kind of exercise, get enough sleep and change your lifestyle to reduce your stress level.

- If you have been suffering with stress for a long time and are feeling constantly tired or imbalanced, have your stress hormone levels checked by a qualified practitioner.

PART 3

Build up Your Stress Resilience

When you're feeling stressed and overloaded, slowing down and focusing on rest and relaxation can seem rather indulgent. Yet this is exactly what you need to do. Not only will you feel calmer, you'll be far better able to cope with life's difficulties. However, we're not talking about zoning out in front of the TV or forgetting all your troubles with a session at the pub. Rather, you should make space for activities that deliver real benefits and enhance how you feel. This is key to building stress resilience.

In this section, we will show you how to generate vital energy, including through types of exercise that do far more than give your body a workout. You'll also learn the value of relaxation techniques that help you to switch into a more peaceful state, activating beneficial and revitalising chemicals that enable you to function smarter and expend less precious energy. Making the most of restorative sleep is also covered, as this is vital to building greater resilience to stress. Finally, you'll discover probably the most valuable tool for switching off stress and building resilience – a surprisingly simple yet transformational technique from the HeartMath® system.

CHAPTER 9

Generating Vital Energy

When you're looking for a solution to stress and fatigue, there's more to it than simply eating better and developing a more positive attitude to life. Being stress resilient requires a sense of vitality and energy to deal with difficult situations. While nutrition and mindset both have big parts to play, generating vital energy is another important part of the puzzle.

In Western cultures, vital energy is a relatively new concept. Yet Eastern philosophies have long embraced the notion: Buddhists and Hindus know it as *prana*; the Chinese refer to it as *chi*; Japanese traditions call it *ki*. Each term translates to 'life force' and there are entire medical systems based on generating and distributing this vital energy (such as acupuncture). It's what makes us feel vibrant and alive. And you can generate more vital energy simply by breathing more fully, spending time in the natural world and doing specific vital energy-generating exercises.

Oxygen: are you getting enough?

Oxygen is the most important nutrient of all. It accounts for about 80 per cent of your body's make-up; it is a component of water, fat and protein; and when combined with glucose it is what your body uses to make energy. Deficiency results in death in minutes.

The assumption is that we all get enough oxygen from breathing, yet there is a big difference between 'sufficient' and 'optimal' levels, as we'll see shortly. The *type* of air that you breathe can also have a big impact. A few hours of breathing in city air compared to mountain air provides a vivid example of how air quality can affect your vitality.

New Zealand scientist Dr Les Simpson believes that a lack of oxygen can contribute to such maladies as chronic fatigue syndrome and muscle pain. This is because oxygen is required by all cells to make energy. It is carried around your body in red blood cells via your arteries, and as these arteries become narrower, eventually turning into tiny blood capillaries, the red blood cells release the oxygen so it can pass through the capillary walls and into the surrounding cells. At the capillary/cell interface, the cell receives oxygen and nutrients from the blood, and gives off carbon dioxide and other unwanted by-products of metabolism. These capillaries are only 4 microns wide (for context, a human hair is about 75 microns wide), yet red blood cells are typically 7 microns in diameter. So how, Simpson wondered, do they manage to travel along such a narrow passage? The answer is that they squeeze through. However, some red blood cells are too large to do this, some are too inflexible and others clump together. These can create a log-jam which results in a deficit of oxygen supply to cells, leading to a build-up of lactic acid and poor cell function.

A common symptom of chronic fatigue syndrome (CFS) is muscle pain after exertion (see Chapter 17 for more on CFS). Muscle pain is also a symptom of polymyalgia, an inflammatory condition that is particularly prevalent among older women. A number of researchers have also observed a lack of oxygen in the frontal lobes of the brain of people diagnosed with schizophrenia, and treatment with extra oxygen has been found to help.[1]

How nutrient deficiency impacts oxygen delivery

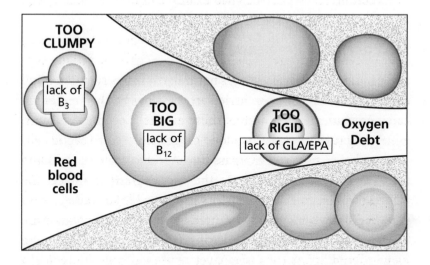

Certain nutrients are essential for healthy red blood cell function: for example, a lack of B_{12} is the most common cause of oversized red blood cells, while a deficiency of essential fats (GLA/EPA) makes them too rigid and therefore unable to squeeze through capillaries. Niacin (vitamin B_3) helps by increasing the electrochemical charge on cells so that they repel each other and don't clump together; it also dilates the blood vessels through the release of histamine. All of us need a good intake of these nutrients every day. However, if you suspect a lack of oxygen at a cellular level may be an issue for you, it's worth consulting a nutritional therapist, who will devise a tailored supplement programme to boost your intake. This will probably include the following:

- 100mg or more of niacin twice a day (this can cause temporary blushing for around 20–30 minutes).

- 150mg of the omega 6 essential fat GLA and 500mg of the omega 3 fat EPA.

- 25–500mcg* of vitamin B₁₂, possibly in a sublingual formula (which is more easily absorbed), or in higher doses or through injections if severe deficiency is diagnosed.

Increase your lung capacity

You can also increase your oxygen intake by increasing your lung capacity. Most people use less than one-third of their potential capacity, but exercise and breathing exercises can increase this, which helps to boost the intake of oxygen, leading to better oxygenation of tissues and extra energy. Aerobic, stamina-building activities such as jogging, swimming, circuit training and cycling all require you to breathe deeper and harder. However, if you have been experiencing a lot of stress, it's wise to stick with more gentle forms of aerobic exercise – such as a brisk walk, gentle jogging, dancing or yoga (see pages 97–8) – as your body might interpret anything too vigorous as an additional form of stress, which will be counterproductive. As long as the exercise you choose stimulates deeper breathing, you will feel the benefit, especially if you breathe from your stomach, as this will help to open up your ribcage and diaphragm and allow in more air. You could also do some daily exercises that focus purely on breathing.

The breath of life

Breathing is something most of us take for granted, yet certain ancient traditions have used breathing exercises for thousands of years to produce conscious, healthful changes in the body.

Our breathing reflects our emotions, and each emotional state has its own distinct breathing pattern. For example, when we are anxious or afraid, our breathing becomes rapid and shallow. Con-

---

* Some people require very high doses of B₁₂ and other B vitamins. The best way to tell if you are one of them is by having your homocysteine level checked, as levels of this natural substance in the blood are a good indicator of B vitamin status and individual requirements (see Resources at the end of the book for more details).

versely, when we are happy and relaxed, our breathing is naturally slow and deep. Working with the breath is a fundamental part of both meditation and yoga. The breath is the link between mind and body – the key to calming the mind and relaxing the body.

By slowing and deepening your breathing, you may also live longer. That is because there appears to be a universal law in nature: the heart of every mammal, including humans, beats 2.5–3.5 billion times in an average lifetime.[2] For people with an average heart rate of 72 beats per minute, that equates to a lifespan of 70 to 80 years. So, slowing your heart rate to 60 beats per minute could add about seven years to your life. Although this has not yet been proven, breathing more fully to slow your heart rate certainly seems sensible. Deeper breathing and a slow pulse are both well-acknowledged signs of health. The stronger your heart, the less often it needs to beat; and the deeper your breath, the more tissues will be oxygenated.

However, there may be more to breathing than that. Yoga philosophy tells us that the air we breathe contains *prana* as well as oxygen. So, by performing conscious breathing exercises, you will accumulate this vital energy and revitalise your body and mind.

Exercise: Boost your oxygen intake

This exercise is adapted from a traditional yoga practice called dirga pranayama, or three-part breath. It's designed to maximise your oxygen intake by utilising all of your lungs' capacity, and also helps to calm your mind and make you feel more grounded. You can do it while sitting comfortably (e.g. on a chair or cross-legged on the floor) or while lying on your back. It takes around five minutes.

1. Close your eyes and check through your body, from head to toes, relaxing any parts that are holding tension.

2. Concentrate on your breathing and focus your attention on your natural inhalation and exhalation.

3. Now start to inhale deeply through the nose, and, with

each inhalation, feel the air filling your belly, so it expands like a balloon.

4. When you exhale, push all the air out from your belly through your nose, bringing your navel back towards your spine to expel every last bit.

5. Repeat these deep belly breaths five times.

6. On your next inhalation, fill the belly as before, then draw in a little more breath, so you feel your ribcage expanding.

7. When you exhale, first let go of the air in your ribcage, then from your belly, drawing the navel back to your spine as before.

8. Repeat these belly and ribcage expanding breaths five times.

9. Now, fill your belly, then your ribcage, then take in a little more breath to fill your upper chest with air, right up to your collarbones.

10. When you exhale, expel the air in reverse order again – first from your upper chest, then your ribcage and finally your belly.

11. Repeat these belly, ribcage and upper chest expanding breaths five times.

12. Now you are practising three-part breath. Continue for a further ten breaths, aiming to make each inhalation and exhalation flow smoothly, without pause.

You can download an MP3 file of this and many of the other exercises outlined in the book at www.patrickholford.com or www.susannah-lawson.co.uk.

There's more to air than oxygen

We are closer than ever to finding a way to measure this invisible *prana* energy. Some scientists think it's connected with charged particles in the air, called ions. These particles have positive effects on us when they are negatively charged – and vice versa. This is why ionisers generate negative ions. High levels of positive ions, the bad guys, are found during strong winds, such as the Mistral that blows along the Rhône valley in France. With it comes PMT (pre-*Mistral* tension) as the wind is rumoured to make the valley's inhabitants grumpy and irritable. Conversely, after a thunderstorm, or close to a waterfall, the air is charged with negative ions, the good guys. These may help us to accumulate vital energy. You can also feel more alive and vital when you spend time walking by the sea, relaxing in a park or strolling through a forest. According to research by Dr Aaron Michelfelder, Professor of Family Medicine at Loyola University Chicago's Stritch School of Medicine, walking in a forest or park reduces levels of the stress hormone cortisol and lowers heart rate and blood pressure.[3] It also increases levels of white blood cells, meaning it boosts your immunity to disease.

Another way to accumulate vital energy is through specific breathing exercises (see the example on page 95). Most yoga and meditation techniques teach a variety of ways to deepen your breathing. In addition to aiding oxygen delivery, this is a great way to calm the emotions and clear the mind. Tension makes the breath shallow, while taking deep breaths reduces tension.

Exercise for vital energy

Energy isn't just about the food you eat and the air you breathe. It's also linked to the state of your body. Without exercise, the body loses muscle tone and accumulates tension and you end up feeling tired. Exercise improves the circulation and oxygenates the blood, which increases your energy levels. But there's more to exercise than simple physical training. Scientific research into yoga and the Oriental exercise systems tai chi and qigong have found a positive health effect that doesn't occur from aerobics classes or running around the park. While excessive aerobic exercise can actually depress the immune system and overstress the body, tai chi and qigong can boost well-being, mood and immunity.[4] Similarly, yoga has been shown to have positive effects on heart rate, blood pressure,[5] and mental[6] and physical performance beyond that expected from physical exercise alone.

In addition to keeping you fit, all of these ancient exercise regimes were designed to generate vitality by removing the blockages caused by accumulated tension. Most of us accumulate stress every day, which manifests in our minds as anxiety and in our bodies as tension. The underlying philosophy of the martial arts of the East and the ancient Indian traditions is that tension blocks the flow of vital energy and halts rejuvenation. Therefore, yoga, tai chi and qigong are designed to break through the blockage, unlock the tension and allow you to return to a state of equilibrium. Unlike body-building, the emphasis is on increasing flexibility and suppleness to allow the *chi* or *prana* to flow.

A growing body of research supports the stress-relieving benefits of these types of exercise: for example, studies have found that tai chi and qigong can reduce levels of stress hormones and decrease heart rate.[7] And doctors at the Boston University Medical Center have found that yoga is especially beneficial for those suffering from stress-related conditions, as it can stimulate the parasympathetic nervous system (as opposed to the sympathetic nervous system, which is triggered by stress) and increase levels of the calming neurotransmitter gamma amino-butyric acid (GABA).[8] Low levels of GABA are common in people with anxiety disorders, depression, epilepsy and chronic pain.

Practising yoga, tai chi or qigong usually requires you to attend a class (see Resources, page 308). However, this can be challenging if you live in a remote location with a lack of good local teachers, or find it difficult to make the time to attend regular sessions. In these circumstances, if you're looking for a quick and extremely effective form of vital energy-generating exercise that you can do at home, we recommend Psychocalisthenics®.

Psychocalisthenics: the holistic workout

This exercise system was developed by Oscar Ichazo, founder of the Arica Institute in New York, an organisation that is dedicated to helping people achieve their full potential. Psychocalisthenics means strength (*sthenia*) and beauty (*cali*) through the breath (*psyche*). It encompasses a routine of 23 exercises that can be done in less than 20 minutes. The breath is the driving force, as each of the exercises is guided by a precise deep-breathing pattern.

Psychocalisthenics is unique because it combines movement, breath control and exercise – a perfect fusion of Eastern and Western philosophies – to generate vital energy. At first glance, it looks like a hybrid of yoga, dance, tai chi and martial arts. This is hardly surprising as Ichazo is a master of both martial arts and yoga. 'In the same way that we have an everyday need for food and nourishment, we have to promote the circulation of our vital energy as an everyday business,' he says. Ichazo first developed Psychocalisthenics (often shortened to Psychocals) in 1958, and it has since been taken up by thousands of people all over the world.

Advocates of Psychocals give it glowing reports. 'This is exercise pared to perfection. I wasn't sweating buckets as I would after an aerobics class but I could feel I had exercised far more muscles. I was feeling clear-headed and bright rather than wiped out,' said natural health expert Jane Alexander, when she reviewed the routine for the *Daily Mail*.

One of the things we like most about Psychocals is that you don't have to go anywhere, wear special clothes, or buy any expensive equipment. Once you've learned the routine, you can do it in around 16 minutes in your own home, guided by the DVD or a talk-through music recording. The best way to learn it is to do a one-day training course. These are held frequently in various locations throughout the UK (see Resources, page 307). You can learn it from the DVD, of course, but there's nothing like having someone there to tell you what you're doing right or wrong and offering advice on how to perfect your technique. There's also a fascinating book called *Master Level Exercise*, which explains the basis of Psychocals and how each exercise revitalises a different part of the body or mind (see Resources, page 307).

Redefining vitality

As we've discussed, vitality, the very real experience of feeling full of energy, is more than just the consequence of your diet and physical fitness. The extra factor is harder to measure, but no less tangible. Vital energy is often described as the energy we draw in from the universe and, depending on how receptive we are, it has the power to nourish us at a fundamental level. As mentioned before, yoga, tai chi, qigong and other martial arts are all designed to make us more receptive, as is acupuncture, which works by unblocking channels of energy, called 'meridians', through which this vital energy is said to flow. You can also feel more energised and alive in natural surroundings because vital energy is that hidden ingredient that connects us with each other and with the world around us.

According to traditional Chinese medicine, vital energy comes to us from the food we eat and the air we breathe, but we are convinced that there is more to this than just absorbing nutrients, oxygen and negative ions. We are sure that eating organic, fresh food, prepared conscientiously, has a profoundly different effect than eating processed fast food, such as a hamburger made from grossly mistreated animals and reconstituted chips made from pesticide-laden potatoes. This difference cannot be explained by nutritional content alone. Similarly, we believe that it isn't just *what* we breathe but *how* we breathe that's important.

Summary

In summary, to maximise your overall energy and resistance to stress, we recommend you boost your vitality in the following ways:

- Be conscious of your breath and give yourself the opportunity to breathe more deeply through regular energy-generating exercise and/or deep-breathing exercises in order to boost your oxygen intake and reduce tension.

- Spend as much time as you can in clean air. If you are a city dweller, take regular trips to the countryside and choose holidays in the mountains or by the sea.

- Include some form of stress-relieving exercise in your weekly routine, such as yoga, tai chi, qigong or Psychocals.

- If you suffer from chronic fatigue syndrome or suspect you may not be utilising oxygen effectively, visit a nutritional therapist. They will help you address any deficiencies in the nutrients that are essential for efficient oxygen circulation.

Note: Psychocalisthenics® is a registered trademark of Oscar Ichazo, used with permission.

CHAPTER 10

Rapid Relaxation
Techniques that Work

When you are feeling stressed and overwhelmed, it's easy to perpetuate a negative emotional state by pushing yourself harder in an attempt to catch up or get more done. However, what you really need to do is the opposite and slow down. We sometimes hear clients say, 'I don't have time to relax,' but relaxation isn't a treat to fit in when you have a spare moment. It's essential to your health and well-being.

The relaxation response is the physiological opposite to the 'fight or flight' stress response. It activates your parasympathetic nervous system, which works to calm you down and restore equilibrium after your sympathetic nervous system has instigated a stress reaction.

Scientists have discovered that the long-term practice of regular relaxation activities can also change the expression of genes involved in the body's response to stress. As well as increasing overall 'wellness', this can counteract the adverse clinical effects of stress in such conditions as hypertension, anxiety, diabetes and ageing. A 2013 study by the Benson-Henry Institute for Mind–Body Medicine at Massachusetts General Hospital took the research one step further by identifying how this works in practice.[9] It examined the expression of more than 22,000 genes in 51 healthy adults, both before and after they undertook relaxation techniques such as meditation and yoga. Analysis revealed that the pathways involved with making energy, particularly the function of mitochondria (the engines that generate energy in every cell), became more efficient during the relaxation response. Pathways controlled by the activation of a protein called NF-κB – known to have a prominent role in inflammation, stress, trauma and cancer – were suppressed after the relaxation response. The expression of genes involved in insulin pathways was also significantly altered.

Moreover, in addition to bringing about biochemical changes that provide long-term health benefits, relaxation activities can improve your mood. Meditating for just half an hour a day, for example, can reduce anxiety, depression, stress and pain, thereby improving quality of life, according to a 2014 review published in *JAMA Internal Medicine*.[10]

How to choose the type of relaxation that's right for you

So it's clear that incorporating regular relaxation into your daily routine not only increases your immediate sense of well-being but enhances your long-term health. There is no shortage of classes and techniques to help you relax. The challenge is finding the one that works best for you – and then doing it regularly. When working with clients, we usually suggest approaches based on their dominant mind state. For example:

- If you feel wired, agitated or angry, you are likely to find calming techniques, such as meditation, deep breathing and guided imagery, most helpful.

- If you are depressed, introverted or spaced out, activities that energise your nervous system, such as yoga, tai chi, qigong and psychocals, are especially beneficial. (You can find details of these exercises in the previous chapter.)

Use your breathing to activate relaxation

In Chapter 12 you will learn how a simple breathing and focus technique can dramatically reduce stress and improve well-being. But you can also use nothing more than your breathing to activate an immediate relaxing and calming influence. As soon as you notice yourself starting to feel stressed or overwhelmed, focus on your breathing. Aim to breathe a little more deeply, and with each breath in imagine that you are inhaling calm and peace. Then, when you breathe out, exhale any feelings of anxiety and tension. Feel your shoulders relaxing and wiggle about a bit to release any tension in your body. A few minutes of this can make you feel much more relaxed and better able to face the challenges of the day.

Tune in to the benefits of meditation

Meditation has been growing in popularity in the West as a way to switch off from the stresses of modern life and find inner peace. There's an ever-expanding body of research that supports claims of multiple health benefits from regular practice. You don't need to have any religious beliefs to meditate, and it can be an ideal way to make space for yourself in an otherwise hectic day.

There are many different techniques – from mindfulness and kindness-based practices to transcendental and Zen approaches, and more besides. Essentially, though, most of them teach similar skills – the means to find a calm centre within yourself and observe your thoughts and emotions while recognising that these are not who you truly are. 'When I understood that there was a part of me that could watch all these churning thoughts and feelings, it was a revelation,' said one of our clients, Emma. 'I realised that there was more to me than my physical, mental or emotional aspects and that was deeply liberating.'

Dr Elizabeth Hoge, a psychiatrist at the Center for Anxiety and Traumatic Stress Disorders at Massachusetts General Hospital and an assistant professor of psychiatry at Harvard Medical School, believes that mindfulness meditation can be especially helpful for those suffering with stress, anxiety and frequent worries. 'Mindfulness teaches you to recognise, "Oh, there's that thought again. I've been here before. But it's just that – a thought – and not a part of my core self,"' she explains.

When it comes to reducing stress, meditation certainly seems to be effective. A 2014 review looking at its impact on healthy people found that, 'Of the 17 studies, 16 demonstrated positive changes in psychological or physiological outcomes related to anxiety and/or stress.'[11] An earlier review – which analysed 47 trials with some 3515 participants – found that mindfulness meditation can also ease pain, as well as anxiety and depression. The researchers concluded: 'Clinicians should be prepared to talk with their patients about the role that a meditation program could have in addressing psychological stress.'[12]

Studies have found that kindness-based meditation can reduce negative and increase positive emotions when compared with standard types of relaxation.[13] Moreover, it seems that meditation can also reduce age-related cognitive decline,[14] insomnia, post-traumatic stress disorder and fatigue. It can even have a positive effect on the behaviour of infants born to mothers who meditate during pregnancy.[15]

The best way to learn is from an experienced teacher. You're likely to find classes in most areas (look for adverts in health-food shops, or ask local yoga teachers for a recommendation). Find someone whose philosophy appeals and who has their feet firmly on the ground (rather than their head in the clouds). Ideally, you should feel more grounded, aware and calm – not spaced out – after you meditate.

Exercise: Visualise a calming energy boost

Using visual imagery to focus your mind is another form of meditation and can be a useful tool to help you relax. There is a huge range of themes to choose from and numerous recordings you can download from the internet or buy on CD to guide you. Once you've got the hang of it, you can also make up your own, using calming images that you find particularly meaningful or restful. The trick is to stay focused on the exercise and not let your mind wander into areas that trigger stressful thoughts (recalling an argument, difficulties at work, your overwhelming to-do list, etc.). If you find your mind wandering, take a deep breath and return to your calming image.

Many of our clients find this visualisation exercise useful:

1. Sit down somewhere quiet where you won't be disturbed and make yourself comfortable, then close your eyes.

2. Picture yourself standing on a beautiful beach. No one else is around so the only sound you can hear is the lapping of the waves at the water's edge. The sand beneath your toes is soft and golden and you can feel the warm sunshine on your face.

3. You see a comfortable chair at the water's edge. Walk towards it and sit down. Sink back into the chair and feel it take your weight so you are fully supported.

4. Stretch your legs out so you can put your feet in the water. Feel the cool sea washing over your toes. Now picture that vast sea, and appreciate the huge volume of nourishing energy it contains.

5. You realise that you are connected to that energy, and as you breathe in you feel it rising up through your feet and filling your whole body.

6. Each time you breathe out, gradually let go of anything that doesn't nourish you – stressful thoughts, anxiety, ailments, concerns, worries. Imagine releasing them into the sea bit by bit and watching them dissolve into nothing.

7. Continue with this visualisation for whatever length of time feels most comfortable (ten minutes is usually a good guideline – but shorter or longer might suit you better). Then prepare to leave the chair at the water's edge, knowing that you will remain filled with the sea's nourishing energy even when you leave the beach behind. Know too that you can return at any point in the future.

8. Give yourself a few moments to bring your attention back to the room and slowly open your eyes and adjust.

> You can download an MP3 file of this visualisation exercise from
> www.patrickholford.com or www.susannah-lawson.co.uk.

If you like visualisation, you may also enjoy yoga nidra, an ancient yoga exercise designed to induce full-body relaxation and a deeper sense of consciousness. One of Patrick's favourites is Swami Jakananda's *Experience Yoga Nidra* CD (available to download via iTunes), which offers both 20-minute and 45-minute exercises, plus a handwritten guide.

Practise emotional stress release

There are times when a particular stressful event can overwhelm you and make it hard to focus on anything else. At such a time, using the emotional stress release (ESR) technique can be helpful. This simple yet effective exercise can quickly reduce the distress you feel and help you gain a wider perspective. It requires you to gently touch two points on your forehead just above your eyebrows that activate reflexes to bring more blood to the frontal lobes of your brain. As we explain in Chapter 12, your brain's frontal cortex is responsible for creative thinking and problem-solving, so stimulating these points while focusing on a specific issue that's causing you to feel stressed or anxious can help to alleviate negative feelings.

ESR points

Exercise: Emotional stress release

Here's how to practise ESR:

1. Close your eyes and lightly touch the two ESR points (see previous page) with each hand, using the tips of your fingers.

2. Focus on the issue that is causing you distress, or simply the feeling of anxiety or tension if you cannot pinpoint a specific problem.

3. Recall as much detail as you can: for example, run through the event or problem from start to finish, see it in your mind's eye, remember what people said and the expressions on their faces; most importantly, feel the emotions that the event triggered in you.

4. As you continue to touch your ESR points lightly, you should notice that it becomes harder to hold on to the imagery, feelings and memories. As they start to fade, keep bringing them back to mind.

5. After a few minutes, you will find the incident or feeling fades away completely and your mind begins to wander.

6. Remove your fingertips from the ESR points and open your eyes. You should feel calm and rebalanced because the stress trigger or negative emotion has been defused.

This exercise can be practised at any time of day, but it is especially useful at night if you wake up with stressful thoughts whirring around your mind that seem impossible to shift. If you are in a public place and don't want to draw too much attention to yourself, you can use one hand to touch both ESR points (in the same way as you might position your hand over your forehead to assess if you have a temperature).

Practise progressive relaxation

This technique requires you to focus on and consciously relax each part of your body, starting at your toes and running upwards to your head. It may seem like a lot to remember, but it's a natural progression from one body part to the next, so it's easy to follow. For guidance, you can download instructions from www.patrickholford.com or www.susannah-lawson.co.uk, or find a CD of progressive relaxation exercises.

Exercise: Progressive relaxation

1. Start by lying on your back on a bed or the floor and close your eyes. Focus on your breathing and allow your breaths to deepen slightly.

2. Concentrate on your feet and sense their weight. Consciously relax your toes, then your ankles, and feel them sink into the bed or the floor.

3. Move your focus to your calves. Again, sense their weight. Consciously relax them and feel them sink into the bed/floor.

4. Now focus on your knees. Sense their weight and let them sink into the bed/floor.

Repeat this for each part of your body as you move up towards your head. Your focus could flow something like this:

Upper legs and thighs, then buttocks and pelvis.

Abdomen (above your pelvis but below your chest).

Chest.

Hands, lower arms, then upper arms.

Shoulders, then neck.

Face and skull, then mouth and jaw. Pay particular attention to your jaw muscles and unclench them if they are tense.

Eyes. Sense if there is tension in your eyes or eyelids. If there is, consciously relax them and feel the tension melt away.

Cheeks. Consciously relax them and feel the back of your head sink further into the bed/floor.

Finally, scan through your whole body once again. If you come across any part that is still tense, consciously relax it and let it sink deeper into the bed/floor.

This exercise can be particularly helpful just before you go to sleep.

Exercise: Toe tensing

Tensing and relaxing your toes can help to draw tension from the rest of your body and help you relax. Do it while lying down – either before you go to sleep or if you are able to take a break and get horizontal during the day.

1. Lie on your back and close your eyes.

2. Focus your attention on your toes.

3. Flex all ten toes towards your head. Hold and slowly count to ten.

4. Release your toes, so they relax, and slowly count to ten again.

5. Repeat the flex and release cycle ten more times.

Case study: A relaxation convert

Ron is a 27-year computer programmer who came to see Susannah for help with his eczema. He also suffered with tension-related headaches and insomnia, which he believed were due to his stressful job and difficult working relationship with his boss. Ron adopted an anti-inflammatory diet and supplement programme and his skin started to improve. But the real breakthrough came once he was able to focus on relaxation as an antidote to his daily stress. Using the

Emotional Stress Release technique to break the cycle of running through problems over and over again in his head was, he said, 'like an amazing magic trick'. Alternating a visualisation exercise with progressive relaxation each evening when he went to bed also helped him to fall asleep more easily and stay asleep until morning. His tension headaches reduced from almost daily to a few of times a month at most. 'I honestly thought this all this relaxation stuff was a load of fluffy rubbish, but it's made an enormous difference to how I feel, function and look,' says Ron. 'I'm a true convert!'

Summary

Most days, we spend much of our time accumulating stress. So, for balance, you should spend some time releasing that stress. Don't think of relaxation as a lazy, indulgent waste of time. A huge body of scientific research supports both the short- and long-term benefits of regular relaxation and the notion that releasing stress is essential for our health. So pick a technique that works for you and commit to doing it regularly; ideally every day.

It's no bad thing if you fall asleep during an exercise, as that indicates you are relaxing and letting go of stress. But staying focused and awake should be the goal. If you can't find an exercise on these pages that works for you, keep searching for something that feels right. For instance, the HeartMath® Quick Coherence® technique is another excellent tool for reducing stress (see Chapter 12). Calming exercises such as tai chi, qigong and yoga (see Chapter 9) are also ideal routes to relaxation and may be more suitable if you like to 'do' rather than simply 'be'. There are also numerous experts in stress management who can provide one-to-one coaching (see Resources for more details).

CHAPTER 11

The Power of Sleep

Sleep is essential 'nourishment' for your body and mind. People who are stressed often suffer from sleep-related problems, and a lack of sleep is itself a stress factor.

According to the 100% Health survey, the UK's largest study into the connection between dietary habits and markers for health, 55 per cent of the population have difficulty sleeping or suffer restless sleep, while 43 per cent wake up feeling tired. In the Sleep Council's Great British Bedtime survey (2013), only 30 per cent of men and 22 per cent of women said they sleep very well. Almost half (47 per cent) said that stress and worry keep them awake at night. The majority also reported getting five to six hours of sleep a night, with only 22 per cent enjoying the recommended seven to eight hours.

Sleeping problems are often referred to as insomnia, although this can mean different things to different people. It is commonly defined as experiencing regular periods when you:

- Have difficulty falling asleep (on average taking more than 30 minutes to nod off).

- Wake up frequently during the night and have difficulty getting back to sleep.

- Wake up too early in the morning and are unable to return to sleep.

- Wake up tired or exhausted, which can persist throughout the day, making you feel irritable, anxious or depressed.

Lack of sleep not only makes you more prone to stress, but long term it increases your risk of poor health: for example, research shows that you're more than twice as likely to feel anxious and depressed if you don't get adequate sleep.[16] Your blood may also begin to clot abnormally, putting you at increased risk of heart attack or stroke.[17] A chronic sleep debt also almost doubles your chance of being obese,[18] and it's linked with diabetes, too.[19] As if all this wasn't enough, lack of sleep triggers the stress response and increases an inflammatory marker called CRP, which is a strong predictor of heart disease.[20]

Clearly, if sleep is a problem for you, it needs to be addressed if you want to reduce your stress, improve your health and decrease your risk of disease. But before we look at how you can enhance your slumber, we first need to understand why it's so valuable.

The stages of sleep

Ideally, we should all spend just under a third of our lives asleep. This is not unproductive downtime; rather, it is vital for keeping our bodies in a good state of repair and helping our brains to process and assimilate our daytime activities.

If you enjoy an undisturbed sleep pattern, once you've drifted off you enter a period of light sleep which deepens as you become disengaged from your surroundings. Your body temperature starts to drop a little and your brain waves slow down. If all's well, after about 30 minutes you enter a period of deep sleep when your heart rate slows, your blood pressure drops and your breathing becomes slower. This is the most restorative stage, when tissue repair and regeneration occur. After about 90 minutes you shift to a period of REM (rapid eye movement) sleep, which is when most dreaming occurs. This stage is believed to be particularly important for psychological health and well-being. Then you move back and forth between deep sleep, lighter sleep and REM, with the latter stage ideally accounting for around 25 per cent of your total sleep time.

Statistically, the amount of sleep that correlates with the longest lifespan is between seven and nine hours each night.

Particularly as we get older, there is a higher correlation between too few (less than five) and too many (more than nine) hours of sleep and increased mortality. Seven hours a night is linked to the lowest death rate.[21] However, quality is just as important as quantity of sleep. Many people, as they age, experience more fragmented and lighter sleep and don't spend enough time in deep or REM sleep. As well as causing daytime fatigue, this can impact on your mood and make you more prone to depression and anxiety.

Why an eight-hour sleep might not be natural

Good news for night risers – nocturnal waking is not necessarily unnatural or bad for you. The American historian Roger Ekirch spent 16 years studying the sleeping habits of our ancestors and uncovered many references to segmented sleeping patterns consisting of two distinct periods of sleep, with a period of activity between.[22] His research suggests that it was commonplace for people to get up in the middle of the night for an hour or more to read, write, pray, have sex or talk to companions. However, this practice started to die out during the late seventeenth century, when the first appearance of street lighting made socialising at night safer and so people started going to bed later.

Many sleep psychologists concur that waking at night can be a natural part of human physiology, and that not everyone will be able to sleep concurrently for seven or eight hours. If you believe this is the case for you, then the key is not to become anxious but to engage in some sort of relaxing or calming activity until you feel ready to go back to sleep again. Ekirch uncovered many accounts of people using the time to meditate on their dreams, for example. Reading, writing a journal or doing a HeartMath® exercise (see Chapter 12) could also be a positive use of your time.

Sleep and repairing the body

During the night, and especially during the deep and REM sleep phases, your brain produces higher levels of growth hormone. This hormone helps to repair and regenerate your body's tissues. When you're stressed, the consequently high levels of cortisol suppress growth hormone, diverting energy away from repair and into coping with the energy demands of the stressful situation. This impedes tissue repair and effectively accelerates the ageing process.

Sleep experts recommend you should aim to reduce stress before going to bed. For example, the Sleep Foundation recommends 'a regular, relaxing bedtime routine such as soaking in a hot bath or listening to soothing music'. So, if you tend to work late, argue with your partner or watch thrillers or crime dramas in the evening, you may want to assess if these activities are helpful, especially if you routinely have problems sleeping.

Throwing a few handfuls of magnesium-rich Epsom salts into a warm bath and wallowing for 20 minutes, or using calming essential oils, such as lavender, can really aid relaxation.

Sounds of sleep

New York psychiatrist Dr Galina Mindlin uses 'brain music' – rhythmic sound patterns derived from recordings of her patients' own brain waves – to help them overcome insomnia, anxiety and depression. The recordings sound rather like classical piano music and appear to have a calming effect similar to yoga or meditation. A small double-blind study from 1998, conducted at Toronto University, found that 80 per cent of those undergoing this treatment reported benefits.[23]

Another study found that specially composed music induced a shift in brain-wave patterns to alpha waves, associated with the deep relaxation you feel before you fall asleep, and that this induced less anxiety in a group of patients going to the dentist.[24]

Many of our clients have also reported excellent results with John Levine's *Silence of Peace* CD (see Resources, page 310), which induces alpha brain waves that help to quieten the mind and encourage restful sleep.

Increase your chances of a good sleep

If you feel very stressed and fatigued during the day but find your exhaustion lifts around 10 or 11 p.m., as you get a second wind, don't be tempted to start doing all those chores you felt too tired to tackle earlier in the evening. The extra energy is usually the result of a burst of cortisol, as your body struggles to function and regulate energy to keep you going in what it perceives to be an emergency situation. However, as we discovered in Chapter 8, if this continues over the long term, you will fast-track yourself to burnout and exhaustion. So go to bed before the second wind hits and save your adrenal glands from unnecessary extra work.

Once you are in bed, spending a few minutes doing a simple HeartMath® exercise (see page 129) or following a relaxation routine (see page 109) can help to bring your body into the sort of calm state from which a good night's sleep is more likely to follow.

If you find you frequently wake between 2 and 3 a.m. with a pounding heart or in a sweat, you may be experiencing low blood sugar. Eating a small protein-rich snack (such as an oatcake and nut butter) before you retire might alleviate the problem.

How you wake up in the morning is important, too. Normally, cortisol and adrenalin levels are low during the night. Consequently, your heart rate and blood pressure should be low when you wake up and increase once you get out of bed. If you wake with a fast heart rate and/or high blood pressure, and then experience no increase when you get up, this is indicative of high cortisol levels during the night. (To test this, you need a blood pressure monitor by the bed – see Resources, page 309.)

This kind of 'desynchronisation' occurs in some people and is thought to be a component of seasonal affective disorder (SAD) and other depressions. Under these circumstances, it is best to see a nutritional therapist who can run a 24-hour salivary hormone test to find out what's out of sync and make recommendations to bring you back into balance.

Another cause of high blood pressure and increased heart rate on waking is a condition called sleep apnoea,[25] which is thought to affect between 2 and 4 per cent of people. This is when a person's breathing pattern becomes disturbed during the night, resulting in the improper exhalation of carbon dioxide and a deficiency of oxygen. It is also associated with fewer REM phases and therefore a less restorative sleep. Apnoea is more common in people who snore and it can be brought on by going to sleep after drinking alcohol or by stress. Other factors, including being overweight and suffering with a food or chemical sensitivity, also seem to contribute to the condition. If sleep apnoea is an issue for you, following the guidance below and throughout the rest of this book may help to alleviate it. Alternatively, a nutritional therapist will be able to investigate the problem further and devise a tailored programme (see Resources, page 307).

Sleep and the mind

As far as the mind is concerned, the most critical phases of sleep are the bursts of REM sleep. These tend to last for about 30 minutes and occur on average three to five times a night. If a person is deprived of REM sleep, they don't feel fully rested on waking and they are more likely to get depressed. If and when they do get a chance to sleep, they experience longer periods of REM sleep, which suggests that our minds need time to process what's been happening in our lives.

Most of our dreams occur during REM sleep, and it's believed they are important for mental and emotional health. Once again, high levels of the adrenal hormone cortisol result in less REM sleep, and some antidepressants have the same effect, potentially creating a vicious cycle of poor-quality sleep leading to low mood, with low mood then creating more need for antidepressant drugs. In Chapter 18 we explore the best ways to address mood issues without the need for drugs.

Nutritional solutions to sleep problems

Much of the general advice in this book will help you to address the common biochemical imbalances that can underpin insomnia and sleep issues. But there are also some specific actions that will help you to improve both the quality and the quantity of your sleep (if you are currently sleeping for less than seven hours a night).

Nutrients play a key role in producing the hormones that aid sleep, and in ensuring the body is able to calm down at night. The main sleep hormone is melatonin, which your body makes from another hormone, serotonin. Natural sources of melatonin include porridge oats, sour cherries (e.g. in the form of the juice concentrate Cherry Active), bananas, peanuts, grape skins, walnuts and liquorice. It is also concentrated in herbs such as St John's wort, sage and feverfew. Caffeine suppresses melatonin for up to ten hours,[26] so we recommend none after midday (and this includes regular and green tea) if you have difficulty getting to sleep.

You can buy melatonin as an over-the-counter medicine in the United States, or on prescription in the UK. Alternatively, you can supplement 5-HTP, an amino acid that your body uses to make melatonin. Research shows that supplementing 200mg of 5-HTP half an hour before bed improves sleep.[27] (But don't take 5-HTP if you are also taking SSRI antidepressant drugs, unless under supervision from a doctor or nutritional therapist, as 5-HTP can increase levels of serotonin.)

Several minerals and vitamins are also involved in getting a good night's sleep. Calcium and particularly magnesium are calming and aid muscle relaxation. Being highly stressed or eating a lot of sugar lowers levels of magnesium, which is found in seeds, nuts, green vegetables and seafood; calcium is in these foods, too, and in dairy produce. Try supplementing 400mg of magnesium before bed. This can be especially helpful if you tend to wake up in the night with stiff muscles.

A 2014 study by Oxford University has found that higher levels of omega 3 (an essential fat found in oily fish) in the diet are associated with better sleep, at least in children.[28] Those with higher levels of the omega 3 fat DHA experienced less resistance to falling asleep, fewer parasomnias (disorders such as night terrors, sleep walking and restless-leg syndrome) and less total sleep disturbance. This correlation increased when the ratio of DHA to arachidonic acid – a fat found in meat and dairy products – was higher. While further studies have yet to establish a similar pattern in adults, a significant body of research suggests that omega 3 fats reduce anxiety and improve mood, memory and brain health – all of which will, of course, contribute to better sleep.

If you are overweight, this might also impact on your quality of sleep. A Finnish study tracked overweight sufferers of sleep apnoea between 2004 and 2013 and found that those who reduced their weight by only a moderate amount (5kg) were at least able to prevent the condition worsening, while some even overcame it.[29] Research also shows that those who go to bed late and sleep less are more likely to gain weight than those who have a healthier sleep routine.[30]

A better alternative to alcohol

Many people use alcohol to relax, which promotes the release of the neurotransmitter GABA, switching off adrenalin. But alcohol works in this way for only an hour or so. When the effect wears off, you want another drink. If you go to sleep under the influence of alcohol, it disturbs the normal sleep cycle, which can promote low moods. The net consequence of regular alcohol consumption is GABA depletion, which leads to *more* adrenalin, anxiety and emotional over-sensitivity and poorer-quality sleep. One study found that men who drank more increased their risk of sleeping problems by 25 per cent.[31] And the less sleep you get, the more potent and dangerous are the effects of alcohol: it not only suppresses dreaming REM sleep but decreases the amount of deep sleep, which is when the beneficial growth hormone is released.[32]

In the US and elsewhere (although not in the UK) you can buy GABA in 500mg capsules. Taking one to three an hour before bed helps promote a good night's sleep. A combination of GABA and 5-HTP is even better. In a placebo-controlled trial, supplementing GABA and 5-HTP cut the time taken to fall asleep from 32 minutes to 19 minutes and extended sleep from five to almost seven hours.[33] Taking 1000mg of GABA plus 100mg of 5-HTP is therefore a recipe for a good night's sleep. As GABA consists of two amino acids – taurine and glutamine – these can be supplemented in place of GABA, when GABA is not available, and can be found in some sleep formulas (see Resources, page 312).

Why not sleeping pills?

If you can't sleep and you go to your doctor, the chances are that you will be prescribed sleeping pills, also known as hypnotics. Despite having a long charge sheet of side-effects,[34] these drugs still regularly feature in the top 20 most prescribed drugs in both the UK and the USA. Moreover, they aren't even very useful, according to a report in the *British Medical Journal*, which concluded that there is plenty of evidence that they cause 'major harm' and 'little evidence of clinically meaningful benefit'.[35] Just how marginally effective they are was vividly illustrated in a 2007 study by the American National Institutes of Health, which found that the newer drugs, such as Ambien (a brand name of zolpidem), caused users to fall asleep only 12.8 minutes faster and sleep for just an extra 11 minutes when compared with those taking a placebo.[36]

Sleep hygiene

Essentially commonsense advice, rather quaintly known as 'sleep hygiene', forms part of most sleep regimes. The idea is to create regular sleep-promoting habits to generate more confidence and less to worry about when going to sleep. You are advised to keep your bedroom quiet and dark, to wear comfortable night clothes, not to have a big meal before going to bed, to avoid coffee and alcohol and to exercise regularly but not within three hours of bedtime. It's also worth knowing that certain prescription medications – such as steroids, bronchodilators (used for asthma) and diuretics – can cause insomnia. And if you drink caffeinated drinks, research shows that consumption within six hours of bedtime can have significant disruptive effects on sleep.[37]

Although sleep hygiene is widely recommended, there have been very few studies of it as an individual treatment. Good results have been reported, however, for something similar, known as 'stimulus control therapy'. Essentially, this involves ensuring that only the bed is associated with sleeping. So patients are advised against having naps, to go to bed when they feel sleepy, to get up again within 20 minutes if they haven't fallen asleep, to do something relaxing until they feel drowsy and then try again but to get up once more if they still fail to fall asleep.

Keep artificial light to a minimum in the bedroom because being exposed to bright light can inhibit production of the sleep hormone melatonin, which peaks at around 1 a.m. If you need to get up in the night, use only low-wattage bulbs. There is also a growing body of evidence that suggests electromagnetic radiation from mobile phones and wireless internet connections (wi-fi) can interfere with melatonin production. For example, in one small study, melatonin levels were 44 per cent lower at 2 a.m. in those exposed to mobile phone signals, compared to those who weren't.[38] So it might be worth turning off your mobile and any wi-fi routers at night to see if this improves your quality of sleep.

If all else fails, having a nap in the day might help to reduce some of the health risks of poor sleep. Scientists from the University of Athens and the Harvard School of Public Health studied 23,681 healthy adults aged between 20 and 86 for an average period of six years. They found that those who napped for at least 30 minutes three times a week or more had a 37 per cent lower risk of coronary mortality than those who did not sleep during the day.[39]

Case study: Solving the nocturnal munchies

Robert is a City trader who suffered from stress and insomnia. He was also overweight and suffered from poor concentration at work. He would frequently wake at 3 a.m. in a sweat with heart palpitations; then, once he'd calmed down, he would have a strong urge to eat a Mars bar (which he kept in a mini-fridge by his bed). He sought help from Susannah, who worked with him to improve his diet, swapping his morning triple espresso for a proper breakfast and introducing protein with each meal, plus regular slow-energy-releasing snacks to help avert energy or concentration dips. Robert gradually reduced his caffeine consumption throughout the day, increased his water intake and took a multivitamin and mineral especially formulated for stressful lifestyles. He also learned the HeartMath® technique (see Chapter 12) and practised it daily, which he found not only reduced his feelings of being overwhelmed and unable to cope but improved his ability to think quickly in high-pressure situations. After a week of taking 400mg of magnesium before bed, he also found he was able to sleep through the night. (Although he didn't become a saint – his bedside fridge now contains beer and baby oil!)

Summary

To help yourself get a good night's sleep:

- Prioritise relaxing activities in the few hours before you go to bed, so you reduce your stress levels and get your body into a calm state ready for sleeping.

- Avoid alcohol before bed, and limit any caffeine intake after midday (or preferably avoid it completely).

- Aim to follow a soothing bedtime routine, such as having a warm bath with Epsom salts and lavender oil or listening to relaxing music.

- Once in bed, do some simple relaxation exercises to get yourself ready for sleep.

- If you have difficulty sleeping, supplement 400mg of magnesium before bed, or experiment with 200mg of the amino acid 5-HTP half an hour before bed, or a sleep formula containing both, plus GABA precursors (see Resources).

- Follow a good sleep hygiene routine, ensuring your bedroom is quiet and dark and you are comfortable. Also turn off mobile phones and wi-fi connections at night.

CHAPTER 12

The HeartMath® Solution

Reducing the negative impact of stress is a vital piece of the jigsaw puzzle to achieving optimum health and building resilience. In our experience, no matter how well a client follows their recommended diet or supplement programme, fully reaching their health goals is rarely, if ever, achieved if they remain stressed. This has led us to explore a range of approaches to find a way to help clients tackle stress – from breathing exercises and guided visualisation, to referrals to life coaches and Emotional Freedom Technique practitioners. Susannah analysed some statistics which showed that practising a simple technique from the HeartMath® system could reduce the stress hormone cortisol by 23 per cent in just one month, and increase the rejuvenating hormone DHEA by 100 per cent. Nothing we'd ever seen before could claim such dramatic success in such a short space of time – and all from an exercise that takes just five minutes a day. So she jumped on a plane and flew to California, where the HeartMath technique was developed, to find out more. Later, she trained as a HeartMath practitioner to enable her to teach this technique to her clients back in the UK. This chapter explains how it works.

The HeartMath system is a scientifically validated way not only to reduce stress but, more importantly, to transform the negative emotional and physiological effects you experience when a stressful event occurs. This is crucial because so many stress-relieving activities – for example, listening to music, having a warm bath, massage, drinking a glass of wine – focus on relaxation *after* the event. Yet, by the time you wind down, you've probably already experienced hours of stress and its unpleasant effects. The stress hormone cortisol, for example, stays in your system for hours once it has been released. So it's crucial to learn how to interrupt and transform your *immediate reaction* to stress, and therefore stop the emotional and hormonal fallout that follows.

Of course, some people will claim they thrive on stress. They might say, 'Deadlines motivate me.' Indeed, as long as you truly perceive stress in a positive way – and give yourself adequate time to rest and recuperate – you may not suffer any harmful side-effects. It's when stress leaves you feeling depleted and out of control that it becomes problematic.

By this stage in the book, you are probably already aware that if left unchecked, ongoing stress is very bad news. But if you're still not convinced, take a look at the list below. Do you experience any of the following on a regular basis?

- Find it hard to think straight
- Feel out of control
- Tension
- Anger
- Heightened worries and concerns
- Resentment
- Negativity
- Anxiety
- Irritation
- Feel overwhelmed
- Frustration
- Hostility

If you answered 'yes' to even one of these, then the chances are that stress is having a 'depleting' impact on your emotional state. How you *feel*, to a much greater extent than what you *think*, activates and drives the physiological changes that correlate with the stress response. Thus, the key to optimal health and vitality is directly related to your ability to self-regulate your emotional response.

Simply put, the emotions we tend to label as 'negative' – for example, those listed earlier – disrupt optimal physiological and mental functions and leave you feeling depleted. Conversely, the emotions we label as 'positive' facilitate a wide range of physiological functions, renew our energy and optimise the body's natural regenerative processes. The research that supports these findings calls the latter 'psycho-physiological coherence'; or, more simply, heart coherence.

How emotions affect heart rhythms

When you think of the heart, you probably visualise a physical organ, but you might also think about the emotional qualities we attribute to it: your heart's desire, heartfelt, heartbroken, for example. Interestingly, research by the Institute of HeartMath in California has discovered that the two are interlinked – that is, emotional state has an impact on heart rhythm patterns.

Just as your emotions influence your heart rhythm pattern, the heart communicates with your brain and the rest of your body. This occurs via your nervous and hormonal systems, electromagnetic interactions and other pathways. HeartMath research has been able to demonstrate that the signals your heart sends to your brain can profoundly influence perception, emotions, behaviour, performance and health.[40] Interestingly, there seem to be more connections from the heart to the brain than vice versa.

In studying the science of the heart, the Institute of HeartMath has discovered that your heart rhythms have an impact on your thinking. When your heart rhythm is coherent, you are able to access higher-thinking centres in your brain, so you can think more clearly and see more options or solutions to problems. However, when your heart rhythm pattern becomes incoherent, driven by emotions, this access is inhibited. As a result, you will probably find your reactions slower and you will be unable to think so clearly.

How a positive or 'renewing' emotion affects your heart

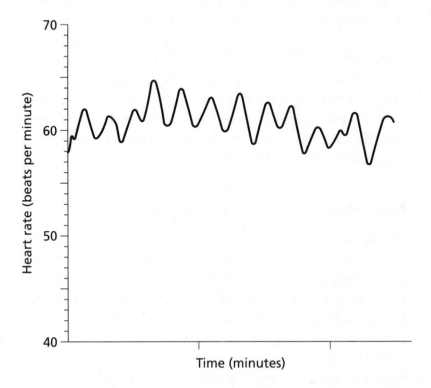

This graph shows the heart rhythm pattern that is typical when we experience a positive feeling such as appreciation or gratitude. This smooth shape is what scientists call a 'highly ordered' or 'coherent' pattern, and it is a sign of good health and emotional balance.

Studies have found that people in a coherent state (i.e. when their heart rhythm pattern is coherent) enjoy improved thinking and performance, whether they are making decisions or playing sport.[41] Over time, coherence also helps to reduce levels of the stress hormone cortisol – which is produced whenever you experience feelings of frustration, anxiety, anger or despair[42] – while increasing the 'vitality' hormone DHEA. Ideally, these hormones should be in balance, but as we saw in Chapter 8, when you experience frequent stress, cortisol can become too high and DHEA depleted. This pattern is found in most major disease states and is also associated with accelerated ageing, brain cell death, impaired memory and learning, decreased bone density, impaired immune function, increased blood sugar and increased fat accumulation around the waist and hips.[43]

How a negative or 'depleting' emotion affects your heart

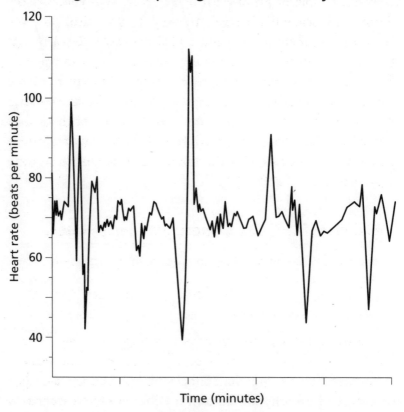

This graph shows the irregular, jerky heart rhythm pattern that is typical when we experience stressful feelings like anger, frustration, worry and anxiety. This is called an 'incoherent' pattern.

Getting coherent with HeartMath techniques

The HeartMath system provides techniques that can be practised daily to help you actively reduce the stress in your life.

The basic premise of the HeartMath system is different from many other approaches to stress relief, which typically focus on calming down and lowering heart rate *after* the stressful event has occurred. With HeartMath tools, you learn a coherence technique that can help you 'reset' your physiological reaction to stress *as the event occurs.*

Just a couple of HeartMath breaths can help you stop the hormonal cascade that triggers the release of cortisol, allowing you to stay coherent (i.e. calm and in balance). Research has found that, when practised regularly, the exercise can help you feel better emotionally and improve your intuition, creativity and cognitive performance.[44] In other words, you become smarter and more resilient under pressure, which is part of the reason why HeartMath has become so popular with senior business executives, as well as with the military and among healthcare professionals.

Exercise: The Quick Coherence® technique

There are three simple steps to practise to get coherent:

1. Heart focus: focus your attention on your heart area, in the centre of your chest.

2. Heart breathing: now imagine your breath flowing in and out of that area. This helps your respiration and heart rhythm to synchronise. So focus on this area and aim to breathe evenly: for example, inhale for five or six seconds and exhale for five or six seconds (choose a timescale that feels comfortable and flows easily).

Take a few minutes to get the hang of the heart focus and heart breathing stages, then introduce step three:

3. Heart feeling: as you breathe in and out of your heart area, recall a positive emotion and try to re-experience it. This could be remembering a time spent with someone you love, walking in your favourite spot, stroking a pet,

picturing a tree or scenic location you admire or even just appreciating that you are able to eat today or have shoes on your feet. If your mind wanders, bring it gently back to the positive experience.

When practised daily for around five minutes these three steps can help you de-stress, feel calmer and become more content. It really is that simple. Your heart rhythm pattern will become coherent and your heart–brain communication will optimise to help you think more clearly. Ideally, find the time to sit down quietly in a place where you will be undisturbed (e.g. first thing in the morning, during your lunch break or when you get home from work) to do this exercise every day. If you do that, it is likely to become habit and you can give it your full attention.

Once you've got the hang of this HeartMath technique, you can use it any time you encounter a stressful event: for example, if you start to feel tense in heavy traffic, overloaded at work or sense you are about to face a difficult emotional situation. Just a few heart-focused breaths can help you stay calm and coherent instead of becoming stressed. (That's why the technique is called the *Quick* Coherence technique.) And you can do it with your eyes open, as you walk or talk – so you have a tool to control stress precisely when you encounter a situation likely to trigger a negative or depleting reaction.

Is it effective? Well, numerous studies have shown regularly practising HeartMath® techniques can have hugely beneficial effects, not only on emotional health and well-being but on physical health markers.

HeartMath: emotional and physical benefits

Research into the benefits of using HeartMath techniques has explored its impact on a wide range of people – from the very young to the elderly, medical professionals to the military, students to chief executives, those suffering from mental and physical health problems to athletes. Time and again these studies have found that regular use of the HeartMath system can produce significant reductions in depression, anxiety, anger, hostility, burnout and fatigue and corresponding increases in caring, contentment, gratitude, peacefulness and vitality.[45]

A study looking at the impact of the daily practice of HeartMath techniques on hormone levels found that after just one month cortisol declined by 23 per cent and DHEA increased by 100 per cent.[46] (The independent lab measuring these hormones thought the subjects must have been on drugs because they had never seen such improvements in ten years of operation, during which they had processed more than 30,000 samples.)

For those suffering with additional health problems, research has shown that practising HeartMath tools and techniques can help to regulate abnormalities. For example, a workplace study of employees with hypertension found that after three months of practising HeartMath techniques, blood pressure dropped an average 10.6mmHg for systolic and 6.3mmHg for diastolic. Participants also reported improvements in emotional health, including reductions in stress symptoms and depression and increases in peacefulness and positive outlook.[47]

In a hospital study, 75 patients suffering abnormal heart rhythms (atrial fibrillation) were taught the HeartMath techniques and practised them for three months. At the end of the study period, 71 reported substantial improvements in their physical and emotional health; 56 experienced such improvements in their ability to control their heart rhythms and hypertension that they were able to reduce their medication; and 14 discontinued medication altogether.[48]

Finally, a small study of type 1 and type 2 diabetics involved teaching a group of 22 participants the HeartMath techniques and monitoring their progress. Six months after the workshop, participants reported significant reductions in anxiety, negative emotions, fatigue and sleeplessness, along with increased feelings of vitality and improved quality of life. Changes in glycosolated haemoglobin (HbA1c – a marker for sugar damage in the blood) were also observed, with increased HeartMath practice associated with a reduction in HbA1c levels.[49]

Measuring your coherence

As you can see, practising HeartMath can really help you reduce stress and improve your well-being. It also helps you develop greater resilience and heart coherence. You can get a firm idea of your state of coherence by measuring not just your heart rate (number of beats) but the pattern of activity that exists between those beats. This is called your heart rate variability or HRV, and it is measured with a simple tool called an emWave® device (the latest version is the emWave 2).

The emWave device has a clip that attaches to your ear lobe to pick up your HRV (your ear lobes register a pulse) and then feeds this data through to a hand-held console that tells you how coherent you are (there is also a mobile phone app). There are three zones: red or incoherent (the state most of us are in); blue for more coherent; and green for fully coherent. There is also a breath pacer to help you regulate your breathing, and different levels and modes, so you can adapt your practice as you get the hang of it. See Resources, page 309 for more details.

Case study: Healing the heart

Pamela was a 55-year-old management consultant who came to see Susannah for help with reducing her high blood pressure, heart palpitations and menopausal symptoms. An adrenal stress index test revealed she was in the 'Maladapted Phase II' stage of stress adaptation, suggesting that she'd been stimulating her stress hormones for some time and was beginning to deplete her reserves. Using the HeartMath® technique alongside a nutritional protocol, Pamela's blood pressure dropped from around 180/139 to 167/101 in four weeks (her GP was also monitoring her progress) and she felt less angry and more positive for much of the time. After eight weeks, her blood pressure had dropped to 140/90 and she had stopped having any heart palpitations. She reported a big improvement in her overall mood and a reduction in menopausal night sweats. She also showed significant progress in her coherence levels and reported enjoying her daily HeartMath practice at home. After 12 weeks, there was a huge improvement in Pamela's stress hormones – her results put her in the 'Adapted' category. Her blood pressure had stabilised at around 135/90 and her GP was very impressed.

Taking HeartMath tools further

In addition to the Quick Coherence technique, which teaches you how to transform stress, the Institute of HeartMath has developed practices for transforming negative attitudes and resolving specific problems. Working with a qualified practitioner, the HeartMath tools can also be used to help overcome such issues as emotional eating, insomnia, chronic pain, anger/conflict resolution, obsessive compulsive disorder and addiction. And with children, HeartMath tools have been used successfully to help manage ADHD, hyperactivity and anxiety. See Resources for how to find a practitioner and for workshop details.

You can visit HeartMath's American site – www.heartmath. org – for more information and research. Doc Childre, Heart-Math's founder, has also written a great book called *Transforming Stress*, which gives lots of useful information about using the techniques and developing your practice.

Note: HeartMath® is a registered trademark of the Institute of HeartMath. emWave® is a registered trademark of Quantum, Intech, Inc. Quick Coherence® is a registered trademark of Doc Childre.

PART 4

Reset Your Mindset

By now, you're aware that stress can result from multiple sources, from lack of sleep to infection, from being overloaded at work to worrying about your finances. We've also looked at the effects your blood sugar, use of stimulants and hormone balance have on your stress and energy levels, and the importance of rest and recuperation. In this section, we're going to explore in more detail the *psychological* side of stress – how your beliefs, rather than specific incidents, can cause you to feel stressed, and the benefits of positive rather than negative thinking. You'll also learn that ensuring your time is well spent can help you to feel less overwhelmed and more satisfied.

By the end of Part 4, you'll have far greater understanding of how your mindset affects your stress and energy levels – and you'll be armed with a host of new ideas for how to reset this in order to support yourself, de-stress and feel happier. You'll also find exercises to help you as you go along.

CHAPTER 13

Uncovering Your
Stress Triggers

If we asked, '*What* causes you stress?', you'd no doubt be able to provide a long list of possibilities. But if we asked you *why*, would you find it so easy to answer? To help you to become clearer, we're going to look in more detail at the psychological side of stress to find out how our beliefs impact on our stress levels and why two people in identical 'stressful' circumstances can have two completely different responses.

In the 1950s, a clinical psychologist called Albert Ellis developed a dynamic approach to tackling problems. He helped people to change their underlying belief patterns and make positive breakthroughs in the way they experienced life's challenges. His model paved the way for cognitive behavioural therapy (CBT), which today focuses on helping people to change negative behaviours without the need to delve deep into their psyches to see how and where the problem originated.

Ellis's work – in particular, his 'ABC' model – has been used widely by those working in the field of stress management. The ABC model enables you to gain insight into how and why you react to stressful events, and to challenge any underlying negative beliefs and replace them with more rational and supportive ways of thinking. However, the ideas that underpin Ellis's work are not new, and he credits various sources across the centuries for inspiration, from the ancient Greeks to Shakespeare.

People are disturbed not by things, but by the views which they take of them.

Epictetus, first-century AD *Greek philosopher*

Everything is what your opinion makes it.

Marcus Aurelius,
second-century AD *Roman emperor and philosopher*

For there is nothing either good or bad, but thinking makes it so.

William Shakespeare, Hamlet, c. *1600*

When it comes to stress, uncovering your often subconscious views, opinions and thinking relating to the situations that cause you to feel upset, anxious, angry, humiliated or undermined – and all those other negative emotions that manifest from stress – can be hugely liberating. This is because, once you are aware of them, you can challenge them and instead adopt more realistic and helpful views that reduce the stress you experience.

The ABC of understanding stress

Ellis's premise is that rather than holding external events to blame for our stress and unhappiness, our interpretation of these events is what triggers our distress. His ABC model runs like this:

- A – Activating event: something happens in the environment around you.

- B – Beliefs: you hold a belief about that event or situation.

- C – Consequence: you have an emotional and/or psychological response to your belief.

To put this into practice, let's consider a client of ours called Rosie. She juggled working part time with looking after her two school-age children. If anything went wrong – the children didn't do their homework, her office computer crashed, a neighbour didn't make time for their usual chat (A) – Rosie felt extremely anxious and often experienced a mild panic attack (C). By keeping a daily record of her stress and anxiety triggers and asking herself, 'Why do I feel this way?', she was gradually able to become aware of a pattern, whereby she believed she had to make sure everyone else was OK. If they weren't, she felt it was somehow her fault (B). When asked if this belief was realistic – could she really be responsible for ensuring everyone else was OK all the time? – she had to admit that it wasn't. 'I feel a huge sense of relief,' she said. By continuing to note her sources of stress and nurture a more realistic approach to the everyday situations she encountered (using the model set out later in this chapter), Rosie was able to reduce the stress levels in her life significantly.

Identify what underpins your stress

By now, you're probably beginning to wonder how your own set of unconscious beliefs might be contributing to your stress levels. Of course, life can present us with some unexpected situations that are extremely difficult and distressing: for example, losing your job, being diagnosed with a serious illness, or the death of a loved one. But our focus here is on the routine, day-to-day events that add to our general stress load. It's these we have the most power to change our reaction to.

Exercise: Identify your underlying beliefs

To help identify your underlying beliefs, think back to the last time you became stressed. Recall in detail the circumstances, what happened and how you felt about it. For example:

- If you were anxious, did you think the situation was terrible or frightening?

- If you were angry, did you feel like an idiot or blame other people?

- If you were embarrassed, did you feel responsible or that you shouldn't have been treated that way?
- If you felt hurt or humiliated but did or said nothing, did you feel you must not make a fuss, that you must just endure it?

It can often help to identify these hidden beliefs by seeing if one of the following cues prompts a response: 'I must ...', 'I should ...', or 'I always ...' For example: 'I must not make a mistake'; 'I should be in control of my children'; or 'I always get things wrong.' There are some further examples in the 'Stress-inducing beliefs' section opposite.

To help get you started, take a piece of paper (or make a copy of 'The stress log' at the end of this chapter), pick one recent stressful incident, so you have a real-life example, contemplate it and answer these three questions:

What stressed me today?	How did I feel?	Why?/Underlying beliefs

Here are some possible responses:

Left my wallet at home	Ashamed, embarrassed	I am useless
My contribution wasn't acknowledged	Angry, snubbed	I must not be ignored
Had slow service in restaurant	Irritated, frustrated	I deserve the best
Friends arrived and house untidy	Mortified, overly apologetic	I should be prepared
Spilled a drink down my dress and boss joked I was a slob	Humiliated, upset	I must look perfect

Stress-inducing beliefs

We all hold beliefs that can be limiting, self-defeating or impossible to live up to – and it's often these, rather than the life events we encounter, that cause stress in our lives. Below are some common examples of these types of belief.

Exercise: Identify your stress-inducing beliefs

Tick or underline the beliefs that resonate with you (or write them down in a workbook). Also think of your own. Delve deep and write down as many as you can.

- ☐ Life should go smoothly
- ☐ I must always make an effort
- ☐ I am indispensable
- ☐ I deserve recognition and/or respect
- ☐ Life should be exciting
- ☐ Doing nothing is boring
- ☐ I must find a solution to every problem
- ☐ I must not let people down
- ☐ My children are a reflection of my worth
- ☐ I must be in control
- ☐ My family should always get along
- ☐ I am important

- ☐ I am stupid
- ☐ My job denotes my status
- ☐ My possessions prove I am successful
- ☐ I am responsible for other people's happiness
- ☐ I must work late to show I am committed
- ☐ My house must be clean and tidy
- ☐ I must always be there for my friends
- ☐ I'm not good enough
- ☐ I'm always to blame
- ☐ Things always go wrong
- ☐ It's my fault if things go wrong

_____

_____

_____

Doors of Compensation

Stressful events don't only generate feelings and emotions within us; they can also trigger behaviours or actions we use as coping strategies. For example, you don't get the recognition you were hoping for at work and you feel undermined and angry. These feelings are unpleasant and uncomfortable, so you go home and eat a huge box of chocolates to make yourself feel better; or you go out and get really drunk; or you pick a fight with your partner and let off steam by being mean to them. These 'Doors of Compensation' were first identified by the psychologist and philosopher Oscar Ichazo. His observation is that when we react to situations we find stressful, the pressure in our psyche increases. To release this pressure, we use one or more of the Doors of Compensation.

The Doors of Compensation

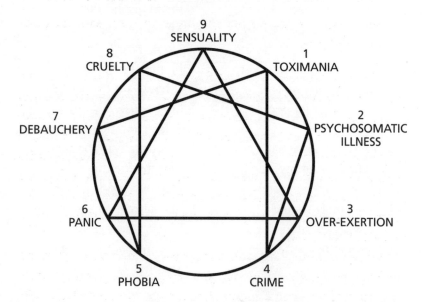

Enneagram: Reproduced with kind permission of the Arica Institute Inc. New York

The nine Doors of Compensation cover:

- Toximania – the use of toxic substances, including cigarettes, alcohol, cannabis and other drugs.

- Psychosomatic illness – being preoccupied with one's mental and physical health and illness.

- Over-exertion – for example, workaholism or excessive sport or exercise.

- Crime – ways of getting even because you don't feel you've had a fair deal.

- Phobia – everything from dislikes to strong aversions.

- Panic – always being in a panic and then spreading it to others.

- Debauchery (excess) – excessive intake of, for example, food; or excess of anything else, such as being endlessly melodramatic or watching three romcoms in a row.

- Cruelty – being mean or using abusive language and behaviour.

- Sensuality – excessive sex and preoccupation with the pleasures of the senses.

While we might all use these compensating strategies at various times every day, the degree to which we use them is also significant. The first degree of use is occasionally, for temporary satisfaction: for example, the odd time you have a couple of drinks after a stressful week. The next degree is when you drink every day and you are anaesthetised by it. The third degree is when you drink habitually, with drunkenness the inevitable outcome, which is debilitating. By this stage, such behaviour denotes a level of addiction.

Understanding how you compensate when you experience difficult emotions, triggered by an event you perceive to be stressful, can add an extra dimension of insight to Ellis's ABC model. For example:

What stressed me today?	How did I feel?	How did I compensate?	Why?/ Underlying beliefs
Left my wallet at home	Ashamed, embarrassed	Drank too much	I am useless
Contribution not acknowledged	Angry, snubbed	Ate a big box of chocs	I must not be ignored
Had slow service in restaurant	Irritated, frustrated	Was mean to my kids	I deserve the best
Friends arrived and house untidy	Mortified, overly apologetic	Smoked too many cigs	I should be prepared
Spilled a drink down my dress and my boss joked I was a slob	Humiliated, upset	Called ex-boyfriend for sex	I must look perfect

We'll incorporate this understanding in the next stage, where we work towards finding a better solution for our stressful reactions.

Taking the next step

Once you have teased out some of the negative or unhelpful underlying beliefs that add to your stress levels by using the ABC model, the next steps, as defined by Ellis, are D and E:

- D – Disputation: dissecting those beliefs to see if they are rational.

- E – Effective new approach: identifying a more supportive way to proceed.

Exercise: Belief reality check

Let's take D next. Take a good, hard look at the under-lying beliefs you have identified to see if they really merit a place in your thinking. Examine each one in turn and ask yourself:

- Is it logical (i.e. does it makes sense, or is it true)?

- Is it realistic (i.e. are my expectations of myself or others fair)?

- What evidence do I have for this belief?

- Is it helpful to me?

Sometimes, it can be helpful to do this exercise with a trusted friend or colleague. Many workplaces also offer coaching sup-port to staff, so if much of your stress centres on your job, it's worth finding out if you can make use of this resource. But most important is that you get honest and impartial feedback, whether it's from yourself or someone else. Aim to deal in facts rather than your interpretation of – or emotional response to – them.

If you find it hard, give yourself some time to reflect and come back to this exercise at a later date. And if you feel out of your depth or find that identifying these beliefs brings up dif-ficult feelings from your past, seek the support of a professional coach or therapist (see Resources). Chapter 19 also suggests some therapeutic approaches that might be helpful (see page 207).

Once you are clear in your mind that your negative underly-ing belief for a particular stressful event is not logical, realistic or helpful, you can proceed to step E and identify a more effective approach that will help you react less stressfully the next time you encounter something similar. It is useful to establish a goal to help you with this.

Exercise: A more effective approach

Take your real-life example and write down the following:

- My goal is to be .... (less stressed, happier, more calm, etc.).

- A more supportive/appropriate/helpful/kinder way to approach this situation that would help me achieve this would be to ....

For example, say you missed a deadline at work and you felt ashamed. You have identified that your underlying belief is that you are not good enough, but on talking this over with a colleague, you accept that this belief is simply untrue. You acknowledge that you've recently been promoted and usually do great work and hit all your deadlines.

Your goal is to be calmer and less reactive, so you ask yourself, 'What would be a more supportive way to approach this type of situation in order to achieve this?' You decide to allow yourself more planning time plus some contingency before you agree to a deadline for future projects. You also decide to share your insight with your boss so that she can see you have learned from the earlier situation and are taking a proactive stance to avoid missing future deadlines.

Again, working with someone you trust can be helpful here. But if you are working through this by yourself, you might like to imagine you are taking on a new role – that of a good friend and coach to yourself. As funny as it sounds, it's a really good idea to switch chairs when you go into 'coach' mode, as if you are talking to yourself, still sitting in the chair opposite. If in doubt, think about how you might respond to a friend sharing the same concerns. Most of us would be supportive, so aim to offer yourself the same kindness to help you find a better solution.

Stress-alleviating thoughts

The American philosopher and psychologist William James (1842–1910) said: 'The greatest weapon against stress is our ability to choose one thought over another.' He was right: another useful tool to help you reach a better solution to life's challenging events is to focus on some stress-alleviating thoughts (SATs) to counter your stress-inducing thoughts (SITs).

The SATs versus SITs approach was developed by Professor Stephen Palmer and his colleague Michael Neenan at the UK Centre for Stress Management. It involves applying a more helpful and rational perspective to a stressful situation, so that you can find a more effective – and less stress-inducing – way forward. Think of it as the kind of advice you might give to a friend in a similar situation: take a deep breath and stay calm; get all the facts before you react; ask for more time so you don't feel pressurised; and so on. Some more examples are given on page 149.

If you are struggling to find a new stress-alleviating way of thinking, you may find the reminders below helpful. Chapter 12 also provides an excellent technique to help you become more receptive to finding better solutions to life's challenges.

Reality check: tips to help you find a new perspective

- Is this situation really so terrible? Will it still matter in a week, a month, a year? Aim to get a more realistic perspective.

- We are human and everyone makes mistakes. Remember that many successful people say their greatest triumphs came from learning from their biggest mistakes.

- We can't like everyone and everyone can't like us. If you don't get a positive response from someone, that doesn't mean you are unlikeable or a failure.

- Just because you feel a strong emotion, that doesn't mean the event merits it. You can react strongly because of a strong negative belief you attach to an event.

- A situation is rarely 100 per cent your fault or someone else's fault. Try to see the bigger picture and examine all the contributory factors.

- It would be great if the world was a just and fair place, but life doesn't always work like that. As the cliché tells us, some you win and some you lose.

- Events are rarely completely in our control, so it's a waste of energy to try to make them so.

- Avoiding a problem rarely makes it go away. It's far better to take a proactive stance to reach the best resolution, rather than letting it niggle away at you in the back of your mind.

- It's impossible to avoid all discomfort, difficulty and pain all the time, but things often aren't as bad as we fear.

- Absolutes are hard to live up to – instead of 'must' or 'should', try to shift your thinking to 'can' or 'could' and give yourself more options. For example, rather than 'I must do a perfect job', try 'I could do a perfect job, but I'm short of time today so good enough will be OK.'

- There's no point trying to read people's minds. You cannot possibly work out what someone else is thinking: either ask them or stick to dealing in facts.

Exercise: The stress log

The way you react to stress has developed over many years, so, unsurprisingly, it can take time to embed new, less stress-inducing ways of looking at things. To help you make some positive changes, photocopy the blank stress log that appears at the end of the book (page 300) and use it to record the stressful events or situations you encounter over the next 30 days. Then work through the tools you've learned in this chapter to develop a new, more supportive approach (and have it to hand for whenever new potentially stressful events arise).

To give you an idea of how your stress log might look, we have completed a sample one opposite.

Activating event or situation	Stress-inducing thoughts/beliefs	Consequences (how you feel)	Compensation (what you do)	Reality check (stress-alleviating thoughts)	Effective new approach
Row with partner	He will leave me I am an idiot	Scream, cry and feel desperate	Have an asthma attack	All couples disagree We get along most of the time	Aim to stay calm and listen in future disagreements
Let down by supplier at work	I must not look stupid I should be in control	Angry, critical, threatening	Tear a strip off supplier's receptionist, make her cry	Some things are beyond my control	Stay calm and ask for help to remedy the situation
Not invited to a neighbour's party	What have I done wrong? Nobody likes me	Feel hurt and humiliated	Stay home and eat two tubs of ice cream	We don't know each other very well. They don't have much room	Don't take things so personally

CHAPTER 14

The Power of Positivity

In the previous chapter, you saw how your thinking colours the way you view a situation – and how you can replace stress-inducing thoughts (SITs) with stress-alleviating thoughts (SATs). This requires you to leave behind harsh, inflexible or pessimistic thinking and move to the realm of more positive possibilities.

Certainly, when it comes to boosting your resilience to stress and enjoyment of life, being more positive – and viewing difficult situations as opportunities to learn, change and grow – is a great attribute. As the 'father' of stress research Hans Selye observed: 'Adopting the right attitude can convert a negative stress into a positive one.'

Optimists fare better than pessimists or cynics

A 2013 study by scientists at Concordia University's Department of Psychology found that pessimists have higher baseline levels of stress hormones compared to optimists, and they are less able to regulate hormone levels after they experience a stressful situation.[1] 'On days where they experience higher than average stress, that's when we see that the pessimists' stress response is much elevated, and they have trouble bringing their cortisol levels back down,' explains the study's lead researcher Joelle Jobin. 'Optimists, by contrast, were protected in these circumstances.'

As well as a tendency to higher stress levels, people with a pessimistic attitude are more likely to suffer with depression and anxiety.[2] They also have an increased risk of dying at a younger age than optimists. In a study looking at the death rates of pessimistic versus optimistic women, researchers at the University of Pittsburgh found that after eight years of tracking 100,000 women, those who were optimistic were 14 per cent more likely to be alive than their pessimistic peers.[3]

Cynicism and pessimism often go hand in hand, but cynicism – and particularly the hostile variety, which illustrates a pessimistic state of mental inflexibility – is more harmful than stress, anger or depression. One study showed that while being stressed raises inflammatory markers more than being depressed, being cynical is even more harmful.[4] Another study found that people with the most hostile cynicism and distrust increased their risk of dementia threefold.[5] Further research found hostile cynicism also triggers the most negative changes to DNA integrity, implying earlier demise.[6]

By contrast, an optimistic attitude has been found to increase positive outcomes, even in difficult circumstances. For example, in a study of pregnant mothers classified as medically high risk, those with an optimistic attitude delivered healthier babies with better birth weights than those who were pessimistic.[7]

Optimists, then, clearly have much to be optimistic about. But is optimism or pessimism simply like your eye colour? Is it something you are born with and over which you have no choice or control?

Pessimism isn't in your genes; it's in your beliefs

Research into identical twins by Professor Tim Spector at St Thomas's Hospital in London has found that personality traits, such as optimism or a propensity to depression, can vary greatly in siblings who share identical genes. Indeed, the new science of epigenetics has discovered that genes are not set in stone, but operate more like dimmer switches. They can be turned on or off – or up- or down-regulated – by environmental factors. This means that it's not necessarily your genetic inheritance that determines your glass-half-empty or glass-half-full viewpoint. Your perspective is more likely due to your response to the life you've lived. And while you can't change your past, you *can* change your beliefs.

As we saw in the previous chapter, your beliefs about a specific situation have a greater impact on how you react than the situation itself. Pioneering work by cell biologist Dr Bruce Lipton, author of the excellent book *The Biology of Belief*, has shown that our beliefs have a profound effect on our biology at a cellular level.[8] 'Thoughts, the mind's energy, directly influence how the physical brain controls the body's physiology. Thought "energy" can activate or inhibit the cell's function-producing proteins via the mechanics of constructive and destructive interference,' he explains. In a nutshell, your thoughts alone can have a positive or negative effect on how your body works, even to the extent of switching genes on and off.

This is especially evident in the placebo effect, whereby patients in drug trials who are given dummy pills often experience similar improvements to their counterparts who have received the real pill. Of course, the idea is that neither patient group knows which pills they are taking, but those who believe they are getting the real drug can experience similar results, right down to the side-effects. And it's not just pills that can have a placebo effect.

A study published in the *New England Journal of Medicine* compared three groups of patients who underwent surgery for severe knee pain. Unbeknown to them, two groups had the real procedure but the third had 'fake' surgery.[9] To the amazement of the surgeon leading the trial, the 180 patients across the three groups reported the same improvements: they all claimed a considerable reduction in pain and increased mobility. Follow-up footage on the Discovery Channel showed members of the placebo (fake surgery) group walking unaided and playing sport, activities they were unable to do before their 'surgery'. On finding out the truth some two years later, one member of the placebo group – who could hardly walk before he participated in the trial – said: 'In this world anything is possible when you put your mind to it. I know that your mind can work miracles.'

When it comes to stress, your mindset also has the power

to exert a significant positive or negative effect on your life. Research by American academics that was published in the *Journal of Personality and Social Psychology* found that people who believed that 'experiencing stress facilitates my learning and growth' reported having far better health, greater life satisfaction and superior work performance than those who believed that the 'effects of stress are negative and should be avoided'.[10] This research also found that it's possible to change your mindset – and therefore your reaction to stress.

Change your perception

As Winston Churchill said: 'The pessimist sees difficulty in every opportunity. The optimist sees the opportunity in every difficulty.' Of course, many of us are not 100 per cent one or the other, but if you find yourself struggling to view life mostly positively, then working to shift your perception can reap considerable benefits.

Let's take the example of colleagues Jim and Mark who apply for the same promotion. Neither of them is successful due to their company employing an external candidate instead. On hearing the news, Jim thinks: 'I'm such a failure. Clearly I just don't have what it takes. I'll never progress in my career, so I may as well not bother.' Mark reacts somewhat differently: 'Oh well, that's a shame, but at least I got some interview practice and showed I'm keen to progress. The new person must have great skills and experience, so hopefully I'll be able to learn from him, which will mean I'll have a better chance of success next time.'

These are two examples of the 'explanatory styles' that we use to explain events in our lives. Did it happen because of me (internal) or because of something else (external)? Will it always happen (stable) or can I change the outcome (unstable)? And does this affect my whole life (global) or was it an isolated event (local)? Pessimists tend to view challenging events as internal, stable and globally pervasive, whereas optimists take the opposite view.

Knowing this, psychologists at the Positive Psychology Center at the University of Pennsylvania are conducting experiments to see if it's possible to change your explanatory style – and therefore make the shift from pessimist to optimist. So far, their work has focused on adolescents, as their personalities are more malleable than those of adults, and therefore ideal to test interventions to change. And, indeed, change has been observed. When taught about explanatory styles and new ways to approach problems, many of those studied reported fewer depressive and related symptoms when compared to a control group.[11] More work now needs to be done to see if these results can be replicated in adults, but exponents of positive psychology are confident, and many of those working in this field already have plenty of anecdotal evidence to suggest that this can be achieved.

Get to grips with gratitude

In addition to challenging negative underlying beliefs (which we explore shortly), feeling grateful is a powerful tool to help you increase your awareness of what's good in your life and become more positive. According to Dr Robert Emmons, Professor of Psychology at the University of California and the world's leading scientific expert on gratitude, one of the best ways to cultivate gratitude is to keep a gratitude journal.

Exercise: Keep a gratitude journal

This is a notebook or diary dedicated to recording – ideally on a daily basis – all the things you have to be grateful for. Some days you may struggle to find a single example; other days you might have enough to fill a page. The key is to focus your mind on what you have to be grateful for, even simple blessings, such as the roof over your head, your health, your family, having enough money to buy food, fresh water to drink, a comfortable bed to sleep in, a good friend, a loving pet, fresh air, sunshine, the shoes on your feet. You don't have to come up with anything other than the good fortune of a fortunate life, although identifying new examples from the events of each day is recommended. In his research, Emmons has found that filling in a daily gratitude journal can start to have beneficial effects in just three weeks, including higher levels of positive emotions and greater optimism.[12]

If you struggle with the concept of gratitude, Emmons offers a definition that may help to clarify it:

> First, it's an affirmation of goodness. We affirm that there are good things in the world, gifts and benefits we've received. This doesn't mean that life is perfect; it doesn't ignore complaints, burdens, and hassles. But when we look at life as a whole, gratitude encourages us to identify some amount of goodness in our life. The second part of gratitude is figuring out where that goodness comes from. We recognize the sources of this goodness as being outside of ourselves. It didn't stem from anything we necessarily did ourselves in which we might take pride. We can appreciate positive traits in ourselves, but I think true gratitude involves a humble dependence on others: we acknowledge that other people – or even higher powers, if you're of a spiritual mindset – gave us many gifts, big and small, to help us achieve the goodness in our lives.[13]

Exercise: Count your blessings

As an alternative to keeping a gratitude journal, you could practise counting your blessings on a daily basis, perhaps first thing in the morning as you wake, or last thing at night before you go to sleep. Just run through what you are grateful for today in your head.

Let's start by taking yesterday as an example. Take a moment to think of three things you are grateful for, however big or small. Aim to do this – or write in your gratitude journal – every day. Start with an achievable goal: do it for 30 days then assess the difference it's made in your life. Our bet is it will have a positive impact, so you'll be inspired to continue.

Counting your blessings and experiencing gratitude are essentially the same thing. And whichever way you choose to be thankful for what you have (rather than feeling unhappy about what you don't have), there are rewards. In research comparing four studies published in the *Journal of Personality and Social Psychology*, psychologists found that those who rated themselves – or were rated by others – as grateful had higher levels of vitality, happiness, satisfaction with life, lack of depressive and anxious symptoms, hope and optimism. 'Compared with their less grateful counterparts, grateful people are higher in positive emotions and life satisfaction and also lower in negative emotions such as depression, anxiety, and envy,' conclude the report's authors. 'They also appear to be more pro-socially oriented in that they are more empathic, forgiving, helpful, and supportive than are their less grateful counterparts.'[14]

Don't blame, reframe

Regardless of attitude, some experiences can trigger negative emotions that can bring us down. But there is a difference between an emotional response that helps us to reflect and move on and one that can lead to us feeling bad about ourselves and unable to resolve a situation. For example, if you have upset someone, feeling remorse and regret is likely to lead you to consider how to make amends and learn how to avoid a similar situation developing in the future. By contrast, feeling guilty and ashamed can result in you feeling bad about yourself, and therefore less able to resolve the situation or move on. The key difference here is the distinction between the behaviour (I *feel* bad about acting that way) and making it about you as a person (I *am* bad for causing this). This difference in mindset is an extension of the 'explanatory styles' we explored earlier and it is a natural progression from the previous chapter on stress triggers.

Exercise: Reflect, learn and move on

Next time a situation arises that causes you to feel bad, reflect on the underlying beliefs you have about what's happened. Ask yourself:

- How did my or another person's behaviour contribute to this situation?

- What can I learn from it?

- How can I resolve things and move on?

This process can also be helpful if you find yourself blaming someone else, or the world, for your suffering. Use these three questions to help yourself discover a different interpretation of the situation in which you find yourself – one that empowers not just you but the other parties involved. If you feel resistant, ask yourself, 'Do I want to be right or do I want to be happy?'

Transform the negative

Sometimes, you can still feel trapped by a negative viewpoint. It's as if it's your default position, and trying to change it feels like pushing a boulder uphill. This is where the HeartMath technique described in Chapter 12 is invaluable, as it equips you with the skills you need to transform your reaction to stress and the negative emotions you feel in the moment *and* helps you to be more positive. Just as a specific physical exercise helps you to develop a particular muscle, the HeartMath tool helps you to develop a more positive perspective on life.

We also suggest you review some of the exercises in Chapter 10, especially the ESR technique for releasing negative thoughts (see page 108).

Know it will pass

In her excellent book *Wired for Joy*, Emotional Brain Training expert Laurel Mellin suggests a simple tool to use when you hit an emergency situation and start to feel really stressed, on the verge of freaking out or launching into a full-blown tantrum. She calls it the Damage Control Tool and it's designed to calm down the brain state that perpetuates the strong negative emotions you are feeling and help you regain control. It's easy to master. You simply repeat the following phrases to yourself about 20 times, or until you feel calm:

- Do not judge (myself or others).
- Minimise harm (e.g. don't lash out on impulse).
- Know it will pass.

Next time you're on the verge of screaming at someone, losing the plot or feeling overwhelmed, try repeating this mantra instead. It can help to write down the three points and keep them in your pocket or handbag so you can refer to them quickly in times of need.

Grin and bear it

Finally, when you feel pessimistic, angry or under pressure, forcing yourself to smile can have a positive effect and reduce the impact of the stress response. Researchers at the University of Kansas studied a group of participants in test conditions that required the subjects to complete tasks that were designed to be stressful. Those who were asked to smile throughout experienced lower levels of stress and had lower heart rates on completion.[15] 'The next time you are stuck in traffic or are experiencing some other type of stress, you might try to hold your face in a smile for a moment,' advises Sarah Pressman, one of the scientists involved in the study. 'Not only will it help you "grin and bear it" psychologically, but it might actually help your heart health as well!'

The Serenity Prayer

The famous Serenity Prayer of St Francis can be helpful when a situation is particularly stressful and you are unsure of the best course of action. It asks for:

- The courage to change the things I can.
- The serenity to accept that which I cannot change.
- The wisdom to know the difference between the two.

CHAPTER 15

Prioritise and Time Manage

The feeling of not having enough time to do all the things we need or want to do is one of the most frequent sources of stress people report. Often we end up doing the tasks that shout loudest for our attention at the detriment of those things that would enhance our lives, such as relaxing, spending time with people who really matter to us, having some 'alone' time, or focusing on activities that support our personal or professional development. Yet, the truth is that you can only do one thing at a time, and having the ability to concentrate on that before moving on to the next thing is a hallmark of successful and unstressed people.

Many time management techniques promise to get you better organised and more focused. Some help you to be clear about the tasks you need to do and how to allow sufficient time to achieve them. Others promote the use of calendars and planners to help you schedule your time better. But the essence of time management is very simple and worth developing, especially in this age when there is always so much going on. In this chapter we suggest some of the helpful tools we've encountered over the years and use ourselves and with our clients.

A big source of stress is unfinished business

Do you ever feel overwhelmed because you have too much to do? According to Michael Walleczek, an expert in helping organisations produce paradigm shifts in their productivity, 'The sense of overwhelm is a consequence of having unfinished business.'

When you have endless 'to-do' lists that never seem to get done and just grow longer, this is likely to strike a chord, especially if you find yourself frequently side-tracked on to other tasks.

There is a saying: 'The past is history, the future a mystery. The only time that exists is the present.' How present are you in the present? How often do you find yourself doing one thing while trying to do something else, and worrying about yet another thing? That sort of multi-tasking will drive you crazy and stress you out.

The ability to stay focused in the present is the hallmark of truly efficient and effective people. What is the difference between these two qualities – efficiency and effectiveness? Think about it. Efficiency means doing something right; in other words, doing it completely. Done and dusted. For example, where bills are concerned, allocate them a time – say, every Wednesday evening – when you go through them and pay any that are out-standing. Then put them in a folder. Paid, sent, bill filed. Done. If you follow this routine every week, you won't get stressed about unpaid bills piling up. In fact, you won't need to think about bills at all, aside from on Wednesday evenings, when you'll have to deal with a handful of them, at most.

Having a multitude of things going on, each in a different stage of completion, generates stress. The nature of the human mind is that we are able to focus properly on only one task at a time, so even though our attention can flit rapidly from one topic to another and we might aspire to multi-task, the truth is that doing several things well at once is beyond our capabilities. Realising this is the key to developing efficient time management.

Exercise: Get on top of your to-do list

To start this process on the right foot, allocate some time – maybe one evening this week – to gather together all the jobs you have on your list – those piles of papers you should have read, the bills you have to pay, the projects you should have assessed – and for each of them ask yourself, 'Am I really going to do this, and, if so, when?' Your options are:

- I will do it now and finish it. So do it.

- I will do it later. Allocate a time when you will do it and make a note of this in your diary or on your daily to-do list.

- I will never do it. Bin it.

If you feel overwhelmed, assign each job a priority from 0 to 10, with 10 being both urgent and important and 0 being neither urgent nor important in any way. Then work through your 10s and decide to take action one or two, above. Do the same with your 9s, 8s and so on until you have allocated a time for all of these tasks, then file them in clearly labelled folders, or note actions on a to-do list on your computer under specific days or weeks. Unless you have lots of spare time or not much paper-work, binning anything below 4 or 5 is probably sensible.

Once you've done this exercise you should end up with a clear idea of what really needs to be done and when. Then you can calmly work through each task in turn, completing it before moving on to the next. As new tasks arrive, do them completely immediately, allocate a time when you will do them completely and stick to it, or bin them.

Of course, you will be unable to complete some jobs in their allocated time slot. For example, you might try to book a holiday only to be told that someone needs to get back to you. In that case, make the request, give them a time frame in which to respond – 'I need to know by next Wednesday' – then make a new note for next Thursday: 'Complete holiday booking'.

There may be some things that you feel you want to do, or read, or look into – but in reality you will probably never get round to them. Make a pile of these ideas and if, in three months' time, the pile is bigger than ever, just chuck it out.

Exercise: Manage your 'to-dos' day to day

Another helpful idea is to set up a daily to-do list on your computer with the headings 'Monday', 'Tuesday' and so on, along with headings for 'Next Week' and 'Next Month'. Then, at the end of each week, shift the 'Next Week' items to specific days. That way you can fully focus on urgent tasks and not waste time thinking about future ones. You can also relax in the knowledge that everything is in hand and will get sorted. So that should be one less source of stress and worry.

Time well spent?

If efficiency is doing something right to completion, effectiveness is doing the right thing. If you find yourself frequently in conflict over the different priorities and amount of time you have for all the activities in your life, then take some time out to assess if you've got the balance right. The chances are that the conflict has arisen either because you are not being realistic or because you are allocating too much time to things that aren't especially important and not enough to those that are. That's why reviewing how you spend your time can be worthwhile.

Let's use the example of Tom, one of Susannah's clients. Below is a time log in the form of a pie chart that shows how he spent his time each week.

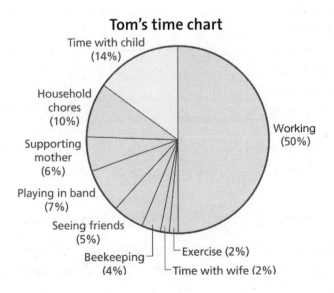

Tom's time chart

Time with child (14%)
Household chores (10%)
Supporting mother (6%)
Playing in band (7%)
Seeing friends (5%)
Beekeeping (4%)
Exercise (2%)
Time with wife (2%)
Working (50%)

Once he had compiled the chart, Tom noticed immediately that he spent more time with his bees than with his wife. No wonder he was having relationship problems! He also realised that his job was taking up half of his life, and that those gardening and DIY jobs his mother kept asking him to do were eating into his precious spare time. Armed with these insights, he was able to make some changes that included reducing his working hours by cutting down on distractions with a weekly priority plan, only attending essential meetings and working from home one day a week. He found his mother a local odd-job man, organised a weekly online shop instead of going to the supermarket, and prioritised a weekly night out with his wife so they could enjoy some quality time together. He also decided to give up his beekeeping, because, while it was something he enjoyed, he realised other things were more important. Finally, he swapped his twice-weekly run for four one-hour sessions of relaxing yoga and started doing a HeartMath exercise (see Chapter 12) each day to de-stress further. Here's his new time plan.

Tom's revised time chart

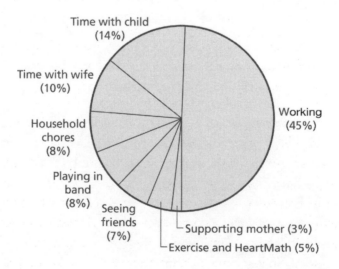

Exercise: Track your time

Now it's your turn. At the end of the book we have provided two blank time charts (see page 301), each with ten segments, with each segment representing roughly ten hours, or about 10 per cent of your waking hours each week (based on you getting roughly eight hours' sleep a night and spending just under two hours each day on personal care, such as getting up and showering, getting ready for bed, etc.). In the first chart, aim to segment your life at the moment into no more than eight key areas, rather than listing numerous smaller activities, which can make the chart harder to review.

Once you've charted your life as it is now, ask yourself:

- Is this the best use of my time?

- Does the time I spend on each activity match the priority it has in my life? (If you're not sure, on a separate sheet list all the key areas in your life and assign them a 0–10 priority rating to see clearly what's most important to you.)

- Are there areas where I can organise things better or take a smarter approach to achieve the same results in less time?

- Are there any activities I'm not doing that would enhance my health and well-being and reduce my stress levels, or any I am currently doing that achieve the opposite?

After giving these questions some thought, fill in the second chart with your ideal division of time for each activity, so you can see what you'd like to work towards. Of course, we appreciate that work might not be a top priority but nonetheless requires sufficient time to enable you to earn enough to pay the bills, so you'll need to be realistic as well as idealistic (at least until you've figured out how to earn more money in less time or have managed to find a job you truly love).

Exercise: Make better use of time

Once you have a clear idea of what will work better for you, note down the changes you can make to help yourself achieve your ideal time balance. These could include working from home more often, sharing out household chores, doing less for other people, or spending more time with the people who matter most to you. (Below are some time-saving ideas you may find helpful.) It is also important to schedule into your diary the important activities that will improve the quality of your life, enhance your energy and help you de-stress, such as a time to exercise or practise the HeartMath technique (Chapter 12). You should view these as equally important to any other diarised item, such as seeing the dentist.

Time-saving ideas

- Can you shorten your working hours without reducing your productivity, for example by better planning, reducing distractions (such as office gossip or drinks after work), or allocating set times to do regular tasks (such as checking and responding to emails every two hours rather than every two minutes)?

- Can you work from home some days to save on commuting time? Or, while you are commuting, can you make better use of your time by catching up on reading, planning your day, responding to the previous day's emails or doing some preparation on your laptop?

- Can you find better ways to organise and share household chores, such as: allocating set nights when you and your partner will take it in turns to cook or agreeing that whoever cooks doesn't do the washing up; ordering your groceries online; cleaning the house instead of going to the gym (and making it an aerobic workout complete with a disco soundtrack) or employing a cleaner; automating your bill paying; and incentivising your children to do specific household chores in return for extra pocket money?

- Spend a few minutes at the start of each day to figure out your key priorities, then work through them one at a time, giving each activity your full attention and completing it before you move on to the next. It can be really motivating to get an early result, so perhaps do the most important – or the most difficult – task first.

- If you are working on one long task, break it down into hour-long chunks and take a short break between each one to help you focus better. Resist distractions but give yourself a reward for each major milestone you complete – for example, a hot drink, a short walk, or a quick chat with a colleague.

- Eliminate time-wasters. If you waste time looking for things, establish a routine that means you always hang your keys on a hook, put your bag on the same chair, leave your mobile phone on your desk, etc. If you get caught up in phone conversations when you're trying to do something else, let your voicemail pick up. Ask friends to call you only after work, or during your lunch break. If people frequently distract you at work, stick a 'Do Not Disturb' sign on your door. Or, if you work in an open-plan office, pop on some headphones (relaxing music optional) to discourage interruptions.

- If you are overloaded at work or at home, either delegate to colleagues or family members or ask for help. If you ask nicely and make it clear exactly what you need, people are usually happy to help if they have the time, especially if you offer to return the favour when they are over-stretched.

It doesn't have to be perfect

We can spend a large amount of time trying to make whatever we do the best it can be – and sometimes that's time well spent. But if you adopt this approach for everything, you're likely to find yourself with insufficient time to do anything properly. In addition to causing you stress and frustration, that will impact on your personal time for relaxing and doing the things you enjoy. So, as we explored in Chapter 13 when we looked at underlying beliefs, if you hear a voice in your head that says, 'It has to be perfect' or 'I must do a great job', encourage yourself to soften a little. Instead, try 'I could do a perfect job, but I have other more important things to do, so today just good enough will be fine' or 'I'll do the best job I can with the resources (or in the time) that I have'.

You probably already understand that cutting yourself a bit of slack is far healthier than driving yourself relentlessly. Pursuing a path that creates stress will not benefit you – or those around you – physically, emotionally or mentally.

Learning to say no

Do you have difficulty saying 'no'? If so, this can be a major cause of lost time and stress. Of course, say 'yes' to whatever is important and appealing to you. But if you find yourself doing this habitually, simply because you feel that refusing would make you look bad, unhelpful, selfish or unlikeable, then you may find yourself at other people's beck and call to the detriment of your own priorities.

If 'yes' is your default setting, buy yourself some time by saying you need to consider the request: for example, 'I'll get back to you on that tomorrow. I just need to be clear on my other commitments.' This is likely to be true, as you often will need to check with others whether you can shift your priorities to accommodate a new request. Also, ask yourself, 'Do I really *want* to do this?' If the answer is 'no', you should decline graciously: for example, 'I'm flattered to be asked but I'm sorry, I've got so many other things on right now, I cannot spare the time to do a proper job.' Or offer an alternative: 'I'm sorry, I can't help you, but you could try . . . ' Showing empathy can also soften your response: 'I appreciate you're in a fix, and I'd really like to help, but I'm sorry, I have another commitment.' Even if that other commitment is spending the evening enjoying a meal out with your partner or playing with your kids, such activities are crucial to your well-being, so don't feel guilty about them. Be true to yourself and your own priorities, even if others don't understand them. As the American author, screenwriter and teacher Scott Stabile says: 'Don't worry if you're making waves simply by being yourself. The moon does it all the time.'

Draw a line between work and personal time

In our digital age of mobile phones and smart devices that provide 24/7 email access, drawing a line between your work and leisure time or home life can be challenging. For many people, there are no clear boundaries, so they feel 'on call' to work commitments all the time and never really switch off. Unsurprisingly, this can be an ongoing source of stress. But managing your time well isn't just about completing all your work-based tasks. It's also about allowing yourself enough time to relax, recharge your batteries and do the things that really matter to you in life, such as spending time with your friends and family and doing activities that enhance your health and well-being. If you find it hard to separate work from other areas of life – and especially if you work at home – you may find the following exercise useful.

Exercise: Leave work behind

Decide in advance what time you are going to finish work each day, then, five minutes before this deadline, get a piece of paper and do a 'brain dump'. Write down all the work-related thoughts that are whirring around your mind, all the jobs you intended to tackle but didn't finish (or even start), all the ideas you are mulling over. If you wish, you can allocate specific tasks to specific days, or put them into next week's list of jobs to do. But as soon as the five minutes are up and you've 'downloaded' everything relating to work onto a piece of paper, stop. Do not take these thoughts and worries home with you.

Next, do something that will help you shift into the following mode – 'me time', 'family time', 'leisure time', whatever it may be. This could be something as simple as turning off your computer or your smartphone. It could be standing up and taking five deep breaths; or drinking a glass of cold water. It could be taking off your tie or putting on some slippers (if you work at home). Find something that marks the boundary between 'work time' and 'you time' and do it every day. That way you will separate the two aspects of your life and move more easily from one to the other.

Summary

To ensure you get the most benefit from this section, here is a summary of the main activities and exercises we suggest:

- Complete the stress log at the end of the book and use it to uncover the underlying beliefs that increase stress in your life. We recommend you review this daily over a 30-day period to tease out all the main triggers, feelings and ways in which you compensate. That way you'll start to identify more effective – and less stress-inducing – strategies you can put into practice to help yourself cope better.

- Either keep a daily gratitude journal or do a daily 'count my blessings' exercise for at least 30 days.

- Fill in the two time charts at the end of the book with your *current* use of time and your *ideal* use of time. Then note down all the ways that will help you move from the former to the latter. Aim to incorporate just two or three new time-saving approaches each week until you have embedded a more efficient approach to ensuring your time is well spent.

PART 5

Troubleshooting Deeper Problems

This section covers some common additional issues that often go hand-in-hand with high-stress and low-energy levels. First, it's worth checking your detoxification potential in Chapter 16; then, if your symptoms suggest this is a stress point for you, review the steps necessary to reduce your toxic load and increase your liver's detoxification capacity.

Chronic fatigue syndrome is discussed in Chapter 17. This is typically the result of a variety of stresses overloading the body that impair normal functioning and make life very challenging. We look at some of the most common underlying causes and offer some pointers to aid recovery.

Low mood and anxiety are covered in Chapters 18 and 19, as these often manifest when you are highly stressed and tired, and then can feed into a vicious cycle where the symptoms perpetuate each other.

Finally, in Chapter 20, we look at stress-related weight gain, a common issue for many people.

As with the previous sections, we offer pointers in each chapter, before going on to pull together what's most important to you in Part 6, where we outline the Stress Cure programme.

CHAPTER 16

Do You Need to Detox?

When high stress and low energy are accompanied by a range of other undesirable symptoms – from headaches and brain fog to increased sensitivity to food and/or chemicals – your body may be telling you it's overloaded. In other words, you are likely to have exceeded your capacity to detoxify. This can place a huge additional stress on your body, so regaining your detoxification ability is an essential part of feeling better and building greater resilience.

While eating the right food and getting sufficient nutrients is one side of the coin, detoxification is the other. Most substances we consume – including food, water and air – contain toxins as well as nutrients, and generate toxic by-products as we use them. Oxygen, for example, turns into carbon dioxide. Even feelings can generate toxins: as we saw in Chapter 2, a stressful thought is all it takes to trigger a cascade of biochemical activity.

From a chemical perspective, much of what goes on in the body involves the breaking down and building up of substances as they are turned from one thing into another. A good 80 per cent of this involves detoxifying potentially harmful substances. Much of this task is performed by the liver, which could be viewed as a clearing house that is able to recognise millions of potentially harmful chemicals and transform them into harmless substances, or prepare them for elimination. Your liver is the chemical brain of your body – recycling, regenerating and detoxifying in order to maintain your health.

External, or exo-, toxins represent just a small part of what the liver has to deal with; many toxins are made *within* the body as by-products during the processing of other molecules. These internally created, or endo-, toxins have to be disarmed in just the same way as exo-toxins do. Whether a substance is bad for you depends as much on your ability to detoxify it as on its inherent toxic properties. People with multiple food sensitivities, for example, eat the same food as healthy people – they have just lost their detoxification potential. If this is the case for you, it's important to regain your capacity to detoxify so you can feel better and increase your energy and ability to deal with stress.

Assessing your detox capability

Multiple allergies, frequent headaches, sensitivity to chemicals and environmental pollutants, chronic digestive problems, muscle aches, inflammation and anxiety are just some of the conditions that can be caused by a breakdown in the body's ability to detoxify.

You can get an instant impression of your detox potential by completing the checklist below, which lists all the symptoms that can be associated with poor detoxification. Add up your total now, then retake the test once you have followed the Stress Cure programme (see Part 6) for a month.

Check your detox potential

- Do you often suffer from headaches or migraines?
- Do you sometimes have watery or itchy eyes, or swollen, red or sticky eyelids?
- Do you have dark circles under your eyes?
- Do you sometimes have itchy ears, earache, ear infections, drainage from the ears or ringing in the ears?
- Do you often suffer from excessive mucus, a stuffy nose or sinus problems?

- Do you suffer from acne, skin rashes or hives?

- Do you sweat a lot and have a strong body odour?

- Do you sometimes have joint or muscle aches or pains?

- Do you have a sluggish metabolism and find it hard to lose weight, or are you underweight and find it hard to gain weight?

- Do you often suffer from frequent or urgent urination?

- Do you suffer from nausea or vomiting?

- Do you often have a bitter taste in your mouth or a furry tongue?

- Do you have a strong reaction to alcohol?

- Do you suffer from bloating?

- Does coffee leave you feeling jittery or unwell?

If you answer 'yes' to seven or more of these questions, you need to improve your detox potential. If you answer 'yes' to between four and seven questions, you are beginning to show signs of poor detoxification and could do with a tune up. If you answer 'yes' to fewer than four questions, you are unlikely to have a problem with detoxification.

If you have a high score, it might be worth getting more information via a test to assess your biochemical detoxification potential. A nutritional therapist (and some doctors) can arrange a hepatic detox profile test to check levels of certain markers (specifically D-glucaric acid and mercapturic acids) from the key liver detoxification pathways (outlined shortly). This can give an indication of how well these pathways are working, and where more support may be needed. (See Resources for more information.)

A hepatic detox profile test is quite different from standard GP tests for liver function, which involve measuring levels of the key enzymes GPT and GOT. If these are high, your liver is really struggling and you have a chronic problem. However, while they are useful in establishing that a problem exists, they don't really identify the best way to help recovery.

Detoxification – a two-step process

As we've established, the main mechanisms for detoxification are carried out by your liver and involve a complex set of chemical pathways that have the ability to recycle toxic chemicals and turn them into harmless ones. This process is known as *biotransformation*. Each pathway consists of a series of enzyme reactions, and each enzyme is dependent on a number of nutrients that, step-by-step, make your internal world safe.

Detoxification can be split into two stages. The first, known as Phase 1, is akin to getting your rubbish ready for collection. It doesn't actually eliminate anything; it just prepares substances for elimination, making them easier to pick up. Fat-soluble toxins, for example, become more soluble. Phase 1 is carried out by a series of enzymes called P-450s. The more toxins you're exposed to, the faster these enzymes must work to pile up the rubbish, ready for collection. The substances created by P-450 enzyme reactions are often more toxic than the original chemicals. For example, many of them are oxidised, generating harmful free radicals.

The function of P-450 enzymes primarily depends on anti-oxidants such as glutathione, N-acetyl cysteine, co-enzyme Q_{10}, vitamins C and E, selenium and beta-carotene, although B vitamins, flavonoids and phospholipids are also important. Substances that kick-start Phase 1 include caffeine, alcohol, pollutants, cigarette smoke, exhaust fumes, high-protein diets, preservatives (such as benzoates), organophosphate fertilisers, paint fumes, damaged trans-fats, steroid hormones and charcoal-barbecued meat.

How the liver detoxifies

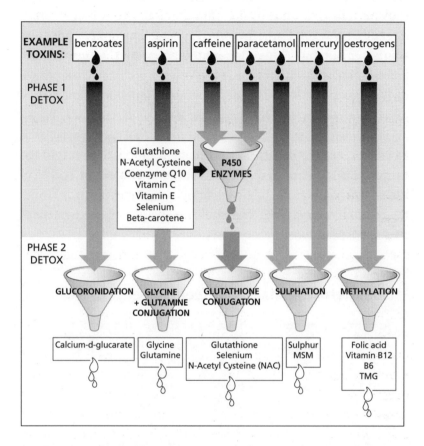

The second stage, known as Phase 2, is concerned with building up rather than breaking down. According to Dr Sidney Baker, an expert in the chemistry of detoxification, around 80 per cent of all the building that the body does is for the purposes of detoxification. The end-products of Phase 1 are transformed by 'sticking' other substances on to them. This process is called conjugation, as in marriage. For example, some toxins have glutathione joined to them (glutathione conjugation). This is how we detoxify paracetamol (acetaminophen): in overdoses involving this painkiller, a person is given glutathione, or its precursor N-acetyl cysteine, to mop up the highly destructive toxins generated by Phase 1 detoxification of the drug.

Other toxins have sulphur stuck to them in a process called sulphation. This is the fate of many steroid hormones, neurotransmitters and, once again, paracetamol. The sulphur comes directly from food. Garlic, onions and eggs, for example, are good sources of sulphur-containing amino acids, such as methionine and cysteine, and without these you've got a problem. Others have carbon compounds, called methyl groups, stuck to them (this is called methylation and it depends on B vitamins, especially B_6, B_{12} and folic acid). Lead and arsenic are detoxified in this way, as is adrenalin. Aspirin has the amino acid glycine stuck to it (glycine conjugation). When these pathways are overloaded the body can use another, known as glucuronidation, which is the primary route for breaking down many tranquillising drugs and the benzoates that are used in food preservation.

Does detoxing make you feel worse?

Sometimes a person who has a high exposure to toxins (perhaps due to diet and lifestyle factors or digestive problems) can have a revved-up Phase 1, because it is used to working hard and fast to get these toxins ready for collection. However, if the next stage of detoxification, Phase 2, isn't similarly upregulated, a toxic backlog can develop, intensifying the range of symptoms outlined in the 'check your detox potential' checklist. A telltale sign of this imbalance can be feeling dreadful when following a general detoxification regime, or even worse when supplementing antioxidants. If this is the case for you, we suggest you consult a nutritional therapist, who will do a more in-depth assessment to determine the best way to rebalance your liver detoxification pathways.

Too many toxins or not enough nutrients?

When your liver's biochemical pathways don't work properly, due to overload or a lack of nutrients, the body generates harmful toxins. An example is homocysteine, a toxic by-product of breaking down the amino acid methionine. Raised levels of homocysteine are associated with increased risk for a range of conditions, including heart disease, osteoporosis, infertility and mental health problems, including dementia.[1] Your level can rise as a result of problems with the sulphation pathway, usually as a consequence of a lack of vitamin B_6, or your methylation pathway, which needs folic acid and B_{12}. Another example is developing sensitivity to exhaust fumes. Sulphur dioxide, a component of exhaust fumes, is detoxified via the sulphation pathway, whose enzymes depend on the mineral molybdenum, which is found in particularly high concentrations in beans. Over-exposure to exhaust fumes, for example due to spending a lot of time in heavy traffic, coupled with a molybdenum-deficient diet, can lead to intolerance.

These detoxifying pathways work together: if one is overloaded, another has the ability to process a toxin. But once the back-up systems are overloaded too, the body is unable to clear toxins. These can then damage and disrupt just about every system of the body, affecting the nervous system, hormone balance, muscles and joints, digestion and immunity. This can be a factor in chronic fatigue syndrome (discussed in detail in the next chapter), in which a person often feels worse after eating or physical exertion because they are unable to detoxify even the normal endo-toxins properly. A common cause of toxic overload is a problem in the digestive tract.

The digestion connection

Digestive dysfunction is a key source of toxic overload and is far more likely to occur when you are under stress. Your 10-metre-long digestive tract stretches from your mouth to your anus, with a series of corrugations, called villi, designed to maximise the surface area. If ironed out flat, your digestive tract would cover a small football pitch! This huge surface area forms a barrier between the 100 tonnes or so of food we consume in a lifetime and our inner world – that is, all that's inside us on the other side of the wafer-thin epithelial cells that line the digestive tract. Only certain digested molecules are allowed through this barrier and into your bloodstream via a rigid selection process that is policed by the immune system. The epithelial cells work hard to transport nutrients from food into the body, so they need to regenerate every four days.

Prolonged stress, marked by high levels of cortisol and low levels of DHEA, shuts down this immune function. Think of it as the bouncers going on strike at a nightclub. The bouncers in this case are called sIgA (secretory immunoglobulin A); they line the digestive tract and their job is to protect us from the entry of undesirable molecules. We lose this protection as sIgA levels fall when we are under stress, which results in large, undesirable molecules finding their way into the body. These stimulate an immune response, which is what food allergies are all about and why people under chronic stress are more likely to develop food sensitivities. (SIgA levels are often measured alongside cortisol and DHEA as part of an adrenal stress test, as described in Chapter 8.)

As we also learned in Chapter 8, too much stress both suppresses the immune system and encourages inflammation, setting the scene for gastrointestinal infections and distress. We react to stress to divert attention towards producing energy for fight or flight, and away from things that aren't essential for short-term survival, such as digestion and immunity. That's why it's harder to digest food when you're feeling stressed and why you become more prone to illnesses and find them harder to shift if that stress is prolonged.

Another reason why uninvited guests get through into the body is that our inner skin, the wall of the digestive tract, can become too permeable, a condition known as gastrointestinal permeability or 'leaky gut syndrome'. This can result from infection, inflammation, low levels of digestive enzymes, too much alcohol, a poor diet or repeated use of antibiotics or non-steroidal anti-inflammatory drugs, such as aspirin or ibuprofen.

How to intoxicate and detoxify the body

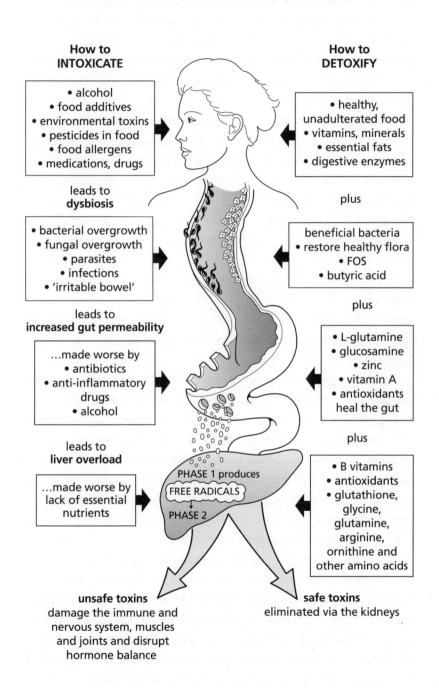

**How to
INTOXICATE**

- alcohol
- food additives
- environmental toxins
- pesticides in food
- food allergens
- medications, drugs

leads to
dysbiosis

- bacterial overgrowth
- fungal overgrowth
- parasites
- infections
- 'irritable bowel'

leads to
increased gut permeability

...made worse by
- antibiotics
- anti-inflammatory drugs
- alcohol

leads to
liver overload

...made worse by
lack of essential nutrients

**How to
DETOXIFY**

- healthy, unadulterated food
- vitamins, minerals
- essential fats
- digestive enzymes

plus

beneficial bacteria
- restore healthy flora
- FOS
- butyric acid

plus

- L-glutamine
- glucosamine
- zinc
- vitamin A
- antioxidants
heal the gut

plus

- B vitamins
- antioxidants
- glutathione, glycine, glutamine, arginine, ornithine and other amino acids

PHASE 1 produces
FREE RADICALS
PHASE 2

unsafe toxins
damage the immune and nervous system, muscles and joints and disrupt hormone balance

safe toxins
eliminated via the kidneys

Once too many toxins and large molecules start gate-crashing through the digestive tract, the body has to work overtime to detoxify and deal with them. Before long, the body's ability to detoxify all of these uninvited guests starts to weaken, resulting in overloaded liver detoxification pathways. By this stage, even the slightest increase in toxins can trigger a host of symptoms, such as fatigue, drowsiness, headaches, body aches and inflammation. For example, when we exercise, muscles tend to produce a toxin called lactic acid (this is what causes stiffness the next day). This is no problem normally, but if a person's detox potential is poor, even a brisk walk can trigger detox overload symptoms (as outlined earlier in the 'check your detox potential' checklist). The same is true of eating a slightly larger meal than normal, or certain foods, especially those that are hard to digest.

How well are you digesting?

You are *not* what you eat. You are what you can digest and absorb. The large food particles that we eat are broken down into tiny food particles that can enter the body. They are on the guest list, so to speak. This digesting is done by enzymes and stomach (hydrochloric) acid. Each day the body should produce around ten litres of digestive juices (yes, *ten* litres!), and if you do not manage to produce enough, the result is indigestion. This can manifest as abdominal discomfort, bloating, excessive flatulence and/or fatigue. Instead of being energised by a meal, you feel tired after eating. Similar symptoms can result if you eat more than your body can digest.

If you suspect you might not be digesting your food efficiently, first make sure you are relaxed before you eat and take time to thoroughly chew each mouthful before swallowing. If you still have problems, go to a health-food shop and buy a digestive enzyme supplement (see Resources). Pick one that contains some amylase (the enzyme that digests carbohydrate), some protease (the enzyme that digests protein), some lipase (the enzyme that digests fat), some lactase (which digests milk sugars), as well as glucoamylase and alphagalactosidase (which digest vegetables, greens and beans). Take one of these with each meal for a week. If your indigestion disappears and your vitality returns, then you've identified the problem ... and the solution. You can keep taking these digestive enzymes for as long as is necessary. However, more often than not, after a month or so they become superfluous, especially if you've made the other dietary changes recommended in this book. This is because you'll be better able to absorb the nutrients required to make these enzymes yourself, so you will kick-start the process into working as it should. It should be noted, though, that some people will always find it hard to digest certain food types, such as beans. In such cases, taking digestive enzymes with a bean-containing meal can make all the difference.

Bacteria in the balance

Inside your digestive tract are three pounds of 300 different strains of bacteria that are essential for your health and vitality. A single course of antibiotics can more or less wipe them out. A big night out when you drink excessive alcohol can have a similar effect. These bacteria make all sorts of nutrients for the body and protect your digestive tract from infection. Of course, there are also harmful bacteria: you may have encountered them on holiday, from food poisoning or just from an unfamiliar environment.

Having the right balance of bacteria is key to digestive health and overall well-being. The symptoms of an imbalance, also called dysbiosis, are much the same as those discussed above for indigestion. If the aforementioned digestive enzymes don't sort you out, you may wish to consider adding beneficial bacteria to your diet. This is especially important if you've been doing anything that might have destroyed them, such as drinking too much alcohol or taking antibiotics.

Fermented foods, such as live yoghurt, miso, pickles and sauerkraut, often contain beneficial bacteria; but if you need to replenish depleted levels, the most efficient way to do so is via a concentrated probiotic supplement which contains the exact strains that should be resident in your gut. The two most important strains are *Lactobacillus acidophilus* and *Bifido bacteria*, so look for products containing these from a reliable supplement company (see Resources). Some supplements even combine digestive enzymes with probiotics.

UFOs of the intestines

More insidious than bacterial imbalance is UFO infestation. Unidentified faecal organisms (UFOs, for short) include a wide variety of harmful life forms that can take up residence in the digestive tract, such as harmful bacteria, fungi, protozoa and worms. These parasites are far more common than is generally realised.

Symptoms of parasite infection can include:

- Abdominal pain and cramps
- Diarrhoea and constipation
- Bloating
- Flatulence
- Foul-smelling stools
- Inflammatory gut problems
- Fatigue
- Headaches
- Food sensitivity
- Weight loss
- Aches and pains
- Fever

This list is by no means comprehensive, but it illustrates how UFO infestation could be the root cause of many common health problems. If you developed any of these symptoms during a holiday in a place where hygiene levels were suspect, or after a course of antibiotics, which has the potential to wipe out your natural defences against parasites, then UFO infestation is a very real possibility.

The best course of action is to have a comprehensive stool test to find out whether you are suffering from UFOs. There are many different parasites, and the best laboratories test for a wide variety as well as for the presence of beneficial and harmful bacteria and yeasts. If a particular parasite is identified, there is usually a specific remedy to deal with it. But this is a complex field and it is definitely best to work with a nutritional therapist or a medical specialist, both of whom will know which tests to carry out (see Resources).

Leaky gut syndrome

Normally healthy foods can become toxic to the body if they are not digested or absorbed properly. As we've seen, during healthy digestion, we break our food down into simple molecules that can readily pass through the digestive tract and into the bloodstream. If, however, we are unable to digest our food properly, or if the gut wall becomes leaky, incompletely digested foods will enter the blood. Once there, they are likely to alert immune 'scout' cells, which treat them as invaders, triggering an allergic reaction. The ensuing battle will generate a complex group of chemicals that themselves are toxins and will therefore need to be cleaned up.

The gut wall can become leaky for a number of reasons in addition to a suppressed immune system and low sIgA. Alcohol irritates the gut lining, as does a gluten protein in wheat called gliadin; a deficiency of cell-building nutrients such as vitamin A, zinc, protein and essential fats can result in a poor gut wall structure; an overgrowth of the wrong bacteria or yeast, such as *Candida albicans*, or any other parasite, can burrow into the intestinal wall, irritating it, causing increased permeability; even abdominal distention, as a result of either bloating or over-eating, can over-stress the gut wall. Certain drugs are particularly damaging to the digestive tract, including antibiotics, aspirin and other anti-inflammatory drugs.

Once the gut wall is permeable, perfectly normal foods can become toxic to the body because they gain access before being completely digested. Instead of boosting your energy, these undigested foods add to the toxic burden of the body and once this is too great, the body can no longer fully detoxify itself. The resulting toxins can generate many of the symptoms listed in the 'check your detox potential' checklist.

There are several simple, non-invasive tests to find out if you have a leaky gut (see Resources). These involve drinking harmless substances and later collecting a urine sample. Depending on what appears in the urine, it is possible to establish the size of the molecules that are passing through the digestive tract. These tests are best done under the guidance of a nutritional therapist, who will then devise a specific diet and supplement programme to heal the digestive tract. Such programmes often include specific supplements of butyric acid, glutamine and essential fats, as well as the vitamins and minerals mentioned in the remainder of this chapter. Glutamine is an amino acid that the epithelial cells use as fuel; taking a heaped teaspoonful (5g), away from food, can help heal the gut, for example after too much alcohol or a course of antibiotics. Some digestive enzyme supplements also provide a basic amount of glutamine.

Promoting good gut health

Irrespective of whether you have digestive problems or a leaky gut, the following dietary and supplementary advice is consistent with keeping your digestive tract in good health:

- Avoid alcohol or have it infrequently and only in moderation.

- Don't take aspirin, ibuprofen or other non-steroid anti-inflammatory drugs on a regular basis.

- Cut down your consumption of wheat products and instead vary your grain intake to include easier-to-digest brown rice, rye bread, oat-based cereals and oatcakes and buckwheat, rice or quinoa pasta. A gluten protein in wheat called gliadin is especially irritating to the digestive tract.

- Eat fermented foods such as live yoghurt (unless dairy intolerant), miso, sauerkraut and pickles.

- Eat seeds and oily fish. The essential fats they contain are used structurally in the digestive tract, and act as natural anti-inflammatory agents.

- If you are suffering from indigestion, try taking a digestive enzyme supplement with each main meal, perhaps with probiotics.

- Make sure your supplement programme includes 15mg of zinc, 10,000iu (3300mcg) of vitamin A, plus antioxidant nutrients.

Time for a detox?

Reducing your dietary toxic load and increasing your intake of the nutrients that support detoxification can give your body a well-deserved break. In much the same way as you can feel revitalised after a holiday, a week or two's detox can help your body to feel more energised, less stressed and better equipped to deal with life's challenges. Beware of regimes that talk about a 'healing crisis', however. This can occur when you encourage the body to detoxify but don't support the liver with the proper nutrients to do the job (for example, as a result of fasting). The headaches, nausea and general ill-feeling that can occur are often signs of intoxication.

Patrick's *9-Day Liver Detox* book provides a fully guided programme with more background on detoxification, daily menus, recipes and a shopping list. This is well worth following in full if you scored high on the 'check your detox potential' checklist. However, we provide a brief account of the key dietary and supplement steps here. As the book's title indicates, an ideal timescale is nine days, generally two weekends and the week in between.

Step 1: Lessen the toxic load

Obviously, the first step to detoxifying the body is to remove or lessen the toxic load. Some foods are nearly all toxin-generating, while others support detoxification. Most, however, have both good and bad aspects. The foods that are *definitely* good for detoxification include:

- Vegetables – all are good, but artichokes, beetroot, broccoli, Brussels sprouts, carrots, cauliflower, chicory, cucumber, kale, peppers, pumpkin, red cabbage, spinach, sprouted seeds and beans, sweet potato, tomato and watercress are *great*. White potatoes and avocado should be eaten in moderation.

- Fruit – the most beneficial fruits with the highest detox potential include fresh apricots, berries (all types), citrus fruits, kiwi, mango, melon (cantaloupe and watermelon), papaya, peaches and red grapes. Go easy on bananas – a maximum of one a day. Dried fruit is best avoided throughout the nine days.

These foods should make up the bulk of your detox diet. Needless to say, choose organic wherever possible so the body doesn't have to detoxify the pesticides.

The following foods are generally good for you, but may contain low levels of toxins. They should therefore make up no more than a third of your detox diet:

- Grains – brown rice, corn, millet, quinoa, buckwheat and oats.

- Fish – wild or organic salmon, trout, mackerel, herring and sardines.

- White meat – organic, skinless chicken, turkey and wild game.

- Oils – use olive oil for cooking and in place of butter, and cold-pressed seed oils for dressing (organic, cold-pressed flax oil is best for this).

- Nuts and seeds – a large handful a day of raw, unsalted nuts and seeds should be included in your diet. Try grinding them up and sprinkling them over a fruit salad. Include almonds, Brazils, hazelnuts, pecans, pumpkin seeds, sunflower seeds, sesame seeds, chia and flax seeds.

The following foods, while usually acceptable in moderation, are best avoided during your detox because they can be difficult to digest or detoxify, and they might mildly irritate the gut:

- Gluten grains – barley, rye and wheat (including spelt and kamut, although the latter, an early form of wheat, seems to have an anti-inflammatory effect).

- Animal products – milk and all other dairy products, eggs and organic red meat.

The following should be avoided *at all times*:

- Non-organic red meat, refined foods, such as white bread/pasta/rice, sugar and any foods to which it has been added, salt and any foods to which it has been added, hydrogenated or partially hydrogenated fat, artificial sweeteners, food additives and preservatives. (A good general rule is: 'If you can't pronounce it, avoid it!')

- Also avoid as much as possible fried foods, pesticides, exhaust fumes and non-prescribed medications – most contain harmful substances that require detoxification.

Step 2: Hydrate

Ensuring you get enough fluid to hydrate the body and help excrete toxins via the urine is essential. Needless to say, alcohol is out while you are detoxing, as it's a major toxin for the body. The same is true of fizzy drinks, including colas and squash. Also avoid any sources of methylxanthines, a family of chemicals that includes caffeine, tannin, theobromine and theophylline. Of course, this means no chocolate, coffee or black tea. Limit green tea to two cups a day, using the same tea bag.

Drink plenty of:

- Water – filtered is best and avoid fizzy water. Aim to drink two litres a day, drinking at regular intervals, but no more than a single glass with meals, as this can impede digestion.

- Fresh fruit juices – in moderation, ideally freshly juiced and always diluted with an equal quantity of water.

- Cherry Active – this cordial-style drink can be diluted with water, contains no sugar and is especially rich in antioxidants, which support your body while detoxifying. Alternatives are Blueberry Active and Beet Active.

- Herbal teas – there is a huge variety to choose from, so sample a few until you find those you like. Red bush (rooibosch) tea is a good source of antioxidants and it's caffeine free, as are berry and rosehip teas. You could also try making your own mint or ginger and lemon tea.

- Dandelion coffee can be drunk as a coffee replacement and is beneficial for the liver. You can buy it powdered or in ready-to-grind chunks for a cafetiere.

Step 3: Boost your intake of detox nutrients

Supplementing the nutrients that help the body to detoxify is a great way to speed up the benefits of this rejuvenating diet. The nutrients needed to support Step 1 of detoxification are vitamins B_2, B_3, B_6, B_{12}, folic acid, glutathione, branched chain amino acids, flavonoids and phospholipids, plus a good supply of antioxidant nutrients to disarm the dangerous intermediary oxidants that are created during this phase.

Step 2 of detoxification can be stimulated back into action with the amino acids glycine, taurine, glutamine and arginine. Cysteine, N-acetyl cysteine and methionine are precursors of these nutrients (i.e. the body can convert them into the others).

Detoxification-supporting formulas that contain a good balance of these nutrients are widely available (see Resources for some suggestions). Take these alongside a daily multivitamin and mineral and extra vitamin C (1000mg with each meal).

If you suspect that your low energy and reduced resilience to stress may be connected with detoxification, and you notice a definite improvement in the first week, keep going for as long as you can, and certainly until you feel better. Then gradually reintroduce some of the foods that you were eating in limited quantities or avoiding altogether in Step 1. The *9-Day Liver Detox* book explains how to do this in a systematic way.

A nutritional therapist will be able to carry out a more detailed detoxification assessment and provide a more personalised programme. They may also recommend a food intolerance test, such as those that are listed on www.yorktest.com and www.lorisian. com. These tests identify any foods or drinks against which your body produces IgG antibodies, indicating intolerance. Nutritional therapists use them to devise specific diet and supplement programmes that are designed to maximise your detoxification potential.

CHAPTER 17

Solving Chronic Fatigue

While general fatigue is incredibly common, with 81 per cent of the 55,000 respondents in our 100% Health survey reporting low energy levels,[2] severe chronic fatigue syndrome (CFS), formerly known as ME, is much rarer, probably affecting one in a hundred people.[3] However, it does appear to be on the increase.

Long-term stress can lead to what's called adrenal fatigue, whereby you feel tired most of the time. It's like your get up and go just got up and went. CFS takes this to a new level, with sufferers often unable to work due to debilitating tiredness that is not relieved by rest.

Chronic fatigue syndrome didn't officially exist until 1997, when a joint report published by the Royal Colleges of Physicians, Psychiatrists and General Practitioners abandoned the term 'myalgic encephalomyelitis' (ME) – meaning inflammation of the sheath of nerve cells in the brain – and agreed instead on the new name. At the time, the report's authors admitted they still had little idea what caused CFS or how to treat it. Some seventeen years later (at the time of writing), many members of the medical profession are still confused, although a diagnostic procedure has now been developed.

In 2007, the British National Institute for Health and Clinical Excellence (NICE – now the National Institute for Health and Care Excellence) released new diagnosis guidelines which state that CFS should be considered if a person has disabling fatigue that had a specific onset (i.e. it has not been present throughout life), is persistent or recurrent, occurs after exertion with slow recovery and cannot be explained by other conditions. In addition, the sufferer will have one or more of the following symptoms for which no other medical explanation can be found:

- Difficulty sleeping
- Muscle and/or joint pain
- Headaches
- Painful lymph nodes
- Sore throat
- Difficulty thinking, poor concentration and failing short-term memory, as well as difficulties finding the right word, planning and organising
- General malaise or 'flu-like' symptoms
- Dizziness or nausea, or
- Palpitations without any identified cardiac problems

However, even if a correct diagnosis is made, NICE states that 'there is no known pharmacological treatment or cure for CFS/ ME'. Instead, it advises healthcare professionals to focus on management strategies, such as providing advice on sleep hygiene, relaxation techniques and the importance of eating a 'well-balanced diet'. As you probably realise by now, such an approach is far from optimal.

What causes CFS?

CFS may not be a new condition: it bears many similarities to vaguely defined syndromes, both epidemic and sporadic, described in the medical literature since the late eighteenth century. For instance, it shares much in common with a Victorian condition known as neurasthenia. There are also similarities with post-viral fatigue syndrome, fibromyalgia, hypothyroidism, multiple sclerosis, autoimmune disorders and pesticide exposure.

Victims of Gulf War syndrome – now believed to be the result of exposure to organophosphate pesticides, coupled with the intake of nerve-gas protection tablets – also show the same pattern of health problems.

However, exactly what's behind the apparent increase in CFS cases remains something of a mystery. While there appears to be no single underlying cause, it is common for sufferers to have disturbed immune system function, and an infectious agent is usually present. The Epstein-Barr virus (the agent that causes glandular fever) is often linked to CFS. However, too many cases of CFS test negative for this virus for it to be a likely cause for most sufferers. Rather, the virus may be an opportunist, taking advantage of CFS sufferers who are already immune-compromised *before* they come into contact with it.

Too many toxins, not enough nutrients

One of the greatly overlooked factors in CFS is nutritional deficiency. The usual assumption is that if you eat a well-balanced diet you get all the nutrients you need, yet scientific studies have found significant improvement in CFS patients who are given magnesium,[4] vitamin B_{12},[5] or essential fats (both omega 6 seed oils and omega 3 fish oil combinations).[6] Deficiency of many nutrients, including B vitamins and vitamin C, results in fatigue, and one very real possibility is that people with CFS have especially high nutrient requirements.

The most likely possibility is that CFS is a product of twenty-first-century living – with its combination of high stress, poor diet, toxin and 'anti-nutrient' exposure and overuse of drugs. Anti-nutrients encompass a range of substances that deplete nutrients from the body, or heighten the body's need for them – from exposure to toxic metals such as mercury, lead and aluminium to chemicals in detergents, alcohol and pesticides. These factors, plus infections and food intolerances, may be enough to overload the body's defences, resulting in CFS.

While most conventional medical practitioners are at a loss

to explain the condition, nutritional scientists have pioneered a highly effective treatment using a combination of diet and supplements, designed to improve gut and liver function and boost immunity. This approach is based on a new understanding of the sequence of events that leads to CFS. Imbalances in digestion and absorption always seem to be involved, leading to an imbalance of gut bacteria and a proliferation of harmful bacteria, fungi or other pathogens. This can result in damage to the gut wall, leading to increased gut permeability, which in turn can trigger allergies and immune reactions. This can overload the liver's detoxification systems (see Chapter 16). An infection may be the trigger for full-blown CFS, or it can result from a gradual weakening of the gut, liver and immune systems.

Evidence of detoxification problems

Research by Dr Jeffrey Bland and his colleagues at the Institute of Functional Medicine in the United States tested 30 CFS patients for liver detoxification abnormalities (as described in Chapter 16), then devised a nutritional strategy that was designed to correct them. Using their metabolic screening questionnaire (similar to our 'check your detox potential' checklist in Chapter 16), the researchers recorded a decline of more than 50 per cent in symptoms over the 21 days of the study.[7] This improvement was confirmed by further liver function tests.

In later research, Bland and his colleagues identified that a significant proportion of CFS patients show a particular type of imbalance in liver detoxification: the first phase is very speedy, generating toxins, but the second phase is sluggish, resulting in an inability to clear those toxins.[8] With this in mind, it's a good idea for people with CFS to have their liver function assessed and treated using specifically designed nutritional support.

Other factors that may be involved are food allergies and intolerances (often the consequence of leaky gut syndrome), adrenal exhaustion, thyroid problems and blood sugar imbalances, all of which have been discussed in earlier chapters.

It's mitochondria, not hypochondria

A key focus for new research has been exploring how the body's mitochondria – the tiny engines within each of our cells that make energy – can become deficient. These microscopic powerhouses are necessary for every bodily function, so if they malfunction, the result can be extreme fatigue.

Dr Sarah Myhill, a GP who specialises in the treatment of CFS, has pioneered research in this area and she has treated hundreds of sufferers successfully. Her approach addresses many of the areas outlined earlier, but, crucially, she also assesses patients for mitochondrial dysfunction, which appears to be a common feature among all CFS sufferers, no matter what other underlying causes exist.

Over the past few years, a new test has been developed which makes it possible to measure mitochondrial dysfunction, and also to assess which of the many nutrients necessary for energy production in the mitochondria are in short supply. Magnesium is one such key nutrient, which may explain why earlier research often found it to be deficient in CFS sufferers, but co-enzyme Q_{10}, vitamin B_3 (niacin) and acetyl L-carnitine are also important.

In a study of 138 patients with CFS by Dr Myhill and Professor Norman Booth of Oxford University, mitochondrial dysfunction was identified in every single case.[9] They also found that the level of dysfunction correlated to the degree of fatigue. As Dr Myhill observed: 'These patients do not suffer from hypochondria – the problem is mitochondria.' This must have been a great relief to sufferers likely to have been dismissed as malingerers by other members of the medical profession.

If you suffer with CFS, you can arrange to have a mitochondrial function profile test through a nutritional therapist with experience in this field, or via Dr Myhill's own practice in Wales (see Resources for more information).

CFS recovery: a multi-factorial approach

The debilitating fatigue and other symptoms of CFS appear to arise when the body fails to adapt to a set of circumstances that may include sub-optimal nutrition, chronic stress and exposure to toxins, as well as poor digestion, poor detoxification, hormonal imbalances, immune dysfunction and depleted mitochondrial function.

While there is a growing body of research that demonstrates how different nutritional and biochemical approaches can be successful in addressing CFS, it's clear that there is no 'one size fits all' strategy. A targeted approach that can identify and help rebalance specific imbalances is therefore the route we recommend. If you suffer with CFS, it's likely that you'll need the guidance of a nutritional therapist to do this successfully. However, there are some initial steps you can take yourself:

- Assess your detoxification potential, as outlined in Chapter 16, and follow a two-week (or longer) programme to reduce your toxic load and support liver detoxification. Ensure that you supplement the suggested nutrients to provide your liver with the tools it needs to function effectively.

- Balance your blood sugar by ensuring you eat protein with every meal and snack. This might mean adding more meat, fish or nuts to your detox programme, and/or including eggs.

- Avoid any foods to which you suspect you might be allergic: for example, if you feel more bloated, get a headache, produce more mucus or have stiff or achy joints after eating certain foods.

- Optimise digestion by supplementing a digestive enzyme (see Resources) with each meal and aim to be relaxed and free from stress whenever you eat.

- Ensure you pace yourself so that you conserve the little energy you have.

- Prioritise good-quality sleep, so aim to go to bed early and follow the advice in Chapter 11.

- Supplement a daily energy-supporting formula that includes magnesium, co-enzyme Q_{10}, vitamin B_3 and acetyl L-carnitine, plus an all-round antioxidant formula. See Chapter 22 for more details.

CHAPTER 18

Correcting Mood Imbalances

Stress and depleted energy are often accompanied by low mood and lack of motivation. While stress is rarely the sole cause of these symptoms, it can certainly be a contributory factor. In the same way as we have seen that hormone imbalances are key to understanding the chemistry of stress, imbalances in other chemical messengers – neurotransmitters – are key to understanding the chemistry of mood disorders.

Mood check

Score 1 for each 'yes' answer:

- Do you often feel downhearted or sad?
- Do you often feel worse in the morning?
- Do you find it difficult to face the day?
- Do you sometimes have crying spells, or feel like crying?
- Do you have trouble falling asleep, or sleeping through the night?
- Is your appetite, or desire to eat, poor?
- Do you feel unattractive and unlovable?
- Do you shun company and prefer to be alone?
- Do you often feel fearful?

- Are you often irritable or angry?

- Do you find it difficult to make decisions?

- Is it an effort to motivate yourself to do things you did more easily in the past?

- Do you feel hopeless about the future?

- Do you derive less enjoyment from activities that once gave you pleasure?

If you scored less than four, you are basically normal, even if you do occasionally feel a bit blue. Following the advice in this chapter will help keep your mood good and balanced.

If you scored between four and eight, your mood needs a boost. Following the advice in this chapter will help you improve how you feel.

If you scored more than nine, you are depressed and need some help. As well as following the advice in this chapter, consider seeing both a nutritional therapist and a psychotherapist.

Natural mood boosters

Serotonin is the key mood-boosting neurotransmitter, which is why most antidepressant drugs try to boost its activity in the brain. However, as you are now beginning to realise, everything in the body and brain is made from the food we eat, and serotonin is no exception. It is made from an amino acid called tryptophan. This is then converted into another amino acid – 5-hydroxy-tryptophan (5-HTP) – which in turn is converted into serotonin. Tryptophan can be found in many protein-rich foods, such as meat, fish, beans and eggs. (5-HTP is found in high concentrations in the African griffonia bean, but this is not a common feature of most people's diets.)

Merely not getting enough tryptophan is likely to make you

feel depressed. Over the course of a single day, Dr Philip Cowen, from Oxford University's Department of Psychiatry, gave 15 volunteers who had histories of depression but were currently fine, a drink that was nutritionally balanced aside from the fact that it excluded tryptophan. (The volunteers were not allowed to eat or drink anything else.) Within just seven hours, 10 of 15 noticed a worsening of their mood and started to show signs of depression.[10]

Both tryptophan and 5-HTP have been shown to have an anti-depressant effect in numerous other clinical trials, with 5-HTP apparently the more effective of the two amino acids.[11] Indeed, in a recent head-to-head trial with fluoxetine (the active ingredient in Prozac), 5-HTP was found to be just as effective as the drug.[12] However, 5-HTP has far fewer, if any, side-effects. If you suffer with low mood, start by taking 100mg of 5-HTP every day, in two doses of 50mg. You can build up to a maximum of 300mg a day if required. Exercise, exposure to sunlight and reducing your stress level also tend to promote serotonin activity.

Finally, though, a note of caution: if you take large amounts of 5-HTP in addition to SSRI antidepressants, this could theo-retically make you produce too much serotonin, so we don't recommend combining the two. Moreover, some people get mild nausea when they start supplementing 5-HTP. If you suffer from this, lower the dose. It's also worth remembering that 5-HTP doesn't suit everybody, and it is most effective for those with low serotonin levels. At the Brain Bio Centre Clinic (see Resources), specialist practitioners always measure serotonin levels first before prescribing 5-HTP, and we recommend this approach.

Get enough sun exposure, exercise and vitamin D

Vitamin D is known as the 'sunshine vitamin' because around 90 per cent of our supply is synthesised in our skin by the action of sunlight. Vitamin D deficiency is implicated in low mood and depression, particularly if you feel worse during the winter.

You are most at risk of suffering vitamin D deficiency if you are elderly (our ability to make it in the skin declines with age), dark-skinned (requiring up to six times as much sunshine as light-skinned people to make the same amount of vitamin D), overweight (vitamin D may be inaccessible as it is stored within your fat tissue), or tend to shy away from the sun (by covering up and using sun-block, although of course you should never risk your skin health by getting sunburned). Getting enough *safe* sun exposure, supplementing vitamin D and eating oily fish, eggs and full-fat dairy products all help to boost your reserves.

A healthy daily intake is 30mcg. Eating oily fish three times a week as well as six eggs each week, and spending half an hour outdoors each day, will give you about 15mcg (more in the summer, less in the winter, if you live in the UK or at a similar latitude). So it's worth supplementing 15mcg (600iu) daily, and possibly 25mcg (1000iu) during the winter months.

Exercising outdoors has a double benefit because regular exercise itself boosts mood, in addition to exposing you to sunshine. So, if you are feeling down, go for a brisk walk in the park.

Balance your blood sugar and try chromium

There is a direct link between mood and blood sugar balance. All carbohydrate foods are broken down into glucose, and your brain runs on glucose. The less even your blood sugar supply, the more uneven your mood. A high sugar intake has been implicated in aggressive behaviour, anxiety, depression and fatigue, not to mention lowered intelligence and academic performance.[13] A high intake of sugar and refined carbohydrates (meaning white bread, pasta, rice and most processed foods) is also linked with depression because these foods not only supply very little in the way of nutrients but use up mood-enhancing B vitamins: turning every teaspoon of sugar into energy demands B vitamins. Moreover, your blood sugar balance affects the delivery of tryptophan into the brain, thereby impacting on the production of serotonin.

The best way to keep your blood sugar level is to eat a low-glycemic load (low-GL) diet (see Chapter 4).

Chromium is vital for keeping your blood sugar level stable because insulin, the hormone that clears glucose from the blood, can't work properly without it. It also boosts serotonin levels.[14] In studies conducted on stressed (and therefore depressed) animals, chromium made them both less stressed and less depressed.[15] This is thought to be because chromium supplementation lowers the level of the adrenal stress hormone cortisol while boosting the level of serotonin.

People classified with 'atypical' depression (with symptoms of daytime sleepiness and grogginess, carbohydrate cravings, weight gain and emotional reactivity) have been shown to benefit from supplementing high-dose chromium (usually 400–600mcg a day), with many experiencing relief in a matter of days.[16] Chromium has also been shown to alleviate pre-menstrual mood swings[17] and reduce the propensity to binge-eating.[18] If you suffer from any of these conditions, it's well worth a try.

Is your food affecting your mood?

Sometimes eating a food to which you are unknowingly allergic can make you feel tired and depressed. We're not talking about classic allergies here, the kind where you react immediately and often violently: for example, vomiting after eating shellfish or having an anaphylactic reaction to peanuts. Rather, the symptoms are more insidious and harder to link to your diet. As well as making you feel down and tired, some foods can trigger anxiety, headaches, bloating, diarrhoea, constipation, muscle pain, joint stiffness, skin problems, rhinitis, sinusitis – the list of potential symptoms is almost endless, as each of us reacts in our own unique way. Such allergic reactions – or intolerances – involve another type of immune response, often linked to an immune marker called IgG.

Keeping a detailed food diary and then rotating the foods you eat most often to once every three days can help you to identify reactions. If this seems too difficult and time-consuming, you can use a home-based pin-prick blood test that allows you to identify an IgG reaction to a wide range of different foods (see Resources, page 311). For a more detailed guide, see *Hidden Food Allergies*, written by Patrick and Dr James Braly, which provides a step-by-step approach to identifying and dealing with allergies. The most common are wheat, gluten, dairy, yeast, citrus fruits, eggs, shellfish, soya and members of the nightshade family (potatoes, tomatoes, peppers and aubergines).

Increase your omega 3 fats

Surveys have shown that the more fish the population of a country eats, the lower is their incidence of depression. There are two key omega 3 fats, the beneficial fat found in fish: EPA and DHA. Research suggests that the former is the more potent natural antidepressant because it is thought to boost serotonin. Increasing your intake of omega 3 has also been associated with less anxiety and aggression in many studies, so there's a good chance that keeping your level high will give you more stress resilience. The best food sources are oily fish (herring, mackerel, salmon, trout, sardines and anchovies).

Studies have also shown that taking fish oil supplements that are high in EPA improves mood more than taking antidepressant drugs, and without the side-effects. A recent meta-analysis confirms that 'the use of omega-3 is effective in patients with diagnosis of major depressive disorder and on depressive patients without diagnosis of major depressive disorder'.[19] You need to take in the region of 1000mg of EPA for a significant mood boost. This equates to two high-potency EPA-rich fish oil supplements a day, which can be prescribed by your doctor.

Increase your intake of B vitamins

As we learned in Chapter 5, B vitamins are vital for energy and dealing with stress, but they also help us stay free from anxiety and depression. This is primarily because they are needed for an essential biochemical process called methylation, which is key to making and balancing neurotransmitters.

People with either low blood levels of the B vitamin folic acid or high blood levels of the toxic amino acid homocysteine (a sign that methylation is not occurring properly, probably because of insufficient B_6, B_{12} or folic acid) are more likely to be depressed and less likely to get positive results from antidepressant drugs. Several research studies have proven this association.[20] For instance, one group of researchers found that women with a high homocysteine level – above 15 (the ideal is 7 or less) – were twice as likely to suffer from depression as those who had normal levels.[21] Meanwhile, another study found that more than half of the participants with severe depression had high homocysteine levels.[22]

Low levels of B vitamins are also an excellent predictor of low mood. For example, a study in the *European Journal of Clinical Nutrition* reports that men with the highest blood levels of folic acid – that's the B vitamin in greens and beans – halve their risk of depression.[23] Similarly, scientists at the University of York and Hull York Medical School analysed the results of 11 more studies, involving a total of 15,315 people, and concluded that the lower a person's folic acid levels, the greater is their risk of depression.[24] Having low levels of folic acid and B_{12} and a high level of homocysteine therefore seems to put you at high risk of depression.[25] Moreover, one study found that having a low level of B_6 has a similar effect;[26] while two found that you are likely to feel better, faster, if you increase your B_{12} level.[27] Among older people, giving supplements seems to improve mood.[28]

Supplementing extra B vitamins also helps conventional antidepressants to work better. In one study, depressed people were given either an SSRI antidepressant with folic acid or the SSRI with a placebo: 93 per cent of those taking the SSRI with the folic acid had a greater than 50 per cent drop in their depression score, compared with just 63 per cent who took the SSRI with the placebo.[29]

You can test your level of homocysteine with a simple pin-prick kit (see Resources), or a nutritional therapist can arrange a test for you. If your level is high, the correct dose of B vitamins and other nutrients can reduce it (the test results should include a guide to appropriate doses). The relevant nutrients are vitamin B_2, B_6, B_{12}, folic acid, zinc and trimethylglycine (TMG).

Given that deficiency in vitamins B_3 and B_6, folic acid, zinc and magnesium is linked to depression, it makes sense to eat wholefoods, fruits, vegetables, nuts and seeds that are high in these nutrients and supplement a multivitamin and mineral with high levels of them.

Low mood action plan

By now, you can see that there are lots of steps you can take to support yourself if low mood is an issue for you. A summary of all the key actions covered in this chapter is given in Part 6, which you can then build into your 30-day Stress Cure programme.

CHAPTER 19

Natural Solutions to Anxiety

Anxiety is the way stress is often expressed emotionally, and it affects many people to varying degrees. In our 100% Health survey, two out of three (66 per cent) respondents admitted they became anxious or tense easily, while 39 per cent said they often felt nervous or 'hyperactive'.[30] For some, extreme anxiety and panic attacks occur with such frequency that they become debilitating and life limiting.

Anxiety check

Answer each question in turn and score two points for the symptoms you experience frequently, one for those you experience occasionally, and zero for those you experience rarely or never.

- Do you feel fearful and panic easily about things?
- Do you feel anxious and nervous?
- Are you restless and unable to keep still?
- Do you easily become irritable or angry?
- Do you find your breathing becomes fast and shallow?
- Do you experience shortness of breath and feel you are lacking oxygen and/or hyperventilate?

- Do you feel overwhelmed and unable to think straight?

- Do you suffer from a sense of impending doom?

- Do you have heart palpitations?

- Do you have a dry mouth?

- Do you perspire excessively?

- Do you feel the need to urinate more frequently than other people?

- Do you suffer with night terrors and/or disturbing dreams?

A score of less than six is normal, although clearly zero would be ideal. Following the general advice for reducing stress and balancing energy levels will probably help you to feel more stable if you answered 'yes' to any of the questions.

If you scored between six and twelve, you are probably suffering an imbalance. The advice in this chapter will help you to improve how you feel.

If you scored 13 or more, you must be finding it hard to live with your anxiety. As well as following the advice in this chapter, review Chapters 10 and 13, and consider seeing both a nutritional therapist and a specialist who can offer you some psychotherapeutic support.

What causes anxiety and how to overcome it

As well as feelings of fear and an inability to think straight, symptoms of anxiety can include a pounding heart, dry mouth, excessive perspiration, insomnia, fatigue, headaches and muscle tension. Dealing with the normal challenges of daily life can trigger any one of these: for example, walking into a room of strangers, getting stuck in traffic, travelling to an unfamiliar place, or having to give a presentation. But anxiety can also occur with no obvious cause, leaving sufferers frustrated that they cannot seem to control these reactions. As we'll see, willpower alone is not the answer. Researchers working in the field of neuroscience have found that emotions operate at a much higher speed than thoughts, and they can frequently bypass the mind's linear reasoning process entirely.[31] The part of the brain that is involved in emotional processing – the amygdala – evolved before the cognitive (thinking) part. It is highly attuned to potential danger, so is hyper-sensitive to possible threats.

In practice, this means that a threatening event can set a pattern for future reactions. And, because this trigger is often held in the subconscious, it can be hard to identify. So, for example, witnessing an angry exchange between your parents as a young child may make you terrified of anger and confrontation as an adult. Also, if you experience a particularly challenging period that causes you to feel extreme stress or anxiety, your amygdala can become hyper-reactive and search for other potential triggers. This means you can find yourself in panic mode before your rational brain is able to evaluate the situation and decide if such a response is really necessary. This state is known as 'emotional hijacking'.

In Chapter 12, we explored the HeartMath system and showed how this simple, three-step breathing technique can help you to disperse feelings of anxiety, panic and stress and enjoy a more positive experience of life. This tool also helps you to deal with anxiety in the moment. Partner it with a nutritional approach to stabilise any biochemical imbalances that can make you more prone to anxiety and you have an effective strategy that will help you to feel better fast and make frequent anxiety and panic things of the past.

Before outlining what will be useful, we should mention what to avoid. While you are working towards adopting a consistently calmer way of being, steer clear of activities that significantly raise your heart rate, as these may confuse the brain into thinking you're in an emergency situation. Opt instead for relaxing activities that raise your natural energy levels, such as yoga or tai chi (see Chapter 9). Likewise, avoid stimulants that get your heart racing – coffee, tea, cigarettes, fizzy drinks, energy drinks, chocolate and caffeine pills.

In pursuit of GABA: the antidote to anxiety

Most people, when faced with an intense or constant feeling of anxiety, will either 'self-medicate' with alcohol or cannabis or ask their doctor for a course of tranquillisers, now often known as 'mood stabilisers'. These so-called solutions are more widespread than many realise. For example, in Britain, with a population of 63 million, consumers pop something like 10 million tranquillisers, puff 10 million cannabis joints and knock back 120 million alcoholic drinks each week.

All three of these drugs – alcohol, cannabis and tranquillisers – boost the neurotransmitter GABA (gamma-amino-butyric acid), the brain's peacemaker, which helps to turn off adrenalin production and calm you down. This is why that pint of beer or glass of wine makes you feel so sociable, relaxed, happy and less serious – at least for an hour, as your GABA level rises. But once that hour is up and your GABA starts to decline you will start to feel irritable and disconnected. At this point most people's solution is to have another drink, then another. The trouble is that after a session of drinking, GABA levels become very suppressed, leaving you grumpy and irritable.

Most of us avoid this by drinking in the evening and going to sleep while still under the influence. Unfortunately, though, alcohol also disturbs the normal cycle of dreaming, and it's dreaming that regenerates the mind. So, when you wake up in the morning, you're mentally tired, grumpy and irritable because of your low GABA, and dehydrated and sluggish because your body is still detoxifying the alcohol from the night before. The net effect is that alcohol, in the long run, makes you *more* anxious, not less. The same is true for cannabis, which, if habitually smoked, also reduces drive and motivation.

Tranquillisers are not the answer

The most well-known anti-anxiety drugs are all members of the benzodiazepine family of tranquillisers: Valium (diazepam),

Librium and Ativan. These are highly effective at reducing anxiety in the short term, but highly addictive in as little as four weeks. For this reason, doctors are strongly advised not to prescribe them for more than a month at a time. However, 3 per cent of the people questioned in a 2001 poll conducted by the British television programme *Panorama* – equivalent to 1.5 million people in the UK as a whole – admitted to taking tranquillisers for more than four months. Of these, 28 per cent had been on them for more than ten years![32] Eight years later, a report by the National Addiction Centre at King's College London found that a third of tranquilliser prescriptions were for more than eight weeks.

Thankfully, these highly addictive drugs are less likely to be prescribed these days because they have been replaced by newer (and more profitable) non-benzodiazepines such as zolpidem, eszopiclone and zaleplon, which are supposedly safer. However, even leaving aside the addictive nature of these drugs, a recent study reported that patients prescribed zolpidem, temazepam and other hypnotics to reduce their anxiety and aid sleep suffered a fourfold increase in mortality when compared with matched patients who were not prescribed such drugs. 'Even patients prescribed fewer than 18 hypnotic doses per year experienced increased mortality, with greater mortality associated with greater dosage prescribed,' reported the study's lead author Dr Kripke, an expert in insomnia from California. There was also a 35 per cent overall increase in incidence of cancer among those prescribed high doses.[33]

The sad truth is that tranquillisers and hypnotics, much like alcohol, *increase* anxiety and depression in the long run, in addition to becoming addictive. Tranquillisers have this effect because they open up the brain's receptor sites for GABA, which makes the brain more sensitive to it. So, at first, you feel more relaxed and less anxious. The next day, however, you can feel 'hung over'. And the more often you take them, the more you need to produce the same effect. Then, if you cut them out, you can get rebound anxiety and insomnia. Luckily, there is an alternative.

How to unwind with natural relaxants

States of anxiety are associated with too much of the stress hormones adrenalin and cortisol. In Chapters 4, 6 and 7, we discussed how blood sugar ups and downs and our over-reliance on stimulants such as caffeine and nicotine can stress us out. So the first step towards reducing anxiety is to balance your blood sugar by eating slow-releasing carbohydrates and avoiding – or at least considerably reducing your consumption of – stimulants and alcohol. These simple measures will significantly reduce your anxiety.

However, some people need a little extra help to learn how to exit the adrenalin state. The breathing and meditation techniques described in Chapter 10 are useful here, as is reframing your approach to stressful situations (see Chapter 13). If you believe the root cause of your anxiety is embedded deep in your subconscious, there are also psychotherapeutic approaches that will help you to access and release negative programming, such as the Emotional Freedom Technique (EFT), Eye Movement Desensitisation and Reprocessing (EMDR), hypnotherapy and Time Line Therapy (see Resources for details on all of these).

On the biochemical side, natural GABA promoters – amino acids, minerals and herbs – will ensure that you produce and release sufficient GABA whenever it is needed. GABA not only inhibits the production of excess adrenalin, noradrenalin and dopamine, but works together with serotonin to keep your mood good. For these reasons, having adequate levels of GABA in your brain is associated with relaxation and happiness, while having too little is associated with anxiety, tension, depression and insomnia.[34]

As its name suggests, gamma-amino-butyric acid is an amino acid, which means it can be supplemented. However, the European Union has decreed that it must be classified as a medicine, which means it is no longer available over the counter in member countries. If you live in the UK or EU, you can buy GABA supplements on the internet from the United States and elsewhere, though. If you can find a reputable supplier, supplement 500–1000mg once or twice a day as a highly effective natural relaxant.

However, while GABA is not addictive, it should be noted that it can have side-effects when taken in large quantities. There is no reported downside to taking up to 2g a day, but 10g a day has been known to induce nausea or even vomiting, and to raise blood pressure. So use GABA wisely, especially if you already have high blood pressure. Start with no more than 1g a day, and do not exceed 3g a day.

Some GABA supplements also contain the amino acid theanine, which can help you feel calm and alert at the same time. Research suggests that 50mg naturally stimulates alpha-wave activity in the brain, which is associated with a relaxed but alert mental state.[35] Therefore, supplements containing both theanine and GABA can help you feel more relaxed and less 'edgy'.[36]

Taurine: GABA's best friend

Taurine is another relaxing amino acid, similar in structure and effect to GABA. Many people think it is a stimulant because it is used in so-called 'energy drinks', but it is not. It actually helps you relax and unwind after the production of high levels of adrenalin, much like GABA, but it has many other uses as well, including alleviating insomnia, depression and even the 'high' phase of manic depression.

Taurine is highly concentrated in fish, eggs and meat, so vegetarians and vegans are more likely to be at risk of deficiency. While the body can make it from the amino acids cysteine and methionine (provided you've got enough vitamin B_6), if you are prone to high levels of anxiety you may benefit from supplementing this relaxing amino acid. Try 500–1000mg of taurine twice daily, together with the same amount of glutamine, another amino acid which supports GABA production, for a natural GABA boost. There are no known adverse effects when these are taken in reasonable doses, and some supplements that are marketed as relaxants provide this combination (see Resources).

Valerian: nature's Valium

The herb valerian (*Valeriana officinalis*) is an excellent antidote to anxiety. Derived from the dried rhizomes and roots of an attractive perennial with pretty pink flowers, it grows throughout Europe in wet soils. This natural relaxant is useful for the treatment of several disorders, such as restlessness, nervousness, insomnia and hysteria, and it has also been used as a sedative for 'nervous stomach'. Valerian enhances the activity of the brain's GABA receptors in a process that is similar to the tranquillising action of Valium and other prescription drugs, but without the unwelcome side-effects. Between 50 and 100mg twice a day should be an effective relaxant, while twice as much 45 minutes before retiring should help to promote a good night's sleep. Since valerian potentiates sedative drugs, including muscle relaxants and antihistamines, don't take it if you are on prescribed medication without your doctor's consent. Valerian can also interact with alcohol as well as certain psychotropic drugs and narcotics.

Hops and passion flower

Hops (*Humulus lupulus*) are an ancient remedy for a good night's sleep; they are probably included in beer for precisely that reason. They help to calm nerves by acting directly on the central nervous system, rather than affecting the brain's GABA receptors. You will need to take about 200mg per day to notice any effect, and it works best in combination with valerian and other herbs, such as passion flower (*Passiflora incarnata*). The latter was a favourite of the Aztecs, who used it to make relaxing drinks. It has a mild sedative effect and promotes sleep, much like hops, with no known side-effects at normal doses. You will need to take 100–200mg a day. Combinations of these herbs are particularly effective for relieving anxiety and can help break the pattern of reacting stressfully to life's challenges.

Magnesium: relaxing mind and muscles

Magnesium is another important nutrient that helps us relax, so deficiency, which is very common, is a problem. It relaxes the muscles as well as the mind, so symptoms of deficiency include muscle aches, cramps and spasms, in addition to anxiety and insomnia. Low levels are commonly found in anxious people and supplementation can often help. Seeds and nuts are rich in magnesium, as are many fruits and vegetables, especially kale and spinach. We recommend eating these magnesium-rich foods every day and supplementing an additional 300mg, to bring total consumption up to about 500mg. If you are especially anxious and can't sleep, supplement an extra 500mg in the evening.

The histamine/copper connection

While blood sugar problems and low magnesium levels are common causes of stressful reactions, they are not the only biochemical imbalances that can lead to anxiety. The late Dr Carl Pfeiffer, who pioneered nutritional approaches to mental health issues, found that many of his patients who experienced extreme fears, phobias and paranoia had very low histamine levels. Many also had high levels of copper – a toxic element in excess – which can depress histamine levels. These low-histamine patients, Pfeiffer found, shared several common characteristics, such as plentiful body hair, a tendency to be overweight, a high pain threshold and a suspicious nature. They also did really well on large supplements of niacin, folic acid and B_{12}, plus vitamin C, zinc and manganese, which help to lower levels of copper.

If you have these symptoms, it's well worth having your mineral levels checked (see Resources). If you find you do have high levels of copper, or any other toxic mineral, then we advise seeing a nutritional therapist who will be able to devise a programme to reduce them. If you experience extreme fears and anxiety, you may also benefit from supplementing large amounts of niacin, folic acid and B_{12}. Again, this should be done only under the guidance of a nutritional therapist.

Adrenalin dominance?

Michael Platt, an American doctor specialising in hormone problems, has been working with patients who suffer from anxiety issues and panic attacks for many years. He has developed a theory that too much adrenalin – a state he calls 'adrenalin dominance' – is a contributory factor in both. Other symptoms can include restless leg syndrome, increased urination frequency, interstitial cystitis, night sweats and waking, cold hands and feet, and fibromyalgia. He reports success using bio-identical hormones, and in particular progesterone cream. Platt claims that a small amount of this cream (30–100mg – the equivalent of a quarter-teaspoonful) applied to the thin skin on the inside of the arms can avert a panic attack in seconds (see Resources). He also advocates a low-GL diet to balance blood sugar and ensure the brain receives adequate glucose, as a dip in blood sugar is the most common trigger for the release of adrenalin.

Lactic acid: pushing the panic button

Panic attacks are characterised by extreme feelings of fear, and they are surprisingly common. Symptoms often experienced during a panic attack include palpitations, rapid breathing, dizziness, unsteadiness and a feeling of impending death. People who suffer with agoraphobia – the fear of being alone or in a public place – often know that they could go outside or be on their own, but they are afraid of suffering a panic attack if they put themselves in such a situation. As 'psychological' as this sounds, there is often a biochemical imbalance behind people's anxiety attacks: too much lactic acid. When muscles don't get enough oxygen, they make energy from glucose without it. The trouble is that lactic acid is produced as a by-product during this process. And, as strange as it might seem, lactic acid can induce anxiety attacks in people who are prone to them.[37]

One way to increase lactic acid levels is to hyperventilate. Many people will do this when they're experiencing an anxiety attack. Hyperventilation changes the acid level of the blood by altering the balance of carbon dioxide, and the body responds by producing more lactic acid. The solution is to breathe into a paper bag during a hyperventilation attack and concentrate on breathing deeply for a minute. This helps to redress the balance.

Blood sugar dips can also bring on hyperventilation and increase lactic acid, so keep your blood sugar level by eating little and often.

A more advanced and highly effective breathing technique is Buteyko breathing. This is good for general anxiety but especially beneficial for people who often hyperventilate and have panic attacks, both of which can be exacerbated by a lack of carbon dioxide induced by over-breathing.[38] Buteyko breathing can be taught in a workshop or during a one-to-one session, and several books explain the technique (see Resources, page 305).

Another approach that works for some people is to supplement the amino acid glycine during a panic attack. Glycine switches off noradrenalin, thus reducing the feeling of panic. The best way to get it into the body quickly is to break open four capsules (usually 500mg each) and put them under your tongue. (Sublingual absorption is faster than taking a pill orally.) You can keep doing this every few minutes, up to a maximum of 10g. No side-effects have been reported at these doses.

Finally, vitamin B_1 deficiency stops the body breaking down glucose properly, again promoting lactic acid. So make sure you supplement a good B complex or multivitamin. Also, have yourself checked for food allergies, as these are the most common biochemical imbalances that can lead to panic attacks.

An integrated approach works best

While high levels of anxiety are often the result of psychological factors, by balancing blood sugar, reducing stimulants, ensuring optimal nutrition and judicially using natural anti-anxiety herbs and nutrients, you can break the habit of reacting with fear and anxiety to life's inevitable stresses. Addressing the potential underlying triggers for anxiety is also important.

In terms of supplements, a combination of relaxing amino acids and herbs is often the most effective way to reduce high levels of anxiety. The synergistic action of nutrients and herbs such as GABA or taurine plus glutamine, valerian, hops and passion flower also means that the doses for each can be lower than if they were taken individually, so always look out for combined formulas (see Resources for reputable suppliers).

An instant way to switch off anxiety

If you experience a panic attack or extreme anxiety, dipping your face into a basin of very cold water for 30 seconds (while holding your breath, of course) can instigate what's known as the 'dive reflex'. This has a rapidly calming effect because cold water stimulates your vagus nerve, which is a key part of your parasympathetic nervous system (PNS). The PNS works in partnership with your sympathetic nervous system (SNS), which is involved in the stress response. So, after a stressful event has passed, it's your PNS that takes over to calm you down and restore your body to business as usual. But triggering the dive reflex activates the PNS *immediately*, so you feel calmer and less stressed in a matter of seconds. Splashing your face with icy water, or pressing your face on to an ice pack, can have the same effect for some people, and it works better if you also lean forward and hold your breath for 30 seconds. The only word of caution is that this procedure should not be attempted by anyone with a slow heart rate or low blood pressure, as it decreases your heart rate.

You can find a summary of our key recommendations for dealing with anxiety in Part 6.

CHAPTER 20

Targeting Weight Issues

It's ironic that the people with the most stored potential energy as fat are almost always the people who feel most tired. At one level, this shows that energy-giving food, instead of giving energy, can drain vitality. However, stress can also play a key factor in weight gain, especially when fat stores are concentrated around the middle. What's more, when you feel stressed, one way to compensate is to over-eat, or to eat and drink harmful substances as a way of 'numbing' difficult feelings. We explained this with the 'Doors of Compensation' model in Chapter 13.

The cortisol connection

When you feel tired, it's natural to want to give yourself an energy boost, and reaching for something starchy or sweet, or a stimulant, is the fastest way to do this. The problem is that over time this leads to disrupted blood sugar levels, as we saw in Chapter 4. Low blood sugar is perceived as a stress by the body, because without a sufficient supply of glucose – our primary fuel – we cannot function and our brain cannot work properly. So we produce the stress hormone cortisol to activate the release of glucose stored in our liver and muscles. If these stores are used up, cortisol can also prompt the liver to convert fat – and, when necessary, protein – into sugar for fuel in a process called gluconeogenesis.

If an imbalance in blood sugar persists – and your life provides plenty of opportunities to trigger the stress response, raising cortisol still further – your body understandably thinks you are in the midst of an emergency situation. So, to ensure you are ready to tackle these frequent perceived 'fight or flight' scenarios, cortisol stockpiles sources of fuel and locates them around your middle, close to where it can call upon your liver to convert them to sugar when required. Research reveals that deep abdominal fat has *four times* more cortisol receptors when compared to surface subcutaneous fat.[39] This makes sense if you're often in a situation that requires you to call upon your energy reserves to enable you to fight or flee. But stress in our modern lives rarely requires us to expend energy as our ancestors did. We don't even have to stand up to watch the news, fret about the traffic or get caught up in workplace politics, so our energy stores, like us, just sit there.

Storing fat for a rainy day

In Chapter 8, we explained how hormones work together in a complex dance to help us remain balanced in mood, energy and alertness. You need insulin to transfer sugar from your blood and into your cells to make energy, but when your cells are fully loaded, that insulin puts any extra sugar into storage as fat. There are two reasons for this. First, having too much sugar in your bloodstream is dangerous because sugar damages your arteries, so your body protects itself. Second, we are programmed to store food as fat for a rainy day. This is known as the 'survival of the fattest'. Our ancestors who were genetically best programmed to do this were the ones who survived. Unfortunately for our waist-lines, rainy days are few and far between these days, so we just keep storing the excess sugar as fat, and especially as abdominal fat.

High cortisol levels also contribute to insulin resistance, which makes us even more prone to put on weight (see Chapter 4 and especially the checklist on page 31).

The key to rebalancing your hormones – and losing weight – is to regain blood sugar control and reduce stress (or at least your reaction to it), which is what this book is all about. The great news is that the best and most sustainable solutions for controlling your weight – and losing some of it, if you need to – are also solutions for increasing energy and stress resilience.

Exercise smarter

At a basic level, the more calories you eat and the less you exercise, the more weight you will gain. Muscle burns fat and therefore the more lean muscle you have – which is a direct consequence of 'resistance' exercise – the more you will be able to burn off fat. It is especially important to do exercise that builds abdominal (core) and upper-body strength, as well as aerobic or endurance exercise that raises your heart rate. This speeds up your body's metabolism for several hours, which helps to burn fat.

However, a word of caution: if you are suffering with high stress levels, strenuous cardiovascular exercise is not good news. A study conducted by the University of Stavanger in Norway found that when a group of obese people adopted dietary modifications and engaged in regular, vigorous keep-fit activity, they failed to lose as much weight as was expected.[40] The scientists concluded that this could be related to cortisol, since the level of the stress hormone rose among the participants and they became more stressed. 'It's often said obese people should change their diet and exercise to lose weight. But they may also need to deal with stress,' observed Associate Professor Brynjar Foss, who led the study.

Exercise such as yoga, brisk walking or Psychocalisthenics can raise your heart rate without stimulating stress hormones, and yoga also incorporates resistance elements that can help to build more muscle. See Chapter 9 for more ideas on how to choose an exercise that both builds muscle and boosts your metabolism while also reducing your overall stress levels. Some simple techniques build muscle in as little as 15 minutes a week. (Go to www.patrickholford.com and put 'build muscle' in the search box, or Google 'peak 8'.)

As well as practising the right kind of exercise, getting enough sleep is important. A chronic sleep debt almost doubles your chances of being obese[41] and it is linked with diabetes. According to one large study that ran for 16 years, women who slept for fewer than six hours a night were more likely than sound sleepers to put on at least 33 pounds.[42]

Is your thyroid impacting on your weight?

As we explored in Chapter 8, your thyroid hormones – which are important for controlling your body temperature, increasing your metabolism and regulating your weight – are affected by high cortisol levels. Other factors can also impede thyroid function, such as deficiency in the nutrients required to convert the thyroid hormones into active compounds (see page 82), or exposure to environmental toxins. As well as weight gain (which in this case typically concentrates around the hips and thighs), symptoms of low thyroid function (also called hypothryroidism) include fatigue, feeling cold, constipation and indigestion, dry skin, hair loss, poor resistance to infection, low mood, loss of libido, irritability, poor memory and loss of focus and concentration.

If your thyroid is clinically underactive, your doctor might prescribe thyroid hormones to be taken directly. However, blood tests are often unable to detect sub-clinical low thyroid function, so it might be better to go by the symptoms. You can also get an indication of your thyroid function via the Broda Barnes temperature test. If your temperature on waking but before rising in the morning is consistently below 36.5 °C, your thyroid might be underactive.

Thyroid health relies on specific nutrients in the diet, most importantly iodine, which is abundant in seafood and seaweed, and tyrosine, an amino acid found in all protein-rich foods, plus zinc and selenium. Several combination formulas supply these nutrients in the correct balance (see Resources). It may also be wise to visit a nutritional therapist for additional support if you believe low thyroid function is an issue for you.

The low-GL approach to weight loss

As you have no doubt realised by now, your appetite, weight and energy level are all largely controlled by your blood sugar balance. If your blood sugar rises too high, perhaps as a consequence of eating or drinking too many fast-releasing carbohydrates in a meal or snack, the excess is converted into fat. Your blood sugar then dips, which triggers hunger. So, before long, you will be gaining weight *and* feeling hungry most of the time. If this continues, you are also likely to develop insulin resistance.

In an attempt to combat weight gain, many people make the mistake of choosing 'low-fat' foods, not realising that they are full of fast-releasing sugars, which really pile on the pounds. As we saw in Chapter 4, the best way to balance blood sugar is to eat a low-GL diet. When you want to lose weight, doing this and limiting your overall intake to no more than 40 GL points a day will shift you from a fat storer to a fat burner. In numerous clinical studies, this approach is both the most effective in the short term – burning more fat than either low-fat or high-protein, low-carb diets, such as Atkins – and more effective and sustainable in the long term.[43]

The beauty of eating a low-GL diet is that most people don't feel hungry. This is because you eat regularly and can have decent portions. A low-GL diet is also easy to follow. There are just three golden rules:

1. Eat no more than 40 GLs a day.

2. Eat protein with carbohydrate.

3. Graze, don't gorge.

Your intake breaks down into 10 GLs each for breakfast, lunch and dinner, plus 5 GLs each for a mid-morning and a mid-afternoon snack – so you eat (or graze) regularly instead of gorging at one or two big meals. The easiest way to make combining proteins and carbs part of your daily life is to keep your food in the following proportions:

- A quarter of each main meal should be protein.

- A quarter of each meal should be slow-releasing carbohydrate: starchy vegetables or other starchy foods, such as wholegrain rice or pasta.

- Half of each meal should be non-starchy vegetables or salad.

At-a-glance GL plate

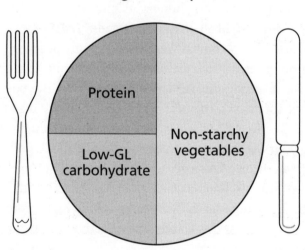

Chapter 4 goes into more detail about these various food types. Here, you just need to remember to limit them to no more than 40 GL points a day. You can find a full list of foods, with portion sizes and GL points, in the low-GL counter at www.patrick holford.com (click on 'low GL' to access).

To highlight the benefits of this approach, below we have set a low-GL diet against a typical diet. The numbers after each item denote the GL points.

Low-GL daily diet		Typical daily diet	
Breakfast		*Breakfast*	
30g (1oz) bowl of porridge	4	Bowl of cornflakes	21
Half a grated apple	3	Banana	12
Small tub of natural yoghurt	1	Milk	2
Milk	2		
Sub total:	10	Sub total:	35
Morning snack		*Morning snack*	
Punnet of strawberries	1	Mars bar	26
Lunch		*Lunch*	
Substantial tuna salad and three oatcakes	11	Tuna salad baguette	15
Afternoon snack		*Afternoon snack*	
Pear and a handful of peanuts	4	Packet of crisps	11
Dinner		*Dinner*	
Tomato soup, salmon, sweetcorn and green beans	12	Pizza with Parmesan and tomato sauce, plus salad	23
Good day total:	38	Bad day total:	110

Take a good look at the food listed on the left. Imagine you ate that breakfast, rather than the one on the right. It would definitely be more filling, wouldn't it? But it's not just that: by eating it, you will cut your propensity to turn glucose into fat by a third! The great news about eating the low-GL way is that you can eat *more food* and still lose weight. And it's all delicious. You can learn more by reading Patrick's *Low-GL Diet Bible* or *Low-GL Diet Made Easy* books.

Supplements that work

Slimming pills rarely deliver the results they promise, and those that do often act like stimulants, speeding up your metabolism and giving you short-term weight loss but long-term problems. However, there are three nutritional supplements that are extremely effective and therefore recommended if you are trying to lose weight. They are hydroxycitric acid (HCA for short), 5-hydroxy-tryptophan (5-HTP) and the mineral chromium.

HCA

HCA is extracted from the dried rind of the tamarind fruit (*Garcinia cambogia*), which you may know from Indian and other Eastern cuisine. It works by inhibiting the enzyme that converts sugar (or glucose) into fat – ATP-citrate lyase – thereby slowing down the production of fat and reducing appetite. Evidence of HCA's fat-burning properties has been accumulating steadily since 1965.[44] For example, participants in one eight-week, double-blind trial reported a 5.4 per cent drop in both body weight and body mass index with a daily dose equivalent to 2,800mg of HCA a day. It also has no toxicity or other safety concerns.

We recommend taking 750mg of HCA a day, especially during the first three months of any weight-loss diet. Most supplements provide 250mg per capsule, so take one capsule three times a day, ideally from 30 minutes before to immediately before a main meal. It is widely available.

5-HTP

The two most powerful controllers of your appetite are your blood sugar level and your brain's level of serotonin, the 'happy' neurotransmitter. Serotonin is often deficient, especially in those on weight-loss diets, with a low level frequently leading to depression ... and increased appetite (which is why many depressed people over-eat). If you are low in serotonin, one of the quickest ways to restore normal levels, and normal mood and appetite, is to supplement your diet with 5-HTP. It also helps to reduce sugar cravings. In one study, 20 obese volunteers took either 5-HTP or a placebo for 12 weeks. During the first six weeks, the volunteers could eat whatever they liked. During the second six weeks they were recommended a low-calorie diet. In both phases, those taking 5-HTP consistently ate less, felt more satisfied and consequently lost more weight.[45]

We recommend you supplement 50mg of 5-HTP with your morning and afternoon snacks, as taking it with some carbohydrate helps to increase its effectiveness. However, do not take it if you are also taking SSRI antidepressant drugs, as this could lead you to produce too much serotonin. Some people also experience mild nausea when they first supplement 5-HTP.

Chromium

For insulin to work properly, it needs a good supply of chromium. As we've seen, many people struggling with weight issues are 'insulin resistant', which makes them more prone to storing sugar as fat. The average daily intake of chromium is below 50mcg, while the optimal intake – certainly for those with a weight and blood sugar problem – is around 200mcg or more. (Diabetics can benefit from as much as 600mcg.) Numerous studies have shown more weight loss and/or less appetite when chromium is supplemented.[46]

Chromium is found in wholefoods and is therefore higher in wholewheat flour, bread or pasta than in refined products. (Refined carbs can have up to 98 per cent of their chromium removed in the refining process – another reason to stay away from over-processed products.) Beans, nuts and seeds are other good sources, and asparagus and mushrooms are especially rich in it.

Most good multivitamins and minerals will contain 30mcg of chromium, but you can help maintain blood sugar control and hence reduce sugar cravings more quickly by taking 200mcg twice a day for the first three months of a weight-loss programme (ideally with your mid-morning and mid-afternoon snacks). Chromium works better when taken alongside cinnamon, or more specifically an extract of cinnamon called Cinnulin®.[47] Some supplements combine the two.

Case study: Reducing stress to lose weight

When Alison, a 48-year-old teacher, visited Susannah for some nutritional advice, she was at the end of her tether. 'I am getting fatter and fatter, yet I am eating less than I ever have,' she lamented. A thorough investigation revealed that she had elevated cortisol levels and her symptoms of feeling cold, depressed and tired pointed to sub-optimal thyroid function, despite her thyroid hormones testing in the 'normal' range when checked by her GP.

Susannah advised a strategy that focused first and foremost on increasing Alison's resilience to stress, via a regular HeartMath exercise, daily relaxation and prioritising time for sufficient sleep. Alison also adopted a low-GL diet to improve her blood sugar balance and supplemented selenium, zinc and the amino acid tyrosine to boost her thyroid function.

Alison lost six pounds within four weeks, and – with some additions to her programme – almost two stones within three months. 'I can't believe how much better I look and feel,' she said. 'I no longer want to hide away at home under the duvet. And for the first time in ages, I feel excited by all the possibilities my life has to offer.'

You can find a summary of our key recommendations for weight loss in Part 6.

PART 6

Take Control: Your 30-Day Action Plan

Now things get exciting. If you have read all the preceding chapters, you are ready to embark on your 30-day Stress Cure programme to reduce stress, increase energy and build greater resilience in your life. In this section, you'll work out the core actions to take with regards to diet and support. You can also devise a plan of the best supplements to take, based on your current needs. And there's a selection of recipes and food ideas to make eating for less stress and more energy come to life.

CHAPTER 21

The Stress Cure Programme

Let's start by identifying where you currently stand in the stress and energy stakes by filling in the chart overleaf. This will also allow you to highlight any other associated factors, such as poor sleep or low mood, that are issues for you. Throughout the book, there have been several checklists, and we want you to fill in your scores for each of them here (the relevant page numbers are referenced to help you locate them). We have also included some additional questions for you to answer. When completed, this chart will allow you to personalise your Stress Cure programme.

For each question, a range is given across four categories – Excellent, Room for Improvement, Attention Required and Urgent Action. On the next line there is space for you to insert your own score or to tick under the option that best applies to you now. Below that, there is space for you to re-score yourself once you have followed the Stress Cure programme for the full 30 days. (If you prefer, you can photocopy the chart and fill that in.)

Stress assessment

	Excellent	Room for Improvement	Attention Required	Urgent Action
Stress score out of 14 (see page 17)	0–1	2–3	4–7	8+
Now:				
After 30 days:				
Insulin resistance score out of 20 (see page 32)	0–1	2–4	5–9	10+
Now:				
After 30 days:				
Stimulant intake (consult inventory on page 58) Units of coffee, tea or energy drinks (including cola) consumed each day	0	1–2	3–4	5+
Now:				
After 30 days:				
Sugary foods/snacks, including chocolate, consumed each day	0	1–2	3–4	5+
Now:				
After 30 days:				

	Excellent	Room for Improvement	Attention Required	Urgent Action
Approximate units of alcohol consumed each week	0–8	9–15	16–21	22+
Now:				
After 30 days:				
Cigarettes/cigars/joints smoked each day	0	1–2	3–5	6+
Now:				
After 30 days:				
Currently, could you live without stimulants?	Yes	At a stretch	No	Never
Now:				
After 30 days:				
Stress hormone balance Using the 'Stress test: which stage are you?' chart on page 84, where in the stress cycle do you estimate yourself to be?	0	1	2	3
Now:				
After 30 days:				

	Excellent	Room for Improvement	Attention Required	Urgent Action
Sleep Which best describes your sleep?	7–8+ hours unbroken	7 hours mostly unbroken	Less than 7 hours or intermittent	Poor
Now:				
After 30 days:				
ADDITIONAL FACTORS **Detox potential** score out of 14 (page 174)	0–1	2–3	4–6	7+
Now:				
After 30 days:				
Mood check score out of 14 (page 199)	0–3	4–5	6–8	9+
Now:				
After 30 days:				
Anxiety check score out of 26 (page 207)	0–3	4–8	9–12	13+
Now:				
After 30 days:				
Weight: Tick which best describes your weight (if unsure, see 'BMI' in Resources)	Within a healthy range	Slightly overweight	Overweight (BMI >25)	Obese (BMI >30)
Now:				
After 30 days:				

Seven steps for stress-free living

The stress assessment you have just completed will give you a good indicator of how well you are coping when it comes to stress, energy and the many related elements that contribute to feeling stressed and tired. If all of your scores are in the 'Excellent' category, congratulations, you can stop reading now! But we suspect that's not the case – otherwise you wouldn't have bought this book. Our goal is to get you into the Excellent category, or at least on your way there, within a month of starting the Stress Cure programme.

At the heart of this programme are the seven steps we outline shortly. These cover all the essential elements for balancing your blood sugar, reducing your dependency on stimulants, boosting your energy levels and improving rest, recuperation and resilience. Often, when clients address these core elements, they find that any other problems resolve, too. However, if you score in the 'Attention Required' or 'Urgent Action' categories for low mood, anxiety, detoxification and/or weight, we provide some additional guidance in the section that follows the seven steps: 'Dealing with deeper problems'.

Some actions and exercises in the main seven steps are useful in more than one step: for example, yoga can be used in both the Energise and the Relaxation steps. When this is the case, you'll see the 'two-in-one' symbol: 2-in-1

Prepare for success

Before you embark on the 30-day Stress Cure programme, we recommend you take several days to plan and prepare so that you are ready to go, and have all you need to support you. For example: line up alternatives to stimulants; order your supplements; do a shop for all the delicious food you're going to cook and eat; and allocate times in your diary for relaxing, generating vital energy and resilience-building activities. This will minimise any additional stress and set you on the road to success.

Step One: Eat for energy

When you are feeling stressed and tired, eating a diet that gives you balanced blood sugar is your number-one priority. In Chapter 4, you learned why stable blood sugar is important and what causes it to lurch out of control. Now it's time to put the key principles into practice and reap the benefits of improved energy, focus and resilience.

Golden rules to banish the blood sugar blues:

- Always start your day with a good breakfast.

- Eat regular meals at regular times.

- Choose slow-releasing, unrefined carbohydrates (wholegrains, beans, vegetables and fruit) over fast-releasing, refined foods (anything white or sweetened) and eat fewer carbs overall.

- Combine carbohydrate-rich foods with protein-rich foods: fruit with nuts, for example.

- Have a snack mid-morning and another mid-afternoon if your energy flags or you crave sugar, stimulants or alcohol.

In Chapter 23, we set out exactly how this works in practice with plenty of delicious and simple recipes for breakfast, lunch and supper, plus energy-boosting snacks.

Step Two: Eliminate stimulants

A crucial part of balancing your blood sugar is to cut out stimulants, as we discussed in Chapter 6. Caffeine, in some shape or form, is usually the biggest culprit here. It not only disrupts your energy levels – causing you to yoyo from energy highs to energy lows – but triggers the release of stress hormones, creating an additional source of stress that contributes to your overall load. Like caffeine, sugar provides a short burst of energy, but then you crash back into fatigue until your next fix. So, if you want stable energy without the dips, caffeine and sugar are best avoided completely during the 30 days of your Stress Cure programme. If that proves too difficult, set yourself a feasible goal: for example, a couple of coffees a week.

As you start to eat regular energy-balancing meals and snacks, your need for stimulants will naturally decline because your energy levels will improve. You will not 'need' a stimulant drink to wake up. Supplementing vital energy nutrients (see Step Seven) will also make a big difference to your energy levels (we look at this in more detail in the next chapter). But if you are a big stimulant consumer, a staged reduction is usually the best approach to avoid withdrawal discomfort (e.g. headaches, low mood, increased irritability and fatigue).

Top ways to beat the stimulant haze:

- With the help of the stimulant inventory in Chapter 6 (page 58), identify your level of addiction to various stimulants.

- At the same time, experiment with caffeine-free, sugar-free and alcohol-free substitutes (see page 63–5), so you will be ready to make the transition and have something lined up to fill the gap.

- If your consumption puts you in the 'Attention Required' or 'Urgent Action' categories in the assessment table at the beginning of this chapter, we recommend a staged reduction: for example, reduce by one or two units each day for the first week; then quit in the second week.

- If your consumption is in the 'Room for Improvement' zone, aim to reduce your intake over two to three days, or just go for it right from the outset, if you're feeling brave!

- Throughout, support yourself by eating to balance your blood sugar and supplementing the nutrients outlined in the next chapter.

- If you are also a smoker, we address that in the 'Dealing with deeper problems' section later in this chapter.

A note about alcohol

Remember, alcohol is a stimulant, although its immediate effect is relaxing. Government guidelines suggest that women should consume no more than two to three units each day, and men three to four units (a unit equates to half a pint of standard beer, *two-thirds* of a small (125ml) glass of wine, or a single (25ml) measure of spirits). Of course, how beneficial or otherwise your drinking is depends on a variety of other factors too – from what you drink to when you drink it, plus your ability or otherwise to detoxify the alcohol effectively. Having a small glass of good-quality organic wine with your supper four evenings a week is rather different to drinking strong lager or spirits on an empty stomach, or polishing off a bottle of wine with your partner every night. Our recommendation is that if you are in the 'Attention Required' or 'Urgent Action' category for alcohol consumption – or if your detox potential score is in either of these categories – you should significantly reduce (and ideally eliminate) alcohol for the duration of the 30-day Stress Cure programme. This will give your liver a break and allow your blood sugar and stress hormones to find a new balance.

Step Three: Generate vital energy

As we saw in Chapter 9, being stress resilient requires harnessing a greater sense of vitality and energy. You can acquire more vital energy simply by breathing more fully, spending time in the natural world and doing specific vital energy-generating exercises. Rather than pounding the treadmill at the gym, or sitting on the sofa watching TV, focus your attention on one or two of the following:

- Include some form of energising and de-stressing exercise in your weekly routine, such as yoga 2-in-1 , tai chi 2-in-1 , qigong 2-in-1 or Psychocals.

- Be conscious of your breath and give yourself the opportunity to breathe more deeply, either by doing one of the above or through some other regular exercise you enjoy, such as brisk walking, gentle jogging or dancing.

- Practise a deep breathing exercise (see example on page 95) as a means to boost your oxygen intake and reduce tension: for example, first thing in the morning, at lunchtime or before you go to bed 2-in-1 . Some forms of meditation and yoga will also teach you to breathe more fully and, in time, you will start to do this subconsciously. Whenever you feel stressed, it is also a good idea to bring your attention back to breathing more deeply.

- Spend as much time as you can in clean air. If you are a city-dweller, take regular trips to the countryside or exercise in a park or by a river.

Step Four: Relax and recuperate

Resting and relaxation are not things to fit in when you've got the time: as we explored in Chapter 10, they are essential to ensure you function at your best. Stress puts you in a state of alarm, so you need to revert to 'business as usual' mode to regenerate and avoid burnout and fatigue. Relaxation activates your parasympathetic nervous system, which switches off your stress-activated sympathetic nervous system, thereby restoring equilibrium. This is a vital part of the Stress Cure programme, so find a form of relaxation that appeals from the following list of options, then set aside 15 minutes three to four times a week to practise it. To ensure you don't forget, and to help you develop this as a new routine, add it to your diary alongside all your other important appointments.

- If you prefer to be 'doing', combine relaxation with exercise that also generates vital energy and make yoga, tai chi or qigong part of your regular routine (see Chapter 9) *2-in-1* .

- Practise a deep-breathing technique to release tension (you'll find an example on page 95). Yoga also aids deep breathing *2-in-1* . This will not only increase your oxygen intake and help to energise you but will dissipate any feelings of anxiety or stress. The HeartMath® technique (see Step Seven) is another good option *2-in-1* .

- Meditate or do a regular visualisation exercise to let go of stress and tension. See page 106 for a visualisation example or make up one of your own.

- Do a relaxation technique such as progressive relaxation (page 109) or toe tensing (page 110), or find another you like. If you enjoy yoga, find a class that concludes with a lying-down relaxation exercise.

You can download instructions for all of the exercises featured in this book from www.patrickholford.com/stresscure or www.susannah-lawson.co.uk under the 'Stress Cure' section.

Step Five: Improve your sleep

Sleep is vital to help you recover from stress and for your body to repair, as you found out in Chapter 11. To help yourself get a good night's sleep:

- Prioritise relaxing activities (such as those outlined in Step Four) in the hours before you go to bed. This will allow you to reduce your stress levels and get your body into a calm state, ready for sleeping.

- Avoid alcohol before bed, and avoid caffeine completely while you're doing the Stress Cure programme. (At other times, preferably avoid and certainly limit caffeine intake after midday.)

- Aim to follow a soothing bedtime routine, such as having a warm bath with Epsom salts or lavender oil or listening to calming music. The CD *Silence of Peace* can be helpful (see Resources).

- Once in bed, do some simple relaxation exercises to get yourself ready for sleep (see Step Four for some examples, or practise the HeartMath technique – see Step Six) 2-in-1.

- If you have difficultly sleeping, supplement 400mg of magnesium before bed, or experiment with 200mg of the amino acid 5-HTP half an hour before bed, or take a sleep formula containing both, plus GABA precursors (see Resources).

- Follow good sleep hygiene: ensure your bedroom is quiet and dark and you are comfortable. Also turn off mobile phones and wi-fi connections at night.

Step Six: Build resilience

Doing some sort of revitalising activity each day that also helps you to cope with stressful events, and minimises the depleting emotions you can feel as a result, will help you to develop greater resilience. Becoming more resilient is like building up a new muscle – a bit of work every day creates a strong resource for you to call on in times of stress.

If you don't currently practise anything – or even if you do – the HeartMath technique (see overleaf) is remarkably effective. But if you already meditate, do oveleaf, tai chi 2-in-1 or some form of other regular activity that puts you in 'the zone' where all feels well with the world or gives you an elevated perspective, then this may be enough. For some, this may be chanting or prayer; for others, it may involve playing music, painting, drawing or sculpting. Whatever activity you do, the key is to be in a calm, positive and 'coherent' state when you practise it. You can measure this state as a pattern of coherent HRV (heart-rate variability). The beauty of the HeartMath technique is that you can use a device called an emWave® to get immediate feedback, so you know whether you are achieving coherence. But there's no reason why you can't use the emWave® to measure your state while meditating, visualising, doing yoga or practising another 'in the zone' activity. In fact, you can use it to discover what brings you into a coherent state most effectively. One user found that stroking her cat worked best for her! (See Resources for more details of emWave technology.)

The goal is to do something regularly – and ideally daily – that connects you to coherence so that it becomes a habitual state that you can return to whenever life's inevitable challenges arise.

Incorporate the HeartMath technique into your daily routine 2-in-1

This surprisingly simple technique is remarkably effective. Not only can it help you to reduce levels of harmful stress hormones, but it can boost revitalising DHEA (see Chapter 12). The Quick Coherence® technique (page 129) is what you need to do. Practising its three easy steps daily for around five minutes, increasing to ten minutes once a week, can help you to reset yourself from stressed to fully functioning, and it can help you to nurture a more positive attitude.

As with all the important actions you take in your Stress Cure programme, we recommend you set aside some time to do this exercise regularly – for example, as soon as you get up, after lunch, in the evening or before you go to bed – and commit to doing it every day.

Step Seven: Supplement supporting nutrients

As we explored in Chapter 5, you need a range of essential vitamins, minerals and other nutrients to support all the energy-making and mood-regulating functions that keep you energised, upbeat and able to deal with stress. A modern, 'well-balanced' diet sadly fails to deliver even the most basic recommended daily allowance for many nutrients, let alone an optimal amount. Remember, stress depletes nutrients so you may well need more for the first 30 days to get yourself back on an even keel. Supplementing alongside eating a nutrient-rich diet is the best way to ensure you have all you need to function at your best. In the next chapter, we set out all the nutrients you should be taking as part of your Stress Cure programme, along with dosage recommendations.

Do your beliefs and choices support your goals?

In Part 4, we explored how beliefs, attitude and time management affect your stress levels. We've not included any specific assessment of the impact these areas may have on you here, as each chapter has questions and exercises to complete as you go along. If you've completed these, by now you'll know whether underlying negative thoughts, a pessimistic approach or feeling overwhelmed by having too much to do are issues for you. But if you score in the 'Attention Required' or 'Urgent Action' categories for the questions on stress, stress hormone balance, sleep, mood or anxiety in the stress assessment chart, we recommend revisiting each relevant chapter to ensure you have taken all you can from it, then working with the stress log (page 148) to embed positive and supportive actions and habits that reduce the stress you're experiencing.

Dealing with deeper problems

If your stress assessment highlighted detoxification issues, low mood, anxiety and/or weight as additional factors – and especially if you scored in the 'Attention Required' or 'Urgent Action' categories for any of them – we include some further recommendations here. Of these four areas, we suggest you tackle the highest scoring first, so as not to overload yourself.

However, if you scored high in all four of these 'deeper problem' areas, we recommend that you address detoxification and digestive issues first, as doing so might well resolve your low-mood and anxiety symptoms and will probably help you to lose weight too. You can always add the extra steps outlined below if you are still scoring highly in any of these areas after 30 days. If you feel overwhelmed at any stage, consult a nutritional therapist. They will help you to prioritise and work out the best programme for your personal requirements.

Do you need to detox?

If you scored in the 'Attention Required' or 'Urgent Action' categories in the detox section, then giving your body a rest with a gentle detox during the 30-day Stress Cure programme is advisable. Chapter 16 provides a full outline of how to do this, with pages 187–89 providing a step-by-step guide to which foods to focus on and which to avoid. Ensure you eat to balance your blood sugar and drink plenty of water and fluids to hydrate (outlined on page 189–90). We also recommend you add some additional nutrients specifically designed to support your liver detoxification pathways (see Chapter 22).

If you are also suffering with digestive issues – bloating, excess flatulence or burping, constipation or diarrhoea, feeling heavy after eating, food sensitivities – then it's worth rereading the pages that discuss these topics (pages 182–87) and assessing if you might benefit from supplementing a digestive enzyme or some beneficial bacteria (probiotics).

Patrick's 9 Day Liver Detox Diet gives detailed information on digestion and how to carry out an effective detox. You could start this after a week of your 30-day Stress Cure programme, once you've got the hang of it. It is designed to be started on a Saturday and completed the following Sunday.

Boost low mood

High stress and low energy, caused by poor blood sugar control, can contribute to mood-related imbalances, so you may find the main seven-step programme is sufficient to boost your mood and restore drive and motivation. However, if you still feel low – perhaps because your problem is more complex – the steps outlined below will provide extra support.

- If your low mood is accompanied by carbohydrate cravings, sleeping problems and a low pain threshold, then you might well be serotonin deficient. You can test for this (see details of the Brain Bio Centre in Resources), but first you could experiment with supplementing the amino acid and serotonin precursor 5-HTP to see if this helps. Start with 50mg twice a day with a carbohydrate snack (such as an oatcake) and build up to 100mg twice a day if required. However, note the caution on page 201.

- If you find your mood is worse in winter, you may be deficient in vitamin D. Boost your intake of eggs, oily fish and full-fat dairy products and spend more time outside in sunlight. Most importantly, supplement at least 15mcg of vitamin D (600iu), and up to 25mcg (1000iu) during the winter months, each day.

- If you suffer with 'atypical' depression (symptoms include daytime sleepiness and grogginess, carbohydrate cravings, weight gain and emotional reactivity), you may benefit from supplementing high-dose chromium (usually 400–600mcg a day). Chromium supplements usually provide 200mcg, so take one with each meal, or one with breakfast and one with lunch.

- If you also suffer with digestive issues and other symptoms for which you can find no cause (e.g. headaches, bloating, diarrhoea, constipation, muscle pain, joint stiffness, skin problems, rhinitis, sinusitis), explore the possibility of food intolerance by reading *Hidden Food Allergies*, co-written by Patrick and Dr James Braly, or consult a nutritional therapist.

You can also test yourself for food intolerances (see Resources, page 311).

- Studies have shown that fish oil supplements high in EPA are better than antidepressant drugs at improving mood, and they have none of the side-effects. You need in the region of 1000mg of EPA for a significant mood boost, which equates to two high-potency EPA-rich fish oil supplements a day. Your doctor might agree to prescribe them.

- Deficiency in B vitamins has been linked to depression, so it makes sense to eat foods rich in B vitamins (wholefoods, vegetables, fish, nuts and seeds) and supplement a multivitamin and mineral with good levels of all eight B vitamins – B_1, B_2, B_3, B_5, B_6, B_{12}, folic acid and biotin. (A multi is included in the core supplement plan outlined in the next chapter.) High levels of homocysteine – a marker in your blood – are also connected with depression and denote low B vitamin status, so it might be worth having yours checked. Some people, especially later in life, absorb vitamin B_{12} poorly and so benefit from much higher supplemental doses. (Low B_{12} results in a high homocysteine level.) You can measure your homocysteine level with a home-based test kit (see Resources, page 312). A nutritional therapist can also arrange this test for you.

Reduce high anxiety

If you suffer with anxiety or panic attacks, then this is likely to be a key priority for you. We therefore recommend that you adopt the seven-step programme as soon as possible, but beware of going cold turkey on stimulants, as rapid withdrawal might have a destabilising effect. Other steps to consider include:

- Steer clear of exercise or activities that raise your heart rate too high and too fast as this can trick your brain into thinking you are in an emergency situation. Focus instead on calming pursuits, such as yoga, tai chi and meditation.

- Learn the HeartMath technique outlined in Chapter 12, as this valuable tool can help you to avert an anxiety attack before it takes hold.

- Boost levels of GABA, the calming neurotransmitter, by supplementing the precursor amino acids taurine (500mg) and glutamine (500mg) twice a day. You can increase these doses to 1000mg of each twice a day if required; or, if you live in the US or Canada, supplement 500–1000mg of GABA itself twice a day.

- Magnesium has a tranquillising effect, so have some handy to calm anxious nerves. Supplement 300mg as required, or 500mg in the evening to aid sleep.

- Alternatively, look for combination formulas containing these nutrients plus calming natural ingredients such as valerian, hops and passion flower (see Resources).

Other factors to consider:

- If you suffer with extreme fears, phobias and paranoia – and have plentiful body hair, a tendency to be overweight, a high pain threshold and a suspicious nature – you may have low histamine levels. We recommend seeing a nutritional therapist (or going to the Brain Bio Centre – see Resources), who will run some tests to determine if this is the case and advise on specific supplements to restore balance.

- If you suffer with panic attacks, pay particular attention to balancing your blood sugar, as dips can bring on an attack. Also, keep a paper bag handy: breathing deeply into it might help next time you experience an attack. If this proves effective, then excess lactic acid might be an issue for you. Buteyko breathing, as described on page 217 (and see Resources), will help with this.

- Try initiating the dive reflex (see page 218) to avert a panic attack.

- Likewise, try rubbing a small amount of progesterone cream into your inner arm. It might relieve anxiety and panic (see page 216).

- If you believe the root of your anxiety lies in past events, investigate psychotherapeutic approaches that can help you to access and release negative programming, such as the Emotional Freedom Technique (EFT), hypnotherapy, the Eye Movement Desensitisation and Reprocessing technique (EMDR) and Time Line Therapy (see Resources).

An extra boost for weight loss

Weight gain, especially around the middle, is one of the hallmarks of long-term stress. It also often goes hand-in-hand with feeling tired much of the time, as we explored in Chapter 20. So, if you are over your ideal healthy weight, following the seven-step programme is the best place to start. However, if you scored in the 'Attention Required' or 'Urgent Action' categories for weight, there are some additional actions to consider. Please note, however, that pushing yourself harder to lose weight, exercising more vigorously or starving yourself will be counter-productive, as you will further stress your body and only exacerbate the problem.

Pay special attention to the following:

- Adopt a low-GL diet and consume no more than 40 GL points a day; always eat carbohydrate with protein; and graze rather than gorge, with three main meals and two snacks (mid-morning and mid-afternoon) each day (see page 225).

- Choose exercise that raises your heart rate but doesn't overly stress you: yoga, brisk walking, gentle swimming or jogging (if you are fit enough) and Psychocals all fit the bill. Yoga also incorporates resistant elements that can help to build more muscle. Consult Chapter 9 for more ideas.

- Ensure you get enough sleep: aim for seven to eight hours of good-quality, uninterrupted sleep every night.

- Chromium can help to reduce sugar cravings and help weight loss, especially when combined with cinnamon. Some supplements contain the cinnamon extract Cinnulin®. Take 200mcg twice a day with your morning and afternoon snacks (see Resources).

- There are some delicious recipes at the back of this book but for a wider selection of low-GL recipes, refer to Patrick's *Low GL Diet Cookbook.*

Other factors to consider:

- If following a low-GL diet does not improve your energy or help you lose weight, get your thyroid checked, especially if you suffer with fatigue, feeling cold, constipation and indigestion, dry skin, hair loss, poor resistance to infection, low mood, loss of libido, irritability, poor memory and loss of focus and concentration. (See page 222 for a basic thyroid temperature test you can do at home.) But bear in mind that many of these symptoms can also occur in people who are adrenalin dominant (see page 216), which your seven-step Stress Cure programme will help to reverse.

- If you suffer with low mood, you might find supplementing 5-HTP helps, in addition to making your appetite easier to control. Take 50mg twice a day with your morning and afternoon snacks.

- HCA slows down the conversion of sugar into fat in your body and has been used successfully in numerous weight-loss trials. Take 250mg three times a day before each main meal (ideally, 30 minutes before). Some supplements contain combinations of chromium, 5-HTP and HCA (see Resources for recommended products).

Quit smoking

Smoking can be a hard habit to kick, especially if you don't deal with the underlying blood sugar imbalance. The average smoker is addicted not only to nicotine but to smoking when tired, when hungry, when upset, on waking, after a meal, with a drink and so on. Improved nutrition based on balancing blood sugar decreases cigarette cravings, so it's best to leave kicking this habit until you've completed the 30-day Stress Cure programme. Thereafter, follow the guidelines in Chapter 7.

Chronic fatigue syndrome

We have not offered a protocol for chronic fatigue syndrome here because we have already outlined various approaches in Chapter 17. All the seven main steps in this chapter should also form part of a recovery programme. But if you are suffering with symptoms and fatigue that are debilitating and stop you from functioning normally, we recommend seeing a nutritional therapist for specialist support. With the right approach, chronic fatigue syndrome can be overcome.

Putting your programme into practice

Now you know what you need to do; and once you've read the next two chapters you'll know exactly what to supplement and how to turn the 'eat for energy' guidelines into easy yet delicious meals. We've deliberately kept the programme as simple as possible, so you don't need to draw up complex plans. But if you feel you'd benefit from making a note of what you're about to do, you can always fill out a chart similar to the example given on pages 252–3. You'll find a blank version in the Appendix, page 302, and you can also download a pdf of the chart to print at www.patrickholford.com/stresscureactionplan.

Getting extra support

If you feel you would benefit from further investigation – such as an adrenal stress test or other biochemical assessment – then we recommend a consultation with a nutritional therapist (see Resources). They will work with you to devise a tailor-made programme to address your key issues.

What next?

After 30 days of following the Stress Cure programme, we are confident you will feel much less stressed, more energised and far better able to be at your best and enjoy life. By making positive changes, such as eating to balance your blood sugar, becoming less reliant on stimulants, sleeping better and doing activities that energise, relax and build resilience, you will have developed new habits that bring big rewards. So we suggest you continue with them. However, once you're at a new, higher baseline, allowing yourself to succumb to one or two of life's temptations won't throw you off balance. So go ahead and enjoy the odd coffee – just don't make a habit out of it. Have a few glasses of wine on a big night out or the occasional thick slice of chocolate cake – but make these the exceptions, not the rule.

After a month, you'll have a far greater awareness of what helps you to function at your best – and what knocks you off balance. And remember, the advice we offer in this book is waiting for you whenever you feel the need to revisit it. We wish you many more months – and years – of stress-less living!

Sample 30-day Stress Cure Programme

1. Eat for energy:

Breakfast	Lunch	Supper	Snacks
Berry booster smoothie	Tortilla	Chicken stir-fry with noodles	Apple & cheese
Poached egg & rye toast	Take-away egg mayo salad	Creamy salmon, leeks & brown rice	Oatcake & nut butter
Easy fruit muesli	Greek salad	Thai baked cod	2 plums and sunflower seeds
			Yoghurt & berries
			Ryvita & cottage cheese
Cinnamon oat pancakes	Take-away lentil soup & oatcakes	Shepherd's pie	Orange & almonds
			Pear & pumpkin seeds
			Crudité & guacamole

2. Reduce stimulants

	Week 1	Week 2	Week 3	Week 4
Caffeine target:	2 teas a day	Green tea instead	0	0
Alcohol target:	6 glasses wine/week	3	0	0
Other:	Fruit and nuts instead of daily chocolate bar			

3. Generate vital energy

Activity/activities:	Brisk walk in park with focus on heavy breathing	Minutes: 30	Days a week: 3

4. Relax and recuperate

Activity/activities:	*Restorative yoga class*	Minutes: *1 hour*	Days a week: *Tuesday*

5. Improve sleep

Steps: *No tea after 4pm; Epsom salts bath with lavender before bed; turn off wi-fi and mobile phone; progressive relaxation exercise in bed.*

6. Build resilience

Activity/activities:	*HeartMath exercise*	Minutes: *5–10*	Days a week: *7*

7. Supplements

Breakfast	Lunch	Supper	Before bed
Multi-vit	*Vit C 1000mg*	*Multi-vit*	*400mg magnesium*
Vitamin C 1000mg	*Co-Q₁₀ 60mg*	*Chill Formula*	
Co-Q₁₀ 60mg			
Awake Formula			

8. Other actions (if applicable):

Request coaching at work to look at underlying beliefs; keep daily gratitude journal; get better organised so able to work from home twice a week

CHAPTER 22

Supplements for Supercharge

Nutritional supplements, taken on a regular basis, make a big difference to your overall experience of energy and resilience to stress. Even if your diet could provide all the recommended daily allowances (RDAs) of nutrients, these levels are far below those that equate to maximum vitality. The better you feel, the more able you are to deal with stress. Also, the more stressful your life, the more nutrients you need. The advice in this book aims to maximise the nutrients you can get from your diet and then explains how to make up any shortfalls through a sensible, balanced use of nutritional supplements.

We appreciate that some people are sceptical about nutritional supplements. Hopefully we have already managed to allay most of that scepticism during the course of this book. If not, we merely ask that you try them during the 30 days of your Stress Cure programme. We are confident that you will soon feel the benefits. The doses we recommend are based on high-quality scientific research and our own clinical experience, and they are often several times higher than the levels that can be found in food. But don't be alarmed, nutrients in supplement form are neither dangerous or toxic; nor do they create dependency. They are simply concentrated food nutrients in pill form.

If you have been brainwashed to believe that you can get all the nutrients you need from a 'well-balanced' diet, consider the following. Before cars and fridges, our ancestors burned twice as many calories and ate twice as much as we do. For example, a worker in early Victorian Britain ate an estimated 3770 calories every day – that's between 50 and 100 per cent more than most people eat today. Also, all of their food was either fresh or cured. Assuming that you don't want to double the amount you eat and then burn it off through extra exercise, the only way to achieve a comparable vitamin and mineral intake today is to supplement, according to research published in the *Journal of the Royal Society of Medicine*.[1]

What's more, in our 100% Health survey, we found that those who both followed a healthy diet and took supplements had the highest energy scores. Also, when we looked closely at the top 100 health scorers, we found that 85 per cent of them took supplements, and that two-thirds took three or more supplements every day.[2]

It's also important to note that what you need in the way of supplements to *restore* balance is more than you need to *maintain* it. So your supplement requirements will decline over time. That's why we recommend reassessing what you need after 30 days if your stress levels have fallen and your energy has improved. It's only then that you will be able to determine what really works for you long term.

The suggestions overleaf give an optimal level of each nutrient in supplement form, assuming you are also eating a reasonably good diet. We recommend you take the core supplement regime (numbers 1 to 4) throughout your 30-day Stress Cure programme. You'll remember that we gave specific supplement recommendations for the different areas outlined in the seven steps in the previous chapter, and many of these nutrients are included in the core regime. Don't worry if the dosage doesn't seem sufficiently high – many nutrients often work in synergy, so when taken in combination (as in the core regime), smaller amounts can be just as effective as high doses. Additional suggestions and modifications for deeper problems are provided after the core regime (see page 260).

Core supplement regime

Your Stress Cure programme should include each of the four following supplements.

1. Multivitamin and mineral

The nutrients listed below should always be present in a good-quality multivitamin and mineral, but check because many multis do not provide enough minerals. At the levels we are recommending, it's unlikely that you'll find everything in just one tablet or capsule – the best multis often advise you to take two a day (morning and afternoon).

Nutrient	Recommended level
B_1	25mg
B_2	25mg
B_3	50mg
B_5	50mg
B_6	20mg
B_{12}	10mcg
Folic acid	200mcg
Biotin	50mcg
Vitamin A*	1000–1500mcg
Vitamin C	200mg
Vitamin D	15mcg
Vitamin E	100mg
Calcium	300–400mg
Magnesium	150–200mg
Manganese	2–3mg
Iron	10mg
Zinc	10mg

| Chromium | 30–50mcg |
| Selenium | 30mcg |

*As retinol or beta carotene. The recommended level is equivalent to 5000–7500iu.

2. Additional boosters

When it comes to making energy, as we saw in Chapter 5, co-enzyme Q_{10} is an important nutrient, so we recommend supplementing it every day if your energy level is low: 30mg will be sufficient if you feel tired. If you feel exhausted, increase your intake to 120mg, ideally in split doses (e.g. one 30–40mg capsule taken three or four times a day). Vitamin C is also key for adrenal and overall health, and as you won't get all you need in a multivitamin, supplement an extra 1000mg twice a day

Nutrient	Recommended level
Co-Q_{10}	30–120mg
Vitamin C	2000mg

3. Extra energy hit

While a good multivitamin will provide optimum levels of key vitamins and minerals, when you are feeling stressed and tired, and/or are weaning yourself off stimulants, it is helpful to have some extra energy support. We therefore recommend taking more of the energy-generating nutrients we have highlighted in earlier chapters. Higher levels of B vitamins, plus amino acids such as tyrosine and adaptogenic herbs, such as ginseng, rhodiola and reishi, will support the natural production of energy and help balance stress hormones when you are under pressure or feeling burned out.

Overleaf, we list these nutrients and the guideline levels to help you find a suitable formula. The exact amounts you'll need will depend on the quality and potency of the extract, so pick reputable brands (see Resources for suggestions). The ideal time to take these nutrients is early in the morning, before breakfast. Note that amino acids such as tyrosine might not be fully absorbed if they have to compete with other amino acids in food, so they should be taken at least 15 minutes before a meal.

Nutrient	Recommended level
Tyrosine	500–1000mg
Ginseng(s) (look for Korean, Siberian or American ginseng, or a combination	200–300mg
Reishi mushrooms	50–100mg OR
Rhodiola	100–200mg
Vitamin B_5	50–100mg
Vitamin B_3	25–50mg
Vitamin B_6	15–30mg
Folic acid	50–200mcg
Vitamin B_{12}	5–10mcg

*'Siberian' ginseng is not from the same plant family as Korean and American ginseng, but, like them, it acts as an adaptogen.

Moringa is a herb from Africa, where it is taken either as a powder or in teas, for a general health and energy boost. It does have a noticeable effect within minutes. Studies show that it has an incredibly high number of nutrients, ranging from amino acids to carotenoids and flavonoids, as well as vitamins and minerals. It is also a very potent antioxidant, helps to stabilise blood sugar and helps boost immunity.[3] It is caffeine-free and a very good all-rounder. Try having a heaped teaspoon a day or drinking Moringa tea.

4. Calm in a capsule

Nutrient	Recommended level
Taurine*	250–750mg
Glutamine*	250–750mg
Theanine	50–100mg
Magnesium	100–400mg**
Hops extract	50–200mg
Valerian	50–100mg***
Passion flower	100–200mg
5-HTP	50–200mg

*If GABA is sold over the counter in your country, supplement 500–1500mg instead of taurine plus glutamine.

**You are aiming for a total of 300mg of magnesium, including whatever is in your multivitamin and mineral.

***Valerian is often available only on its own. When taken in higher doses (e.g. 300mg) it acts as a sedative. Obviously, this is good if you need to switch off and go to sleep, but not advisable if you are about to drive a car or need to concentrate at work.

If you feel frazzled and find it hard to wind down, supplementing amino acids that boost the production of GABA, such as taurine and glutamine, can help to shift you from stressed to rest, without making you sleepy. They are especially useful if you find it difficult to relax at the end of the day, and whenever you feel particularly stressed. Other calming natural agents include magnesium (often referred to as nature's tranquilliser), the amino acid theanine (which helps you to feel calm but alert), and plants such as hops, valerian and passion flower. Note, however, that valerian can make you feel sleepy, so don't take it during the day if you need to remain alert. Tryptophan or 5-HTP is useful too if you feel down and want a mood lift. The ideal time to take these nutrients is towards the end of the day.

Above is a summary of these nutrients, and the recommended

doses. If you can find a single formula that combines many of them, go for the lower end of the dosage spectrum, as their effects can be heightened when they are taken in combination. And do not supplement 5-HTP if you are also taking an antidepressant without first consulting your GP or a nutritional therapist.

30 days and beyond

This core regime provides all the nutrients you need to support you during your 30-day Stress Cure programme. The 'extra energy hit' and 'calm in a capsule' recommendations are designed for use throughout the 30 days to help you feel more awake when you need to be alert, and more relaxed when you need to calm down or fall asleep. Once you feel more in balance, either half the dose or stop them completely, although keep them to hand for difficult days and times when you feel anxious or frazzled. After you complete the 30-day programme, we recommend that you continue with the basic multivitamin and mineral and 'additional boosters' listed above as these will provide ongoing support.

Supplements for deeper problems

Detoxification support

If you scored in the 'Attention Required' or 'Urgent Action' categories for detox potential in the stress assessment chart, then reducing your toxic load via a clean diet and taking additional supplements to support liver detoxification are recommended as parts of your 30-day Stress Cure programme. B vitamins are important for keeping the liver detoxification pathways healthy, but we have already included them in the multivitamin and mineral in the core regime, so the focus here is on adding other key detoxification co-factors and antioxidant nutrients, such as calcium gluconate, N-acetyl cysteine, alpha lipoic acid, glutathione, resveratrol, extra co-enzyme Q_{10}, selenium, vitamin A and beta carotene. Several supplements include many of these in a single formulation (see Resources for product suggestions).

If you also have poor digestion, have been suffering prolonged stress, drink heavily and have a high stimulant intake and/or a poor diet, we recommend supporting your digestion by supplementing:

- Digestive enzymes, such as protease, amylase, lipase plus lactase (if you have trouble digesting milk) and alpha galactosidase (if beans and pulses give you wind).

- Beneficial gut bacteria in the form of *Lactobacillus acidophilus* and *Bifidobacterium* (choose a product with a minimum of 2 billion viable organisms and store in the fridge to maintain integrity).

- The amino acid glutamine, which helps to heal the gut lining. (Note this use is different from that recommended for boosting GABA levels, when taken alongside taurine). Aim for 5g (i.e. 5000mg) in either one dose or split into two. Glutamine is best taken on an empty stomach, so many people choose to take it at night. However, it can be stimulating, so swap to first thing in the morning if your sleep is disturbed.

Boosting low mood

The nutrients included in the 'extra energy hit' and 'calm in a capsule' recommendations in the core regime will support improved mood, while the B vitamins in the multivitamin and mineral will encourage a more upbeat outlook. However, you may have noticed that the core regime doesn't include any omega 3 fats, so we recommend adding 1000mg of omega 3 twice a day if your mood needs a boost.

Natural solutions to anxiety

The nutrients included in the 'calm in a capsule' recommendations in the core regime will help to reduce anxiety by supporting your body's production of GABA, the calming neurotransmitter. 'Calm in a capsule' also includes several natural relaxants to help you feel more chilled. If you still feel anxious or continue to suffer from panic attacks, increase the dosage – for example, take one or two combined formulas up to three times a day – until you feel better.

Kick-starting weight loss

If you suffer from stress-related weight gain, you have the option of adding nutrients that will stimulate your cells to burn more of the fuel from your food as energy, rather than storing it as fat. Look for a formula that combines chromium (300–400mcg) with cinnamon (2000–3000mg) or the potent cinnamon extract Cinnulin® (200–300mg), which will help to balance blood sugar and reduce cravings. Split it into two doses after breakfast and lunch, or after lunch and supper.

If you score in the 'Attention Required' or 'Urgent Action' categories for weight, then you might also consider taking a formula that includes 5-HTP (50–100mg) to help suppress sugar cravings (especially if you also experience low mood) and HCA (also called *Garcinia cambogia*) to help inhibit the conversion of sugar to fat in your body (250–750mg with each meal). However, if you are also taking the 'Calm in a capsule' recommendations above, exclude 5-HTP from one formula or the other, or start one and then introduce the second three or four days later. Either way, do not exceed 300mg of 5-HTP in any one day, and certainly do not supplement this nutrient if you are also taking an antidepressant without first consulting your GP or a nutritional therapist.

CHAPTER 23

High-energy Eating

Eating for health and vitality gives you more energy, as well as nutrients that help you to become more stress resilient. What's more, the meals are delicious. Making them doesn't have to be hard work or difficult, either, as we illustrate here with seven days' worth of easy recipes and ideas for tasty breakfasts, lunches, suppers and snacks. We also look at what to choose when you're eating out and suggest smart ideas for takeaway food while you're at work.

And, of course, every meal here follows the low-GL rules that you learned about back in Chapter 4, to ensure your blood sugar remains in balance.

Seven-day menu plan

	Monday	Tuesday	Wednesday
Breakfast:	Berry booster	Poached eggs on wholegrain toast	Porridge with apple and almonds
Lunch:	Roasted pepper and artichoke tortilla	Greek salad	Salade niçoise
Supper:	Sesame chicken and soba noodle steam-fry	Creamy salmon with leeks	Thai baked cod
Snacks:	Apple and a chunk of Cheddar; two oatcakes and peanut butter	Crudités and hummus; pear and small handful of almonds	Two plums or apricots with a small handful of sunflower seeds; small tub of plain yoghurt with berries

Thursday	Friday	Saturday	Sunday
Super-simple breakfast sandwich	Easy fruit muesli	Cinnamon oat pancakes	Vegetable and herb omelette
Barley and vegetable broth	Red lentil and smoked mackerel kedgeree	Hot smoked trout with pesto and watercress open sandwich	DIY salad
Shepherd's pie with sweet potato topping	Cashew and sesame quinoa	Chickpea curry	Stuffed peppers
Apple and small handful of walnuts; two oatcakes with almond nut butter	Cherries or berries and a handful of sunflower seeds; two Ryvita with cottage cheese or mushroom paté	Crudités with guacamole; pear and a handful of pumpkin seeds	Two oatcakes and hummus; orange and a handful of almonds

Breakfasts

Berry booster

This is so simple that a full recipe is not required. In a blender, just whizz up a small tub (120g) of natural yoghurt (cow, goat, sheep or soya), two large handfuls of mixed berries (e.g. strawberries, blueberries, raspberries and blackcurrants – frozen can be used if not in season), a tablespoon of wheatgerm or oatbran and two heaped tablespoons of seeds (e.g. a mix of flax, pumpkin, sesame, sunflower and chia – pre-ground can be used if a smoother texture is preferred). Pour into a glass and enjoy! If you want a sloppier texture, add a splash of fruit juice or water. Serves one.

Poached eggs on wholegrain toast

Poaching is one of the healthiest ways to serve eggs, as the gentle cooking method preserves more of the valuable phospholipids and B vitamins. Serve with cherry tomatoes if desired. Serves one.

> 2 slices of buttered wholegrain toast (rye is preferable)
> 2 organic or free-range eggs
> Freshly ground black pepper
> Pinch of sea salt

1. Lightly toast the bread.
2. To poach the eggs, pour freshly boiled water into a frying pan over a very gentle heat so that there is the merest hint of bubbles and movement. Carefully crack the eggs into the pan and allow to poach gently in the water for about three minutes or until the tops no longer look transparent.
3. Butter your toast. Remove the poached eggs from the pan and allow to drain, then place on the toast. Serve with cherry tomatoes if desired.

Porridge with apple and almonds

Oats release their energy slowly, so oat-based breakfasts can be very sustaining. You can substitute the apple for another type of fruit if preferred (but avoid bananas as they are very starchy). Serves one.

> 4 tbsp porridge oats
> Water or milk/non-dairy milk, or a 50:50 blend for cooking, in a ratio of 2 parts liquid to 1 part oats
> 1 apple, grated or finely chopped
> 1 tbsp flaked almonds

1. Place the oats in a small saucepan. Add double the amount of water, milk, or a blend of the two.
2. Bring to a gentle simmer and let it bubble and thicken for a few minutes, until the oats have swollen.
3. Meanwhile, grate in the apple.
4. Pour into a bowl and sprinkle with almonds before serving.

Super-simple breakfast sandwich

This is one of Susannah's speedy breakfast favourites (she sometimes wraps it up to eat in the car or on the train when running late for an appointment). Again, no recipe is required. Simply toast two slices of rye (or wholegrain) bread, spread with cottage or cream cheese (or mashed avocado) and top with a generous helping of smoked salmon, a squeeze of lemon juice and some freshly ground black pepper.

Easy fruit muesli

Another super-simple idea. Mix together a small cup of porridge oats with a cup of chopped mixed fruit (e.g. apple, pear, plums, apricots), a cup of milk (cow, goat, soya or rice) or natural yoghurt, a tablespoon of ground seeds (as for the berry booster) and a tablespoon of chopped almonds and hazelnuts. Serves one.

Cinnamon oat pancakes

Serve with mixed berries or stewed fruit, and add a dollop of yoghurt if desired. This recipe makes around 12 small pancakes. Leftovers can be reheated. Serves two.

50g (2oz) whole oat flakes, whizzed in a grinder or food processor attachment to form a flour
1½ tsp cinnamon
1 small free-range or organic egg
150ml (5floz) milk or non-dairy milk
Virgin rapeseed oil for frying

1. Put the oat flour and cinnamon in a bowl.
2. Lightly beat the egg and milk together then stir into the dried ingredients to form a runny mixture. If the mixture is not particularly smooth it may be that your blender isn't powerful enough to grind the oats to a fine flour, so blend the mixture quickly with a hand-held blender to make it as smooth as possible. The mixture may thicken if left for a while but you can loosen it by adding a little more milk.
3. Heat a tablespoon of oil in a large frying pan and tip to coat the base, then pour several tablespoons of the pancake mixture into the pan (without allowing them to touch each other). Fry for a minute or so on each side, or until firm and just turning golden (do this in batches so as not to crowd the pan). Place on a plate and cover with a clean tea towel to keep warm while you finish the batch. Serve the pancakes warm, adding stewed fruit and/or natural yoghurt to taste.

Vegetable and herb omelette

You can use whatever vegetables you have in the fridge in this omelette, but spinach, courgette, peppers, mushrooms, onions, green beans, tenderstem and leeks all work particularly well, as do the herbs parsley, chives, basil and coriander. Serves one.

2 handfuls chopped mixed vegetables
1 tbsp olive or rapeseed oil
2 free-range or organic eggs
Sea salt
1 tbsp chopped fresh herbs
Freshly ground black pepper

1. Fry the vegetables in the oil in a medium-sized frying pan, adding a splash of water after a minute and covering with a lid to 'steam fry' to avoid browning. Don't allow the vegetables to lose their colour or get too soft (a maximum of five minutes is usually sufficient).
2. Beat the eggs and add a pinch of salt, then add to the pan.
3. Jiggle the eggs and lift up the sides of the omelette with a heat-proof spatula to allow any runny mixture to make contact with the pan's base.
4. When the egg on top appears set, throw on the herbs and sprinkle with some black pepper, then fold in half and serve immediately, with a slice of rye toast if desired.

Lunches

Roasted pepper and artichoke tortilla

Spanish tortilla is a robust, colourful dish that can be enjoyed as a simple lunch or on a picnic. This version uses antipasti vegetables, but you could also use leftover cooked veg, such as

French beans, courgettes or mushrooms. Delicious hot or cold. Serve with a green salad. Serves two.

150g (5oz) baby new potatoes (around 8), scrubbed clean but not peeled, cut into small cubes
1 tbsp coconut oil or olive oil
2 cloves garlic, crushed
150g (5oz) roasted red peppers (about 2), from the deli, a jar, or roasted at home, cubed
2 tbsp marinated artichoke hearts, drained, chopped into chunks
4 medium eggs
Freshly ground black pepper
Sea salt
½ tsp dried oregano

1. Place the potatoes in a small pan and just cover with cold water. Bring to the boil and simmer, covered, for around ten minutes, or until the potatoes are soft. Drain and set to one side.
2. Heat the oil in a medium-sized frying pan (use a small pan if you are halving the quantities to make a tortilla for one person) and fry the garlic for 30 seconds. Add the potatoes and sauté for five minutes or so.
3. Stir the peppers and artichokes into the pan and reduce the heat.
4. Beat the eggs with the pepper, a little salt and the oregano. Pour evenly over the vegetable mixture in the pan and stir to expose the egg on top to the heat on the base of the pan. Leave the tortilla cooking over a low–medium heat for around six minutes or until the eggs are set. (The edges and base should be set, with the top still a little soft as it will continue to cook after you remove it from the heat.)
5. Remove the pan from the heat and loosen the edges and base with a palette knife. Turn the tortilla out onto a plate. Serve hot or cold.

Greek salad

Ideal for lunch (at home or to take to work), this classic salad is full of summer flavours and rich in antioxidants from the red onion and ripe tomatoes. You can double the recipe and store in the fridge for up to three days. Eat with a warmed wholemeal pitta bread or a few oatcakes. Serves two.

1 medium red onion, halved then thinly sliced
3 medium tomatoes, chopped into chunks
15cm (6in) cucumber, quartered lengthways then chopped into chunks
1½ tbsp Kalamata olives, pitted and halved
150g (5oz) feta cheese
Freshly ground black pepper

For the dressing:

1½ tbsp extra-virgin olive oil
1 tbsp white wine vinegar
¾ tsp dried oregano
Freshly ground black pepper

1. Put the vegetables and olives in a salad bowl, pour over the dressing and toss gently.
2. Crumble the feta on top and lightly toss through the vegetables.
3. Season with black pepper and chill lightly or serve immediately.

Salade niçoise

A flavour-packed low-GL alternative to the classic French dish. As tuna can be high in mercury and should not be eaten more than once a week, we've suggested eggs and anchovies instead. Mixed pulses take the place of the traditional boiled potatoes to lower the GL and because they make a tasty and interesting change. Serves two.

1 Romaine lettuce, washed, dried and torn into bite-sized pieces
3 spring onions, sliced on the diagonal
6 black olives, pitted and halved
2 eggs, hardboiled (8 minutes), shelled and chopped into smallish chunks
4 anchovies in oil, drained on kitchen towel and sliced into 1cm strips
2 large, ripe tomatoes, chopped
Freshly ground black pepper
1 can (410g) mixed pulses, rinsed and drained
225g (8oz) cooked French green beans, rinsed and drained to remove any salty water

For the dressing:

2 tbsp extra-virgin olive oil
2 tsp lemon juice
½ clove garlic, crushed
Freshly ground black pepper

1. Toss all of the salad ingredients together.
2. Mix the dressing ingredients, pour over the salad and toss again, gently.

Barley and vegetable broth

This is a very hearty, filling soup, yet the GL score is very low, thanks to the high vegetable content and the lentils and barley. Serves two.

1 tbsp mild or medium (not extra-virgin) olive oil, or virgin rapeseed oil, or coconut oil, or 20g butter
1 carrot, peeled and diced

½ leek, thinly sliced
2 sticks celery, finely sliced
1 stalk of thyme
50g (2oz) pearl barley, rinsed and drained
25g (1oz) red lentils, rinsed and drained
600ml (1pt) vegetable or chicken stock
1 tbsp flat-leaf parsley, finely chopped
2 tbsp baby spinach, watercress or rocket, finely chopped
Sea salt
Freshly ground black pepper

1. Heat the oil or butter in a pan and add the carrot, leek and celery. Sweat for around five minutes so that the vegetables start to soften.
2. Stir in the thyme, barley, lentils and stock, bring to a simmer, then cover and cook for around 45 minutes, or until the pearl barley is soft to the bite and the vegetables are very tender.
3. Remove the thyme stalk, stir in the chopped parsley and greens, and season to taste.

Red lentil and smoked mackerel kedgeree

This cross between kedgeree and lentil curry is so moreish that you'll have to stop yourself eating it from the pan. The lentils are very low GL, while mackerel is an excellent source of omega 3s. You can double this recipe and store in the fridge for up to two days. Serves two.

½ tsp turmeric
1 tsp medium curry powder
1 tbsp coconut oil or olive oil
2 cloves garlic, crushed
1 onion, chopped
250g (9oz) red lentils, well rinsed and drained
690ml (25floz) cold water

4 tsp reduced-salt vegetable bouillon powder
1 hardboiled egg (8 minutes), cooled, peeled and sliced
2 small smoked mackerel fillets (75g/3oz in total), skinned and
flaked into pieces (removing any bones)

1. Dry-fry the turmeric and curry powder for a minute in
   a large frying pan.
2. Add the oil and garlic and fry for a further 30 seconds,
   then add the onion and sweat until it softens.
3. Place the lentils, water and bouillon powder in the pan
   and boil, uncovered, for ten minutes.
4. Cover and simmer for 15–20 minutes, until the lentils
   are soft to the bite.
5. Stir in the egg slices and flaked fish just before serving.

Hot smoked trout with pesto and watercress open sandwich

If you don't like pesto, use cottage cheese or olive tapenade (available in jars from good supermarkets) instead. Serves one.

2 slices thin pumpernickel-style rye bread
1 tbsp pesto
1 hot smoked trout fillet, flaked (remove any bones)
1 handful watercress, roughly chopped
Freshly ground black pepper

1. Toast the rye bread (optional) and spread with the pesto.
2. Place the flaked fish on top and scatter with watercress.
3. Season with black pepper and serve.

DIY salad

A simple salad of mixed leaves and chopped raw vegetables can become a nutritious and delicious meal in moments if you add some deli delights, such as artichoke hearts, sun-blushed tomatoes, olives, hardboiled eggs, peppers, anchovies, smoked fish or slices of lean white meat. Fresh herbs can also boost the flavour and they are a rich source of phyto-nutrients (one dessertspoon is the equivalent of one portion of veg). You can also buy ready-cooked grains and pulses like quinoa, spelt and lentils, so you have all you need to hand if you're in a hurry. The combinations below also work well for a lunch on the go (just pack in an air-tight container and remember a fork). Each serves one.

- Cold trout, salmon or a smoked mackerel fillet, flaked through whole grains such as quinoa, brown rice, millet or couscous, with chopped raw vegetables (e.g. cucumber, tomato, red pepper, carrot, cabbage, spring onion). Season with lemon juice, balsamic vinegar, black pepper and chopped fresh herbs.

- Tofu chunks (bought marinated and cooked; or marinate yourself in tamari or soy, ginger, garlic, sesame oil and brown rice syrup, then cook in a medium oven for 20 minutes, turning half way through). Toss with whole grains, as above, or stir into buckwheat noodles with finely sliced cucumber, red pepper, spring onion and seaweed (packets of dried varieties can be found in the Oriental section of many supermarkets). Sprinkle with sesame seeds and serve warm or chilled.

- Toss a tin of mixed beans with sliced chicory, a handful of cherry tomatoes, a finely chopped small red onion, a handful of sweet baby peppers (bottled or from the deli) and a diced hardboiled egg. Season with finely chopped parsley, olive oil, a splash of balsamic or wine vinegar, sea salt and freshly ground black pepper.

- Mix cold (or warm) cooked new potatoes with a flaked smoked mackerel fillet, a diced avocado, a handful of sundried tomatoes and three handfuls of rocket. Dress with olive oil, lemon juice, a clove of crushed garlic (optional) and season with sea salt, freshly ground black pepper and a pinch of paprika.

- Tabbouleh of couscous, bulgur wheat, millet or quinoa with chopped cherry tomatoes, spring onions, cucumber, parsley, mint, olive oil, lemon juice and seasoning.

- Blueberries and crumbled feta cheese on green leaves (e.g. torn Romaine lettuce and lamb's leaf or spinach) with avocado, alfalfa sprouts and radishes. Serve with a mustardy French dressing (four parts olive oil to one part wine vinegar, a dash of French mustard and sea salt and freshly ground black pepper to taste).

Suppers

Sesame chicken and soba noodle steam-fry

Soba noodles are made from buckwheat, a gluten-free seed with an earthy, grain-like taste. They cook quickly (four to six minutes) and make an interesting change from wheat noodles or rice. Serves two.

2 tsp coconut oil or olive oil
2 cloves garlic, crushed
2 tsp chopped fresh root ginger
2 chicken breasts, trimmed of skin and fat and sliced into strips
4 handfuls chopped mixed vegetables (e.g. peppers, carrots, baby corn, mangetout, broccoli)
2 tsp reduced-salt vegetable bouillon powder
2 tbsp water
100g (4oz) soba noodles
2 tsp sesame oil

1. Heat the coconut or olive oil in a wok, add the garlic, ginger and chicken and stir-fry over a moderate heat for two minutes or until the meat is coloured on all sides.
2. Add the vegetables, bouillon powder and water to the wok and cover immediately with the lid. Cook for five to seven minutes to let the vegetables soften and the meat finish cooking, checking halfway through to make sure the water hasn't evaporated. If it has, add another tablespoon or so and replace the lid.

3. Meanwhile, cook the noodles: put in a pan of boiling water, cover and boil for four to six minutes, then drain and rinse under cold water. Take care not to overcook them.

4. Tip the noodles into the wok, add the sesame oil, stir all the ingredients together and serve.

Creamy salmon with leeks

Real comfort food, with a wonderfully creamy sauce, this dish also packs a substantial nutritional punch from the omega 3s, green veg and fibre-rich butter beans. If you're hungry, serve with quinoa or brown rice. Serves two.

2 tsp coconut oil or olive oil
2 courgettes, thinly sliced horizontally
4 leeks, thinly sliced horizontally
75g (3oz) low-fat cream cheese
210ml (7floz) skimmed milk, soya milk or nut milk
2 tbsp cornflour
1 can (410g) butter beans, rinsed and drained
100g (4oz) smoked salmon, torn into strips
4 spring onions, finely sliced diagonally
2 tsp dill, chopped

1. Heat the oil in a large frying pan or wok and sauté the courgettes and leeks until they start to soften and colour.

2. Add the cream cheese and half the milk and stir while the cream cheese melts.

3. Mix the cornflour with the rest of the milk to form a smooth liquid and add to the pan, stirring constantly to avoid any lumps as the sauce thickens.

4. Tip in the drained butter beans, smoked salmon, spring onions and dill and heat through, then serve.

Thai baked cod

Thai seasoning is subtle and delicious. You can use any white fish instead of cod if you prefer. The dish is even better if the fish is left to marinate in the sauce for a few hours before cooking. Serve with brown rice (start cooking this 40 minutes before you plan to eat) and steamed green vegetables (e.g. broccoli, pak choi, spring greens or cabbage). Serves two.

    1 lime, juice and grated zest
    ½ inch ginger root, grated
    1 stick lemon grass, sliced (or 1 tsp lemon grass paste)
    2 cloves garlic, crushed
    1 tsp tamari or soy sauce
    1 fresh chilli, finely chopped
    2 medium cod fillets

1. In a mug, blend the lime juice, lime zest, lemon grass, crushed garlic, ginger, tamari and chilli. (Beware: after you chop chilli, wash your hands immediately.)
2. Rinse the cod fillets, pat dry with kitchen roll and place in a baking dish.
3. Pour over the lime mixture, turning the fish so it is well coated. Ideally, leave to marinate for at least an hour or even overnight.
4. Cover with lid or foil and bake in a preheated oven (200°C/gas mark 6) for 20 minutes or until cooked (this will depend on the thickness of the fillets).
5. Serve with brown rice and steamed green vegetables.

Shepherd's pie with a sweet potato topping

This version of the winter classic replaces ordinary potatoes with sweet potatoes, which are less likely to upset blood sugar levels. Serves two.

250g (9oz) lamb mince
1 carrot, diced
1 clove garlic, crushed
1 leek, finely sliced
1 tbsp tomato purée
225ml (8floz) beef stock
Splash Worcestershire sauce
Freshly ground black pepper
500g (1lb 2oz) sweet potatoes, cubed
Olive oil, rapeseed oil, or a knob of butter for mashing

1. Preheat the oven to 180°C/gas mark 4.
2. Brown the mince in a large, hot pan. Break up with a spoon, then add the carrots, garlic and leek. Let them sweat down a little for five minutes or so.
3. Stir in the tomato purée, stock and Worcestershire sauce and season with black pepper.
4. Bring to a simmer, then cover and cook for 15 minutes.
5. Stir and cook for a further 15 minutes, uncovered.
6. Meanwhile, steam the sweet potatoes for 15 minutes or until tender. Mash (with a little oil or butter if desired).
7. Spoon the lamb mixture into an ovenproof dish and spread the mashed sweet potatoes evenly over the top.
8. Ruffle the top with a fork, then bake for 20–25 minutes or until the top starts to colour and the mince is starting to bubble at the edges. Pop under the grill after cooking for a golden-brown colour if you wish.

Cashew and sesame quinoa

The sesame, tamari and cashews enliven this dish, while the raw vegetables provide extra crunch as well as vitamins and antioxidants. You can double this recipe and store in the fridge for up to three days. It also works cold, so you could take it to work for lunch. Serves two.

140g (just over 5oz) quinoa
360ml (12floz) water
1 tsp reduced-salt vegetable bouillon powder
3–4 tbsp fresh or frozen petit pois
2 tbsp cashew nuts
2 tsp sesame oil
1 tbsp tamari (wheat-free soy sauce) or soy sauce
2 tsp lemon juice
1 large carrot, finely chopped into matchsticks
6 spring onions, finely sliced on the diagonal
Freshly ground black pepper

1. Add the quinoa, water and bouillon powder to a sauce-pan and bring to the boil. Cover and simmer for around 13 minutes, or until all the water has been absorbed and the quinoa grains are soft and fluffy.

2. Add the petit pois and stir through, then remove from the heat. They will cook or soften slightly in the residual warmth.

3. Combine with all the other ingredients, tossing thoroughly to mix all the flavours and allow the quinoa to absorb the liquid seasonings.

Chickpea curry

You can throw together this tasty curry in about five minutes flat, using nothing but store-cupboard staples. It's bursting with valuable nutrients, from the antioxidants in the garlic, onion and curry powder to the calcium and magnesium in the almonds and the phyto-estrogens in the chickpeas. You can double this recipe and freeze the remainder, or store in the fridge for up to three days. Serve with brown rice (but be sure to get this cooking 40 minutes before you plan to eat). Serves two.

1 tsp coconut oil or olive oil
2 cloves garlic, crushed

1 onion, diced
2 tsp curry powder
300ml (½pt) water
2 tsp reduced-salt vegetable bouillon powder
2 tbsp tomato purée
1 can (410g) chickpeas, rinsed and drained
2 tbsp ground almonds

1. Heat the oil in a large frying pan or wok, add the garlic and onion and fry for two minutes.
2. Add the curry powder and cook until the onion softens.
3. Pour in the water and add the bouillon powder, tomato purée, chickpeas and ground almonds. Simmer and stir for a minute or so to let the mixture thicken.
4. Serve with brown rice.

Stuffed peppers

This delicious dish contains a rich stuffing of pine nuts, basil and mushrooms that partners the sweet peppers brilliantly. Tuna provides protein, or you could use borlotti or butter beans for a vegetarian option. Serves two.

1 tsp olive oil, for greasing
2 large red peppers
1 tbsp coconut oil or olive oil
1 medium onion, finely chopped
2 cloves garlic, crushed
150g (just over 5oz) mushrooms, cleaned and sliced
1 tsp reduced-salt vegetable bouillon powder mixed with 2–3 tbsp water
100g (4oz) brown basmati rice, cooked
1 tin tuna (150g drained weight) or 150g tinned borlotti or butter beans
1 tbsp pine nuts
Handful fresh basil, chopped

Sea salt
Freshly ground black pepper

1. Preheat the oven to 200°C/gas mark 6 and lightly grease a baking tray with a little oil.
2. Cut the tops off the peppers (but retain them for later), then remove the seeds and pith as well as any bulbous pieces inside the peppers.
3. Heat the remaining oil in a sauté pan and gently fry the onion and garlic for two minutes. Add the chopped mushrooms and bouillon liquid and fry for a further two to three minutes.
4. In a large bowl, combine this mixture with the cooked rice, tuna (or beans), pine nuts and basil and season with a little salt and black pepper.
5. Stuff the peppers with the mixture and replace the tops.
6. Place on a baking tray and bake for 35 minutes. Serve immediately.

Snacks

In the seven-day menu plan we provided ideas for two snacks each day – one to have mid-morning and the other mid-afternoon – to maintain blood sugar balance and boost your overall nutrient intake. If you don't get hungry at these times, and your energy remains stable throughout the day, you can skip the snacks. Each idea is designed to be easy and portable, and there are no recipes for any of them – they are simply as described in the menu plan (although you can, of course, make your own mushroom paté, hummus or guacamole rather than buying ready-made, if you prefer and have time).

Eating out

Following a healthy diet doesn't mean becoming a slave to cooking. You can still eat out and enjoy someone else doing the cooking and washing up for you. It's just a question of choosing wisely. The low-GL plate (see page 224) serves as an easy reminder of how to structure your meal.

So a portion of meat, fish, eggs, pulses or dairy-based foods should always be eaten with an equal portion of low-GL carbohydrates and twice as much low-starch veg or salad. Often this can be accomplished simply by asking to swap the fries or mash for an extra portion of veg (or asking for a half portion of each), and/or ordering a salad on the side. Many restaurants don't offer wholegrain carbs (such as brown rice rather than white), but it never hurts to ask. New potatoes are the best potato option, as they release their energy slower than chips, mashed or jacket potatoes.

Opting for a protein-rich or salad-based starter over a stodgy, sugar-laden pudding is also a good idea. (Susannah sometimes selects a starter to eat instead of a pudding *after* the main course, usually much to the amusement of her fellow diners!) If you feel you must have a dessert, most restaurants offer fruit as an alternative to the chocolate puddings and cheesecakes. That said, we're not proposing you live like a saint for the rest of your life – as the saying goes, a little of what you fancy does you good! But while you are following the 30-day Stress Cure programme, avoiding energy-depleting refined carbohydrates and added sugar are highly recommended to help you stabilise your blood sugar and increase your energy levels.

Takeaway lunches

Feeding office workers is a huge industry, with sandwich shops and coffee-shop chains often clustering in business districts. However, as with eating out, if you choose well, you can still get takeaway lunches that give you plenty of energy and work within the guidelines of the 30-day Stress Cure programme. Homemade soup plus a protein-rich sandwich on wholegrain bread is often a good option; as is a salad box with plenty of fish, chicken, cheese, eggs, beans or tofu. To cut down on your intake of bread, try asking for an open sandwich or a wrap with some salad on the side; or buy a sandwich plus ready-made crudités (chopped vegetable sticks) with a hummus or yoghurt-based dip. If you like sushi, this is a protein-rich option. Combine it with a salad or extra veg for a vitality boost. Some chains even offer bento boxes – sushi plus vegetables and edamame (soya beans in their pods) – or you can get these to take away from Japanese restaurants.

Looking for more ideas and inspiration?

Many of the recipes featured in this book are taken or adapted from the huge range of delicious recipes in *The 10 Secrets of 100% Health Cookbook* and *The Low-GL Diet Cookbook* by Patrick and the talented cookery writer Fiona McDonald Joyce. If you're looking for more ideas (or want to follow a low-GL diet to lose weight), then these two books make ideal companions as they also contain lots of useful tips on healthy cooking methods, new ingredients to try, menu plans, delicious low-GL desserts, drinks and more.

References

Introduction

1 Mind, 'Mental Health at Work: Populus Survey of Workers in England and Wales', 2013.

2 'Nearly half of adults feel stressed every day or every few days', press release, Mental Health Foundation, 8 January 2013.

3 N. Vogelzangs et al., 'Urinary cortisol and six-year risk of all-cause and cardiovascular mortality', *Journal of Clinical Endocrinology and Metabolism* (2010), vol 95(11), pp. 4959–4964.

4 A.K. Eriksson et al., 'Psychological distress and risk of pre-diabetes and type 2 diabetes in a prospective study of Swedish middle-aged men and women', *Diabetic Medicine* (2008), vol 25, pp. 834–842.

5 L. Johansson et al., 'Midlife psychological stress and risk of dementia: a 35-year longitudinal population study', *Brain* (2010), vol 133, pp. 2217–2224.

6 M. Kivmaki et al., 'Common mental disorder and obesity: insight from four repeat measures over 19 years: prospective Whitehall II cohort study', *British Medical Journal* (2009), vol 339:b3765 (available online at http://www.bmj.com/content/339/bmj.b3765.full).

7 G.M. Louis et al., 'Stress reduces conception probabilities across the fertile window: evidence in support of relaxation', *Fertility and Sterility* (2011), vol 95(7), pp. 2184–2189.

8 H. Kuper et al., 'Job strain and risk of breast cancer', *Epidemiology* (2007), vol 18(6), pp. 764–768.

9 D. Rai et al., 'Psychological distress and risk of long-term disability: population-based longitudinal study', *Journal of Epidemiology and Community Health* (2012), vol 66(7), pp. 586–592.

10 C. Aboa-Eboule et al., 'Job strain and risk of acute recurrent coronary heart disease events', *Journal of the American Medical Association* (2007), vol 298(14), pp. 1652–1660.

Part 1

1 P. Holford et al., '100% Health survey: a comparison of the health and nutrition of over 55,000 people in Britain', Holford & Associates, January 2010 (available online at https://www.patrickholford.com).

2 S. Davies, 'Scientific and ethical foundations of nutritional medicine. Part 1: Evolution, adaptation and health' [editorial], *Journal of Nutritional Medicine* (1991), vol 2(3), pp. 227–247.

3 See https://www.patrickholford.com/advice/supplements-optimum-daily-
   allowances.
4 Facts about Divorce, Divorces in England and Wales, 2012 release, Office of
   National Statistics, 2014.
5 See http://www.mind.org.uk/information-support/types-of-mental-health-
   problems/statistics-and-facts-about-mental-health/.
6 P. Clayton and J. Rowbotham, 'An unsuitable and degraded diet? Part 1:
   Public health lessons from the mid-Victorian working class diet', *Journal of
   the Royal Society of Medicine* (2008), vol 101, pp. 282–289.
7 N.M. Avena, M.E. Bocarsly and B.G. Hoebel, 'Animal models of sugar and
   fat bingeing: relationship to food addiction and increased body weight',
   Methods of Molecular Biology (2012), vol 829, pp. 351–365.
8 C.B. Pert, *The Molecules of Emotion*, Pocket Books, 1999, p.8.
9 J. Cleary et al., 'Naloxone effects of sugar-motivated behaviour',
   Psychpharmacology (1996), vol 176, pp. 110–114; S.A. Czirr and L.D. Reid,
   'Demonstrating morphine's potentiating effects on sucrose-intake', *Brain
   Research Bulletin* (1986), vol 17, pp. 639–642; E. Blass et al., 'Interactions
   between sucrose, pain, isolation distress', *Pharmacology, Biochemistry
   and Behaviour* (1986), vol 26, pp. 483–489; L. Leventhal et al., 'Selective
   actions of central mu and kappa opioid antagonists upon sucrose intake
   in sham-fed rats', *Brain Research* (1995), vol 685, pp. 205–210; A. Moles
   and S. Cooper, 'Opioid modulation of sucrose intake in CD-1 mice',
   Physiology and Behaviour (1995), vol 58, pp. 791–796; E. Cheraskin and
   W.M. Ringsdorf, 'A bio-chemical denominator in the primary prevention
   of alcoholism', *Journal of Orthomolecular Psychiatry* (1980), vol 9(3), pp.
   158–163.

Part 2
1 G. Reaven, 'Role of insulin resistance in human disease', *Diabetes* (1988), vol
   37, pp. 1595–1607.
2 'Diabetes Prevalence by Age Group', http://www.data360.org/dsg.
   aspx?Data_Set_Group_Id=233.
3 J. Rankins, 'Glycemic index and exercise metabolism', *Gatorade Sports
   Science Institute Sport Science Exchange* (1997), vol 10(1).
4 K. Heaton et al., 'Particle size of wheat, maize and oat test meals: effects on
   plasma glucose and insulin responses and on the rate of starch digestion in
   vitro', *American Journal of Clinical Nutrition* (1988), vol 47, pp. 675–682.
5 S. Kalghati et al., 'Bactericidal antibiotics induce mitochondrial dysfunction
   and oxidative damage in mammalian cells', *Science Translational Medicine*
   (2013), vol 5(192):192ra85.
6 P. Holford, C. Trustram-Eve and D. Fobbester, '100% Health survey: a
   comparison of the health and nutrition of over 55,000 people in Britain',
   Holford & Associates, January 2010 (available online at https://www.
   patrickholford.com).
7 E. Cheraskin et al., 'Establishing a suggested optimum nutrition allowance

(SONA)', http://www.enerexusa.com/articles/establishing%20_sona.htm; 'What is optimum?', *Optimum Nutrition* (1994), vol 7(2), pp. 46–47.

8   P. Holford et al., 'The association of various food group consumption with overall health ratings: a survey of 55,570 United Kingdom respondents', *Journal of Orthomolecular Medicine* (2010), vol 25(3), pp. 115–124.

9   G. Block et al., 'Usage patterns, health, and nutritional status of long-term multiple dietary supplement users: a cross-sectional study', *Nutrition Journal* (2007), vol 6(30).

10 E. Cheraskin et al., 'Daily vitamin consumption and fatigability', *Journal of the American Geriatrics Society* (1976), vol 24(3), pp. 136–137.

11 D. Kennedy et al., 'Vitamins and psychological functioning: a mobile phone assessment of the effects of a B vitamin complex, vitamin C and minerals on cognitive performance and subjective mood and energy', *Human Psychopharmacology: Clinical and Experimental* (2011), vol 26(4–5), pp. 338–347.

12 K. Mizunoe et al., 'Antifatigue effects of coenzyme Q_{10} during physical fatigue', *Nutrition* (2008), vol 24(4), pp. 293–299.

13 See P. Langsjoen, 'Introduction to coenzyme Q_{10}', http://faculty. washington.edu/~ely/coenzq10.html.

14 P. Langsjoen et al., 'Treatment of statin adverse effects with supplemental Coenzyme Q_{10} and statin drug discontinuation', *Biofactors* (2005), vol 25(1–4), pp. 147–152.

15 K. Jones et al., 'Coenzyme Q-10 and cardiovascular health', *Alternative Therapies in Health & Medicine* (2004), vol 10(1), pp. 22–30; see also M. Dhanasekaran and J. Ren, 'The emerging role of coenzyme Q-10 in aging, neurodegeneration, cardiovascular disease, cancer and diabetes mellitus', *Current Neurovascular Research* (2005), vol 2(5), pp. 447–459.

16 R. Wunderlic, *Sugar and Your Health*, Good Health Publications, 1982.

17 S. Davies, 'Zinc, nutrition and health', in *Yearbook of Nutritional Medicine*, Keats, 1985.

18 S. Davies et al., 'Age-related decreases in chromium levels in 51,665 hair, sweat and serum samples from 40,872 patients – implications for the prevention of cardiovascular disease and type II diabetes mellitus', *Metabolism* (1997), vol 46(5), pp. 1–4.

19 Y.L. Chen et al., 'The effect of chromium on inflammatory markers, 1st and 2nd phase insulin secretion in type 2 diabetes', *European Journal of Nutrition* (2014), vol 53(1), pp. 127–133; T.C. Drake et al., 'Chromium infusion in hospitalized patients with severe insulin resistance: a retrospective analysis', *Endocrine Practice: Official Journal of the American College of Endocrinology and the American Association of Clinical Endocrinologists* (2012), vol 18(3), pp. 394–398.

20 S. Anton, 'Effects of chromium picolinate on food intake and satiety', *Diabetes Technology and Therapeutics* (2008), vol 10(5), pp. 405–412.

21 K.A. Brownley et al., 'Chromium supplementation for menstrual cycle-related mood symptoms', *Journal of Dietary Supplements* (2013), vol 10(4), pp. 345–356.

22 J. R. Davidson et al., 'Effectiveness of chromium in atypical depression: a placebo-controlled trial', *Biological Psychiatry* (2003), vol 53(3), pp. 261–4; K.A. Brownley et al., 'A double-blind, randomized pilot trial of chromium picolinate for binge eating disorder: results of the Binge Eating and Chromium (BEACh) study, *Journal of Psychosomatic Research* (2013), vol 75(1), pp. 36–42.

23 N. Cheng et al., 'Follow-up survey of people in China with type-2 diabetes consuming supplemental chromium', *Journal of Trace Elements in Experimental Medicine* (1999), vol 12, pp. 55–60.

24 M.F. McCarty, 'The therapeutic potential of glucose tolerance factor', *Medical Hypotheses* (1980), vol 6(11), pp. 1177–1189.

25 J. B. Deijen et al., 'Tyrosine improves cognitive performance and reduces blood pressure in cadets after one week of a combat training course', *Brain Research Bulletin* (1999), vol 48(2), pp. 203–9.

26 C.R. Mahoney et al., 'Tyrosine supplementation mitigates working memory decrements during cold exposure', *Physiology and Behaviour* (2007), vol 92(4), pp. 575–82.

27 H. Beckmann et al., 'DL-phenylalanine versus imipramine: a double-blind controlled study', *Archive fur Psychiatrie und Nervenkrankheiten* (1979), vol 227(1), pp. 49–58;
J. Mouret et al., 'L-tyrosine cures, immediate and long term, dopamine-dependent depressions. Clinical and polygraphic studies', *Comptes rendus de l'Academie des sciences, Serie III, Sciences de la vie* (1988), vol 306(3), pp. 93–8 (in French).

28 R.L. Brent et al., 'Evaluation of the reproductive and developmental risks of caffeine', *Birth Defects Research Part B: Developmental and Reproductive Toxicology* (2011), vol 92(2), pp. 152–187.

29 G. Taylor et al., 'Change in mental health after smoking cessation: systematic review and meta-analysis', *British Medical Journal* (2014), vol 348:g1151.

30 Y. Ohmura et al., '5-hydroxytryptophan attenuates somatic signs of nicotine withdrawal', *Journal of Pharmacological Sciences* (2011), vol 117(2), pp. 121–124.

31 K. Unno et al., 'Anti-stress effect of theanine on students during pharmacy practice: positive correlation among salivary α-amylase activity, trait anxiety and subjective stress', *Pharmacology, Biochemistry and Behavior* (2013), vol 16(111C), pp. 128–135.

32 A. Panossian and G. Wikman, 'Evidence-based efficacy of adaptogens in fatigue, and molecular mechanisms related to their stress-protective activity', *Current Clinical Pharmacology* (2009), vol 4(3), pp. 198–219; S.K. Kulkarni and A. Dhir, 'Withania somnifera: an Indian ginseng', *Progress in Neuro-Psychopharmacology and Biological Psychiatry* (2008), vol 32(5), pp. 1093–1105; L. Huang et al., 'Acanthopanax senticosus: review of botany, chemistry and pharmacology', *Pharmazie* (2011), vol 66(2), pp. 83–97; A. Panossian and G. Wikman, 'Pharmacology of Schisandra chinensis Bail.: an overview of

Russian research and uses in medicine', *Journal of Ethnopharmacology* (2008), vol 118(2), pp. 183–212; A. Panossian et al., 'Rosenroot (Rhodiola rosea): traditional use, chemical composition, pharmacology and clinical efficacy', *Phytomedicin* (2010), vol 17(7), pp. 481–493.

33 T. T. Chu et al., 'Study of potential cardioprotective effects of Ganoderma lucidum (lingzhi): results of a controlled human intervention trial', *British Journal of Nutrition* (2012), vol 107(7), pp. 1017–1027.

34 P. Methlie et al., 'Grapefruit juice and licorice increase cortisol availability in patients with Addison's disease', *European Journal of Endocrinology* (2011), vol 165, pp. 761–769.

35 M. Davydov and A.D. Krikorian, 'Eleutherococcus senticosus (Rupr. & Maxim.) Maxim. (Araliaceae) as an adaptogen: a closer look', *Journal of Ethnopharmacology* (2000), vol 72, pp. 345–393.

Part 3

1 Y. Bloch et al., 'Normobaric hyperoxia treatment of schizophrenia', *Journal of Clinical Psychopharmacology* (2012), vol 32(4), pp. 525–530.

2 S. Cook et al., 'High heart rate: a cardiovascular risk factor?', *European Heart Journal* (2006), vol 27(20), pp. 2387–2393.

3 Loyola University Health System, 'Boost your immune system, shake off stress by walking in the woods', *Science Daily*, 3 October 2013.

4 R. Jahnke et al., 'A comprehensive review of health benefits of qigong and tai chi', *American Journal of Health Promotion* (2010), vol 24(6), pp. e1–e25.

5 D. Cohen at al., 'Lifestyle Modification in Blood Pressure Study II (LIMBS): study protocol of a randomized controlled trial assessing the efficacy of a 24 week structured yoga program versus lifestyle modification on blood pressure reduction', *Contemporary Clinical Trials* (2013), vol 36(1), pp. 32–40.

6 N. Gothe et al., 'The acute effects of yoga on executive function', *Journal of Physical Activity and Health* (2013), vol 10(4), pp. 488–495.

7 P. Jin, 'Efficacy of tai chi, brisk walking, meditation, and reading in reducing mental and emotional stress', *Journal of Psychosomatic Research* (1992), vol 36, pp. 361–370; M. Lee et al., 'Qigong reduced blood pressure and catecholamine levels of patients with essential hypertension', *International Journal of Neuroscience* (2003), vol 113, pp. 1691–1701.

8 C.C. Streeter et al., 'Effects of yoga on the autonomic nervous system, gamma-aminobutyric-acid, and allostasis in epilepsy, depression, and post-traumatic stress disorder', *Medical Hypotheses* (2012) , vol 78(5), pp. 571–579.

9 K. Manoj et al., 'Relaxation response induces temporal transcriptome changes in energy metabolism, insulin secretion and inflammatory pathways', *PLoS ONE* (2013), vol 8(5):e62817.

10 M. Goyal et al., 'Meditation programs for psychological stress and well-being: a systematic review and meta-analysis', *JAMA Internal Medicine* (2014), vol 174(3), pp. 357–368.

11 M. Sharma and S.E. Rush, 'Mindfulness-based stress reduction as a stress management intervention for healthy individuals: a systematic review',

Journal of Evidence-Based Complementary and Alternative Medicine (2014), 22
July, p. 2 [epublished ahead of print].

12 M. Goyal et al., 'Meditation programs for psychological stress and well-
being: a systematic review and meta-analysis', *JAMA Internal Medicine*
(2014), vol 174(3), pp. 357–368

13 J. Galante et al., 'Effect of kindness-based meditation on health and well-
being: a systematic review and meta-analysis', *Journal of Consulting and
Clinical Psychology* (2014), 30 June [epublished ahead of print].

14 T. Gard, B.K. Hölzel and S.W. Lazar, 'The potential effects of meditation on
age-related cognitive decline: a systematic review', *Annals of the New York
Academy of Science* (2014), vol 1307, pp. 89–103.

15 K.P. Chan, 'Prenatal meditation influences infant behaviors', *Infant
Behaviour Development* (2014), vol 37(4), pp. 556–561.

16 M.L. Jackson et al., 'Sleep difficulties and the development of depression
and anxiety: a longitudinal study of young Australian women', *Archives of
Women's Mental Health* (2014), vol 17(3), pp. 189–198.

17 R. von Känel et al., 'Association between polysomnographic measures of
disrupted sleep and prothrombotic factors', *Chest* (2007), vol 131, pp. 733–739.

18 F. Cappuccio, 'Sleep deprivation doubles obesity in both children and
adults', study presented at International Research Festival, 2006; J.E.
Gangwisch et al., 'Inadequate sleep as a risk factor for obesity: analyses of
the NHANES I', *Sleep* (2005), vol 28(10), pp. 1289–1296.

19 S. Patel et al., 'Association between reduced sleep and weight gain in
women', *American Journal of Epidemiology* (2006), vol 164(10), pp. 947–954.

20 A. Ananthaswamy, 'Sleep your way to a slimmer body', *New Scientist*, 26
May 2006.

21 C.E. Hammond, 'Some preliminary findings on physical complaints from a
prospective study of 1,064,004 men and women', *American Journal of Public
Health* (1964), vol 54, pp. 11–23.

22 A.R. Ekirch, *At Day's Close: Night in Times Past*, W.W. Norton & Company,
2005.

23 L. Yai, 'Brain music in the treatment of patients with insomnia',
Neuroscience and Behavioural Physiology (1998), vol 28, pp. 330–335.

24 I. Olszewska and M. Zarow, 'Does music during dental treatment make a
difference?', http://www.silenceofmusic.com/pdf/dentists.pdf.

25 G. Parati et al., 'Obstructive sleep apnea syndrome as a cause of resistant
hypertension', *Hypertension Research* (2014), vol 37(7), pp. 601–613.

26 L. Shilo et al., 'The effects of coffee consumption on sleep and melatonin
secretion', *Sleep Medicine* (2002), vol 3(3), pp. 271–273.

27 T.C. Birdsall, '5-Hydroxytryptophan: a clinically-effective serotonin
precursor', *Alternative Medical Review* (1998), vol 3(4), pp. 271–280.

28 P. Montgomery et al., 'Fatty acids and sleep in UK children: subjective
and pilot objective sleep results from the DOLAB study – a randomised
controlled trial', *Journal of Sleep Research* (2014), vol 23(4), pp. 364–388.

29 H. Tuomilehto et al., 'The impact of weight reduction in the prevention of

the progression of obstructive sleep apnea: an explanatory analysis of a 5-year observational follow-up trial', *Sleep Medicine* (2014), vol 15(3), pp. 329–335.

30 A.M. Spaeth et al., 'Effects of experimental sleep restriction on weight gain, caloric intake, and meal timing in healthy adults', *Sleep* (2013), vol 36(7) [epublished].

31 P. Peppard et al., 'Sleep disorders linked to heavy drinking in men', *Journal of Clinical Sleep Medicine* (2007), vol 3(3), pp. 265–270.

32 V. Coiro et al., 'Alcoholism abolishes the growth hormone response to sumatriptan administration in man', *Metabolism* (1995), vol 44(12), pp. 1577–1580; A. Heinz et al., 'Blunted growth hormone response is associated with early relapse in alcohol-dependent patients', *Alcoholism, Clinical and Experimental Research* (1995), vol 19(1), pp. 62–65.

33 W. Shell et al., 'A randomized, placebo-controlled trial of an amino acid preparation on timing and quality of sleep', *American Journal of Therapeutics* (2009), vol 17(2), pp. 133–139.

34 Common side-effects include 'daytime sedation, motor incoordination, cognitive impairments (anterograde amnesia), and related concerns about increases in the risk of motor vehicle accidents and injuries from falls', according to the *Lancet* (2004), vol 364, p. 9449.

35 'Editorial: Treating insomnia – use of drugs is rising despite evidence of harm and little meaningful benefit', *British Medical Journal* (2004), vol 329, pp. 1198–1199.

36 S. Saul, 'Sleep drugs found only mildly effective but wildly popular', *New York Times*, 23 October 2007.

37 C. Drake et al., 'Caffeine effects on sleep taken 0, 3 or 6 hours before going to bed', *Journal of Clinical Sleep Medicine* (2013), vol 9(11), pp. 1195–1200.

38 S. Jarupat et al., 'Effects of the 1900 MHz electromagnetic field emitted from cellular phone on nocturnal melatonin secretion', *Journal of Physiological Anthropology* (2003), vol 22, pp. 61–63.

39 A. Naska et al., 'Siesta in healthy adults and coronary mortality in the general population', *Archives of Internal Medicine* (2007), vol 167, pp. 296–301.

40 D. Childre and D. Rozman, *Transforming Stress: The HeartMath Solution for Relieving Worry, Fatigue and Tension*, New Harbinger Publications, 2005.

41 *HeartMath Intervention for Counselors, Therapists, Social Workers and Health Care Professionals: Establishing a New Baseline for Sustained Behavioural Change*, HeartMath LLC, 2008.

42 R. McCraty et al., *Impact of the Power to Change Performance Program on Stress and Health Risks in Correctional Officers*, HeartMath Research Center Publication No. 03-014, November 2003.

43 D. Childre and D. Rozman, *Transforming Stress: The HeartMath Solution for Relieving Worry, Fatigue and Tension*, New Harbinger Publications, 2005.

44 R. McCraty and D. Tomasino, 'Emotional stress, positive emotions and psychophysiological coherence', in *Stress in Health and Disease*, Wiley, 2006, pp. 342–365.

45 R. McCraty, *Heart–Brain Neurodynamics: The Making of Emotion*, HeartMath

Research Center Publication No. 03-015, 2003; R. McCraty et al., *Science of the Heart: Exploring the Role of the Heart in Human Performance*, HeartMath Research Center Publication No. 01-001, 2001; R. McCraty et al., *Impact of the Power to Change Performance Program on Stress and Health Risks in Correctional Officers*, HeartMath Research Center Publication No. 03-014, 2003; F. Luskin et al., 'A controlled pilot study of stress management training of elderly patients with congestive heart failure', *Preventive Cardiology* (2002), vol 5(4), pp. 168–172; B. Barrios-Choplin et al., 'An inner quality approach to reducing stress and improving physical and emotional wellbeing at work', *Stress Medicine* (1997), vol 13(3), pp. 193–201.

46 R. McCraty et al., 'The impact of a new emotional self-management program on stress, emotions, heart-rate variability, DHEA and cortisol', *Integrative Physiological and Behavioral Science* (1998), vol 33(2), pp. 151–170.

47 R. McCraty et al., 'Impact of workplace stress reduction program on blood pressure and emotional health in hypertensive employees', *Journal of Alternative and Complementary Medicine* (2003), vol 9(3), pp. 355–369.

48 Study carried out at the Pacemaker Clinic for Kaiser Hospitals in Orange County, California, and featured in the *HeartMath Interventions Manual*, HeartMath LLC, 2008, p. 46.

49 R. McCraty et al., *Emotional Self-regulation Program Enhances Psychological Health and Quality of Life in Patients with Diabetes*, HeartMath Research Center Publication No. 00-006, 2000.

Part 4

1 J. Jobin and C. Worsch, 'Associations between dispositional optimism and diurnal cortisol in a community sample: when stress is perceived as higher than normal', *Health Psychology* (2014), vol 33(4), pp. 382–391.

2 L. Kamen and M.E.P. Seligman, 'Explanatory style and health', *Current Psychological Research and Reviews* (1987), vol 6(3), pp. 207–218.

3 H.A Tindle et al., 'Optimism, cynical hostility, and incident coronary heart disease and mortality in the Women's Health Initiative', *Circulation* (2009), vol 120(8), pp. 656–662.

4 N. Ranjit et al., 'Psychosocial factors and inflammation in the multi-ethnic study of atherosclerosis', *Archives of Internal Medicine* (2007), vol 167(2), pp. 174–181.

5 E. Neuvonen et al., 'Late-life cynical distrust, risk of incident dementia, and mortality in a population-based cohort', *Neurology* (2014), vol 82(24), pp. 2205–2212.

6 L. Brydon et al., 'Hostility and cellular aging in men from the Whitehall II cohort', *Biological Psychiatry* (2012), vol 71(9), pp. 767–773.

7 M. Lobel et al., 'The impact of prenatal maternal stress and optimistic disposition on birth outcomes in medically high-risk women', *Health Psychology* (2000), vol 19(6), pp. 544–553.

8 B. Lipton, *The Biology of Belief: Unleashing the Power of Consciousness, Matter and Miracles*, Mountain of Love/Elite Books, 2005.

9   J.B. Moseley et al., 'A controlled trial of arthroscopic surgery for osteoarthritis of the knee', *New England Journal of Medicine* (2002), vol 347(2), pp. 81–88.

10 A.J. Crum et al., 'Rethinking stress: the role of mindsets in determining the stress response', *Journal of Personality and Social Psychology* (2013), vol 104(4), pp. 716–733.

11 J.E Gillham et al., 'Prevention of depressive symptoms in schoolchildren: two-year follow-up', *Psychological Science* (1995), vol 6, pp. 343–351; J.E Gillham et al., 'School-based prevention of depressive symptoms: a randomized controlled study of the effectiveness and specificity of the Penn Resiliency Program', *Journal of Consulting and Clinical Psychology* (2007), vol 75, pp. 9–19; J.J. Cutuli et al., 'Preventing co-occurring depression symptoms in adolescents with conduct problems: the Penn Resiliency Program', *New York Academy of Sciences* (2006), vol 1094, pp. 282–286.

12 R. Emmons, 'Why gratitude is good', online article on *The Greater Good: the science of a meaningful life*, 16 November 2010, (greatergood.berkeley.edu).

13 R. Emmons, 'What is gratitude?', online article on *The Greater Good* (greatergood.berkeley.edu).

14 M.E. McCullough et al., 'The grateful disposition: a conceptual and empirical topography', *Journal of Personality and Social Psychology* (2002), vol 82(1), pp. 112–127.

15 T. Kraft and S. Pressman, 'Grin and bear it: the influence of manipulated facial expression on the stress response', *Psychological Science* (2012), vol 23(11), pp. 1372–1378.

Part 5

1   P. Holford and J. Braly, *The Homocysteine Solution*, Piatkus, 2003.

2   P. Holford et al., '100% Health survey: a comparison of the health and nutrition of over 55,000 people in Britain', Holford & Associates, January 2010 (available online at https://www.patrickholford.com).

3   K.G. Brurberg et al., 'Case definitions for chronic fatigue syndrome/myalgic encephalomyelitis (CFS/ME): a systematic review', *British Medical Journal* (2014), vol 4(2), e003973.

4   I.M. Cox et al., 'Red blood cell magnesium and chronic fatigue syndrome', *Lancet* (1991), vol 337, pp. 757–760; J.M. Howard et al., 'Magnesium and chronic fatigue syndrome', *Lancet* (1992), vol 340, p. 426.

5   M.L. Pall, 'Cobalamin used in chronic fatigue syndrome therapy is a nitric oxide scavenger', *Journal of Chronic Fatigue Syndrome* (2001), vol 8(2), pp. 39–44.

6   P.O. Behan et al., 'Effect of high doses of essential fatty acids on the postviral fatigue syndrome', *Acta Neurologica Scandinavica* (1990), vol 82, pp. 209–216; B.K. Puri, 'The use of eicosapentaenoic acid in the treatment of chronic fatigue syndrome', *Prostaglandins, Leukotrienes and Essential Fatty Acids* (2004), vol 70(4), pp. 399–401.

7   S. Rigden et al., *Management of Chronic Fatigue Symptoms by Tailored*

Nutritional Intervention Using a Program Designed to Support Hepatic Detoxification, HealthComm Inc., 1997.

8 S. Rigden et al., *Evaluation of the Effect of a Modified Entero-hepatic Resuscitation Program in Chronic Fatigue Syndrome Patients*, Functional Medicine Research Center, 1997.

9 S. Myhill et al., 'Targeting mitochondrial dysfunction in the treatment of myalgic encephalomyelitis/chronic fatigue syndrome (ME/CFS) – a clinical audit', *International Journal of Clinical Experimental Medicine* (2013), vol 6(1), pp. 1–15.

10 K.A. Smith et al., 'Relapse of depression after rapid depletion of tryptophan', *Lancet* (1997), vol 349, pp. 915–919.

11 We have read 27 studies, involving 990 people, most of which proved the efficacy of taking either tryptophan or 5-HTP.

12 P. Jangid et al., 'Comparative study of efficacy of l-5-hydroxytryptophan and fluoxetine in patients presenting with first depressive episode', *Asian Journal of Psychiatry* (2013), vol 6(1), pp. 29–34.

13 P. Holford, 'Sugar and stimulants make you stupid', in *Optimum Nutrition for the Mind*, Piatkus, 2010.

14 J.R. Komorowski et al., 'Chromium picolinate modulates serotonergic properties and carbohydrate metabolism in a rat model of diabetes', *Biological Trace Element Research* (2012), vol 149(1), pp. 50–56.

15 V.K. Dubev et al., 'Possible involvement of corticosterone and serotonin in antidepressant and antianxiety effects of chromium picolinate in chronic unpredictable mild stress induced depression and anxiety in rats', *Journal of Trace Elements in Medicine and Biology* (2014), pii: S0946-672X(14)00119-9 (epublished ahead of print).

16 M. McLeod, J. Davidson et al., 'Effectiveness of chromium in atypical depression: a placebo-controlled trial', *Biological Psychiatry* (2003), vol 53(3), pp. 261–264.

17 K.A. Brownley et al., 'Chromium supplementation for menstrual cycle-related mood symptoms', *Journal of Dietary Supplements* (2013), vol 10(4), pp. 345–356.

18 K.A. Brownley et al., 'A double-blind, randomized pilot trial of chromium picolinate for binge eating disorder: results of the Binge Eating and Chromium (BEACh) study', *Journal of Psychosomatic Research* (2013), vol 75(1), pp. 36–42.

19 G. Grosso et al., 'Role of omega-3 fatty acids in the treatment of depressive disorders: a comprehensive meta-analysis of randomized clinical trials', *PLoS One* (2014), vol 9(5), e96905 (epublished).

20 H. Tiemeier et al., 'Vitamin B_{12}, folate, homocysteine: the Rotterdam Study', *American Journal of Psychiatry* (2002), vol 159(12), pp. 2099–2101; T. Bottiglieri et al., 'Homocysteine, folate, methylation, and monoamine metabolism in depression', *Journal of Neurology, Neurosurgery and Psychiatry* (2000), vol 69(2), pp. 228–232; T. Bottiglieri et al., 'Folate, vitamin B_{12}, and homocysteine in major depressive order', *American Journal of Psychiatry* (1997), vol 154, pp. 426–428.

21 H. Refsum et al., 'Folate, vitamin B_{12}, homocysteine, and the MTHFR

polymorphism in anxiety and depression: the Hordaland Homocysteine Study', *Archives of General Psychiatry* (2003), vol 60, pp. 618–626.

22 T. Bottiglieri et al., 'Homocysteine, folate, methylation, and monoamine metabolism in depression', *Journal of Neurology, Neurosurgery and Psychiatry* (2000), vol 69(2), pp. 228–232.

23 A. Nanri et al., 'Serum folate and homocysteine and depressive symptoms among Japanese men and women', *European Journal of Clinical Nutrition* (2009), vol 64(3), pp. 289–296.

24 S. Gilbody et al., 'Is low folate a risk factor for depression? A meta-analysis and exploration of heterogeneity', *Journal of Epidemiology and Community Health* (2007), vol 61(7), pp. 631–637.

25 J.M. Kim et al., 'Predictive value of folate, vitamin B_{12} and homocysteine levels in late life depression', *British Journal of Psychiatry* (2008), vol 192(4), pp. 268–274; N. Dimopoulos et al., 'Correlation of folate, vitamin B_{12} and homocysteine plasma levels with depression in an elderly Greek population', *Clinical Biochemistry* (2007), vol 40(9–10), pp. 604–608; P.S. Sachdev et al., 'Relationship of homocysteine, folic acid and vitamin B_{12} with depression in a middle-aged community sample', *Psychological Medicine* (2005), vol 35(4), pp. 529–538; A. Coppen and C. Bolander-Gouaille, 'Treatment of depression: time to consider folic acid and vitamin B_{12}', *Journal of Psychopharmacology* (2005), vol 19(1), pp. 59–65.

26 A.M. Hvas et al., 'Vitamin B_6 level is associated with symptoms of depression', *Psychotherapy and Psychosomatics* (2004), vol 73(6), pp. 340–343.

27 A. Coppen and C. Bolander-Gouaille, 'Treatment of depression: time to consider folic acid and vitamin B_{12}', *Journal of Psychopharmacology* (2005), vol 19(1), pp. 59–65; J. Hintikka et al., 'High vitamin B_{12} level and good treatment outcome may be associated in major depressive disorder', *BMC Psychiatry* (2003), vol 2(3), p. 17.

28 S. Gariballa and S. Forster, 'Effects of dietary supplements on depressive symptoms in older patients: a randomised double-blind placebo-controlled trial', *Clinical Nutrition* (2007), vol 26(5), pp. 545–551.

29 A. Coppen and J. Bailey, 'Enhancement of the antidepressant action of fluoxetine by folic acid: a randomised, placebo controlled trial', *Affective Disorders* (2000), vol 60, pp. 121–130.

30 P. Holford et al., '100% Health survey: a comparison of the health and nutrition of over 55,000 people in Britain', Holford & Associates, January 2010 (available online at https://www.patrickholford.com).

31 J.E. LeDoux, *The Emotional Brain: The Mysterious Underpinnings of Emotional Life*, Simon and Schuster, 1996.

32 NOP Poll, *Panorama*, BBC TV, May 2001 (available online at http://news.bbc.co.uk/ hi/english/audiovideo/programmes/panorama/tranquillisers/newsid_1325000/1325909.stm).

33 F. Kripke, R.D. Langer and L.E. Kline, 'Hypnotics' association with mortality or cancer: a matched cohort study', *British Medical Journal* (2012), vol 2(1):e000850 [epublished].

34 I.S. Shiah and N. Yatham, 'GABA functions in mood disorders: an update and critical review', *Life Sciences* (1998), vol 63(15), pp. 1289–1303.

35 L.R. Juneja et al., 'L-Theanine, a unique amino acid of green tea and its relaxation effects in humans', *Trends in Food Science and Technology* (1999), vol OR10, pp. 199–204; A.C. Nobre et al., *Modulation of Brain Activity by Theanine*, report for Unilever by the Department of Experimental Psychology, University of Oxford, 2003.

36 K. Unno et al., 'Anti-stress effect of theanine on students during pharmacy practice: positive correlation among salivary α-amylase activity, trait anxiety and subjective stress', *Pharmacology, Biochemistry and Behaviour* (2013), vol. 111C, pp. 128–135.

37 F.N. Pitts and J.N. McClure, 'Lactate metabolism in anxiety neurosis', *New England Journal of Medicine* (1967), vol 277, pp. 1328–1336.

38 Artour Rakhimov Ph.D., *Normal Breathing: The Key to Vital Health*, (self published), 2009; see also Robert Fried, *The Hyperventilation Syndrome*, The Johns Hopkins University Press, 1987.

39 E.S. Epel et al., 'Stress and body shape: stress-induced cortisol secretion is consistently greater among women with central fat', *Psychosomatic Medicine* (2000), vol 62, pp. 623–632.

40 B. Foss et al., 'Exercise can alter cortisol responses in obese subjects', *Journal of Exercise Physiology Online* (2014) vol 17(1), pp. 67–77.

41 A. Currie & F. Cappuccio, 'Sleep in children and adolescents: a worrying scenario: can we understand the sleep deprivation-obesity epidemic?' *Nutrition, Metabolism, and Cardiovascular Diseases* (2007), vol 17(3), pp. 230–2; J. E. Gangwisch et al., 'Inadequate sleep as a risk factor for obesity: analyses of the NHANES I', *Sleep* (2005), vol 28(10), pp. 1289–1296.

42 S. Patel et al., 'Association between reduced sleep and weight gain in women', *American Journal of Epidemiology* (2006), vol 164(10), pp. 947–954.

43 https://www.patrickholford.com/advice/gl-scientific-evidence.

44 D. Clouatre and M. Rosenbaum, *The Diet and Health Benefits of HCA*, Keats Publishing, 1994.

45 C. Cangiano et al., 'Eating behavior and adherence to dietary prescriptions in obese adult subjects treated with 5-hydroxytryptophan', *American Journal of Clinical Nutrition* (1992), vol 56(5), pp. 863–867.

46 https://www.patrickholford.com/advice/chromium-the-evidence.

47 https://www.patrickholford.com/advice/cinnamon-may-help-weight-loss.

Part 6

1 Paul Clayton and Judith Rowbotham, 'An unsuitable and degraded diet? Part One: Public health lessons from the mid-Victorian working class diet', *Journal of the Royal Society of Medicine* (2008), vol 101, pp. 282–289.

2 P. Holford et al., '100% Health survey', Holford & Associates, January 2010 (available online at https://www.patrickholford.com).

3 A. F. Razis et al., 'Health benefits of Moringa Oleifera', *Asian PacJ Cancer Prev*, 15(20), pp. 8571–8576.

Appendix

Monitoring Charts

In this section you'll find the blank charts mentioned earlier in the book. You can fill these in, photocopy them or copy the layout and information into a journal, with any other information that is relevant to your Stress Cure Programme. You can also download a pdf of the 30-day Stress Cure Programme to print at www.patrickholford.com/stresscureactionplan

Smoking diary

Day _____		
Time Situation	Feeling before	Feeling after

Stress log

Activating event or situation	Stress-inducing thoughts/ beliefs	Consequences (how you feel)	Compensation (what you do)	Reality check (stress-alleviating thoughts)	Effective new approach

Current time chart

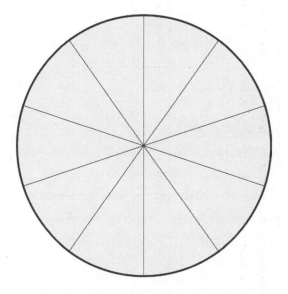

Ideal time chart

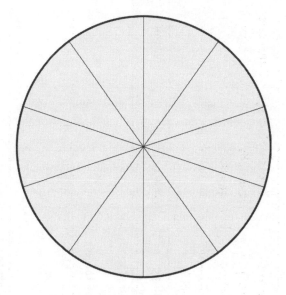

30-Day Stress Cure Programme

1. Eat for energy:

	Breakfast	Lunch	Supper	Snacks

2. Reduce stimulants

	Week 1	Week 2	Week 3	Week 4
Caffeine target:				
Alcohol target:				
Other:				

3. Generate vital energy

Activity/activities:	Minutes:	Days a week:

4. Relax and recuperate

Activity/activities:　　　　　　Minutes:　　　　　　Days a week:

5. Improve sleep

Steps:

6. Build resilience

Activity/activities:　　　　　　Minutes:　　　　　　Days a week:

7. Supplements	Breakfast	Lunch	Supper	Before bed

8. Other actions (if applicable):

Resources

Sources of information and advice

Body mass index (BMI) – you can measure this online at www.patient.co.uk/health/bmi-calculator.

Brain Bio Centre is an outpatient clinic of the charitable Food for the Brain Foundation in London (see overleaf). It specialises in the nutritional treatment of mental health issues, ranging from depression to schizophrenia, anxiety to ADHD. Support is available for people in the UK and all over the world (via Skype). Visit www.brainbiocentre.com or telephone 0208 332 9600.

Breathing and relaxation exercises – you can download free MP3 files of the three-part breath exercise (Chapter 9) and the calming energy boost visualisation and progressive relaxation exercises (Chapter 10) from www.patrickholford.com/stresscure or www.susannah-lawson.co.uk ('Stress Cure' section).

Buteyko method – for more information on this breathing exercise visit www.buteykobreathing.org. Several books also include details of Buteyko, such as *Anxiety Free: Stop Worrying and Quieten Your Mind, Featuring the Buteyko Breathing Method and Mindfulness* by Patrick McKeown.

Emotional Freedom Technique (EFT) is a therapeutic psychological tool that involves tapping on the body's energy meridians while using positive affirmations to clear emotional blocks and embed new positive behaviours. It might sound bonkers, but it can be surprisingly effective! Visit www.emofree.com for more information. There is no central body for EFT practitioners, but some are listed at www. eftregister.com and www.aamet.org, or do an internet search to find one in your local area.

Eye Movement Desensitisation and Reprocessing (EMDR) was developed by the American clinical psychologist Dr Francine Shapiro in the 1980s. It's a well-researched therapy for treating psychological trauma. Visit www.emdrassociation.org.uk for more information and a list of accredited therapists in the UK and Ireland.

Food for the Brain Foundation is a non-profit educational charity directed by Patrick Holford. It aims to promote awareness of the link between learning, behaviour, mental health and nutrition. The website has details on nutritional approaches to anxiety, insomnia and depression, as well as a free cognitive function test that takes 15 minutes to complete. For more information, visit http://www.foodforthebrain.org.

HeartMath® tools – visit www.heartmath.co.uk for details of events, training, HeartMath coaches and products. If you're looking for research and related information, go to www.heartmath.org.

Hypnotherapy uses hypnosis techniques to uncover and resolve underlying issues, or to help a person reach specific goals, such as overcoming panic attacks or low confidence. If you are in the UK, visit www.nationalhypnotherapysociety.org to learn more and find a local practitioner.

Meditation – there are many different meditation techniques and no central register of practitioners, so look out for adverts in your local independent health-food store or centre of complementary therapies to find a teacher in your area. Also ask local yoga teachers for recommendations, or do an internet search. It's important to find someone grounded and experienced whose philosophy appeals to you. Learning with a teacher or in a group can be easier than doing it alone.

Natural progesterone cream – for more information, contact the Natural Progesterone Information Service at www.npis.info and www.bio-hormone-health.com.

Nutritional therapy and consultations – to find a recommended nutritional therapist near you, visit the British Association for Applied Nutrition and Nutritional Therapy at www.bant.org.uk. This website provides details of who to see both in the UK and internationally. If you are unable to find any practitioners in your area, you can always take an online assessment (see below). Or to book an appointment with Susannah Lawson, visit www.susannah-lawson.co.uk or email your details to mail@susannah-lawson.co.uk.

Online 100% Health programme – are you 100% healthy? Find out with a health check and comprehensive 100% Health programme, which will give you a personalised action plan, including diet and supplements. Visit www.patrickholford.com.

Psychocalisthenics® is an excellent exercise regime that takes under 20 minutes each day. It develops strength, suppleness and stamina while also generating vital energy. The best way to learn it is to do the Psychocals training. For further information, see www.pcals.com, which lists training sessions and trainers around the world. Alternatively, you can teach yourself from the *Psychocalisthenics* DVD, available from www.pcals.com. There is also a CD with music and instructions to follow once you have learned the exercises, and a book that explains each exercise. If you are in the UK, you could attend a one-day 'Kath State – The Energy of Inner Fire Training™' seminar, which will teach exercises for awakening, regenerating and revitalising yourself with the *kath* energy (*chi*). See www.pcals.com and select 'Training Information', then 'Integral View' for more information.

Qigong – the Qigong Institute has a list of teachers around the world ('Teachers and Therapists' link), plus much more information and details of research. Visit www.qigonginstitute.org.

Tai chi – the Tai Chi Union lists many UK-based instructors on its website at www.taichiunion.com.

Therapists and coaches – there are many practitioners offering a huge range of talking and support therapies. The British Association for Counselling and Psychotherapy lists UK-based counsellors and therapists at www.bacp.co.uk, as does the UK Council for Psychotherapy at www.psychotherapy.org.uk. If you are looking for a coach, www.lifecoach-directory.org.uk has an extensive UK-wide list, while the Association for Coaching has a directory at www.associationforcoaching.com. Also see EFT and EMDR (page 305–6) and Time Line therapy (below) for details of those who follow psychodynamic approaches. If you need support, it is imperative to find someone with whom you have a good rapport and whose approach you like. Don't be afraid to ask for a trial session to determine whether you can work with a therapist before committing to a full course.

Time Line Therapy uses neuro-linguistic programming (NLP) techniques to help you resolve emotional difficulties and unconscious limiting beliefs and find a more positive way of being. It's an American 'invention', but several UK practitioners also offer Time Line Therapy. Visit www.timelinetherapy.com for more information and a list of practitioners. (Search the whole of the UK as a specific postcode or city search may not yield many results.)

Weight gain and obesity – you can find a number of support services to help keep you on track, motivated and informed at www.patrickholford.com/weightloss. Also see Zest4Life (below).

Yoga – to find a hatha yoga class (which usually includes meditation), visit the British Wheel of Yoga at www.bwy.org.uk. For an iyengar yoga class (which uses props to help with the positions), visit the Iyengar Yoga Association at www.iyengaryoga.org.uk.

Zest4Life is a health and nutrition club, based on low-GL principles, which provides advice, coaching and support for losing weight and gaining health. For more information, visit www.zest4life.eu.

Products

Cherry Active is sold in a highly concentrated juice format. Mix a 30ml serving with 250ml of water to make a deliciously healthy, low-GL cherry juice. Each 946ml bottle contains the juice from over 3000 cherries – that's half a tree's worth! – and provides a month's supply. Cherry Active is also available as a dried cherry snack and in capsules. Other flavours – Beet Active and Blueberry Active – are also now available. For more information and to order, visit www. totallynourish.com.

Blood pressure monitors see www.bloodpressureuk.org, which has a section on how to choose the right monitor.

emWave® technology – you can buy HeartMath emWave® devices, mobile phone attachments and other HeartMath products at www. heartmath.co.uk.

Healthy foods – if you don't live close to a health-food store, www. goodnessdirect.co.uk can deliver a wide selection of products to your door.

Low-GL snack bars – try the tasty GoLower range of protein bars at www.natural-low-carb-store.co.uk or Meridian peanut or almond bars from Holland & Barrett. Siesta carob bars are a sugar-free alternative to chocolate and are available from good health-food shops, or order online at www.goodnessdirect.co.uk.

Probiotics/digestive enzymes/gut repair – probiotics are supplements of beneficial bacteria, with the two main strains *Lactobacillus acidophilus* and *Bifidobacterium*. There are various sub-strains within these two – with some more important in children, and others in adults. There is also considerable variation in the amounts of bacteria in – and the quality of – the numerous products that are on the market. (For example, some labels claim 'a billion viable organisms per capsule'.) For a good-quality product, try Patrick Holford's Digestpro, which also contains digestive enzymes and glutamine. It's available from Totally Nourish. BioCare (see Supplement suppliers, page 312, for details) also has a range of probiotic supplements, including *Bioacidophilus*.

Silence of Peace CD – based on the centuries-old use of specific musical scales and arrangements, the music of John Levine helps you enter a more relaxed and peaceful state of mind. It's excellent for promoting a good night's sleep. To find out more, visit www.patrickholford.com (click 'shop'). It's also available online from major retailers.

Teas Pukka, Yogi and Clipper all have good ranges of caffeine-free teas. Our favourite teas are rooibosch chai, made by Dragonfly and Pukka's liquorice and cinnamon.

Tests

Adrenal stress test measures levels of the stress hormones cortisol and DHEA in saliva at periods throughout the day. It is available from the Biolab Medical Unit in London (www.biolab.co.uk) and Genova Diagnostics (www.gdx.net). Both Biolab and Genova are referral laboratories, so testing can be arranged only via a doctor, nutritional therapist or other registered healthcare professional.

Comprehensive stool test measures digestive markers and levels of both beneficial and pathogenic bacteria, as well as yeasts and parasites. It is available from the Biolab Medical Unit in London (www.biolab.co.uk) and Genova Diagnostics (www.gdx.net). Both Biolab and Genova are referral laboratories, so testing can be arranged only via a doctor, nutritional therapist or other registered healthcare professional.

Food intolerance test – YorkTest Laboratories sells FoodScan, a convenient finger-prick mail-order kit which has the added benefit of a clinical laboratory analysis. Designed as a simple two-step process, the first step is an indicator test that will generate a positive or negative result. If positive, your sample is then upgraded to the second step (FoodScan 113), a comprehensive test that identifies the actual foods (out of a total of 113) that are causing the intolerance and the level of intolerance. In addition, the service includes consultations with a nutritionist and comprehensive support and advice on managing your elimination diet. To order, call YorkTest Laboratories on 0800 130 0580 or visit www.yorktest.com.

Glycosolated haemoglobin (HbA1c) test gives an indication of glucose tolerance over a four-week-plus period and it can be arranged by your GP. It is also available from the Biolab Medical Unit in London (www.biolab.co.uk) or as part of the broader metabolic syndrome profile test at Genova Diagnostics (www.gdx.net). Both Biolab and Genova are referral laboratories, so testing can be arranged only via a doctor, nutritional therapist or other registered healthcare professional.

Gut permeability test provides a measure of digestive tract mucosal permeability and it can be arranged by the Biolab Medical Unit in London (www.biolab.co.uk). Biolab accepts referrals only from registered practitioners, so testing must be arranged via a doctor, nutritional therapist or other registered healthcare professional.

Hepatic detox profile test checks levels of markers from the key liver detoxification pathways. It is available in the UK via Doctor's Data (www.doctorsdata.com), which accepts referrals only via a doctor, nutritional therapist or other healthcare professional.

Homocysteine test – YorkTest sells home-testing kits for homocysteine. To order, call YorkTest Laboratories on 0800 130 0580 or visit www.yorktest.com.

Mineral analysis – your mineral levels can be measured by a hair tissue mineral analysis, which is available from Mineral Check (visit www.mineralcheck.com or call 01622 850 850) or via a nutritional therapist, if you also want comprehensive interpretation.

Mitochondrial function profile is available via Dr Sarah Myhill's practice in Wales. You can call 01547 550 331, but check the website first – www.drmyhill.co.uk – as it has a wealth of information and phone support is limited.

Vitamin D can be tested for £28 if you are in the UK or Ireland (£33 for overseas clients) at www.vitamindtest.org.uk, or a test can be arranged through your doctor.

Supplement suppliers

UK

BioCare offers an extensive range of nutritional supplements, as well as probiotics. Its products are stocked by most good health-food stores and are also available by mail order from Totally Nourish (www.totallynourish.com).

Higher Nature products are available in most independent health-food stores, or visit www.highernature.co.uk, or telephone 0800 458 4747.

Patrick Holford's range includes the convenient Optimum Nutrition Pack (with high-potency multivitamin and mineral, vitamin C and essential fats) and the 9 Day DTX pack (with liver and digestion support). Other combination formulas include Chill Food (with glutamine, taurine, tryptophan, magnesium, hops, 5-HTP and theanine), Mood Food (with 5-HTP, TMG, chromium, zinc, vitamin D and B vitamins), Awake Food (with tyrosine, ginseng and reishi), Cinnachrome, GL Support, Digestpro and Connect (with homocysteine-related nutrients). They are stocked by most good independent health-food stores and are also available by mail order from Totally Nourish (www.totallynourish.com). See www.patrickholford.com/supplementsandtests for more suppliers.

Solgar products are available in most independent health-food stores, visit www.solgar-vitamins.co.uk, or telephone 01442 890355.

Totally Nourish is an e-health shop that stocks many high-quality health products, including home-testing kits and supplements. Visit www.totallynourish.com or telephone 0800 085 7749.

Viridian – for stockists visit www.viridian-nutrition.com or telephone 01327 878 050.

Rest of the world

Australia

Solgar supplements are available in Australia. Visit www.solgar.com.au or telephone 1800 029 871 for your nearest supplier. Another good brand is **Blackmores**.

Kenya

Patrick Holford supplements are available in all Healthy U stores. Visit www.healthy-U2000.com.

New Zealand

BioCare and **Patrick Holford** products are available in New Zealand through Pacific Health, PO Box 56248, Dominion Road, Auckland 1446. Visit www.pachealth.co.nz or telephone 0064 9815 0707.

Singapore

BioCare, **Patrick Holford** and **Solgar** products are all available in Singapore through Essential Living. Visit www.essliv.com or telephone 6276 1380.

South Africa

The original **Patrick Holford** vitamin and supplement brand from the UK is now available in South Africa through leading health-food stores, Dis-Chem and Clicks retail pharmacies. See www.holford-direct.co.za for details of suppliers and products.

UAE

BioCare and **Patrick Holford** supplements are available in Dubai and throughout the rest of the UAE from Organic Foods & Café, PO Box 117629, Dubai, United Arab Emirates. Visit www.organicfoods andcafe.com or telephone +971 4434 0577.

Index